WORLD FOOD POLICIES

WORLD FOOD POLICIES

TOWARD AGRICULTURAL INTERDEPENDENCE

EDITED BY WILLIAM P. BROWNE
AND DON F. HADWIGER

LYNNE RIENNER PUBLISHERS · BOULDER, COLORADO

A Policy Studies Organization Publication

Published in the United States of America in 1986 by
Lynne Rienner Publishers, Inc.
948 North Street, Suite 8, Boulder, Colorado 80302

Library of Congress Cataloging-in-Publication Data

World food policies.

    Bibliography: p.
    Includes index.
    1. Agriculture and state.   2. Food supply.
I. Browne, William Paul, 1945-   .   II. Hadwiger,
Don F.
HD1433.W67   1986   338.1′9   86-3869
ISBN 0-931477-79-4

Distributed outside of North and South America and Japan by
Frances Pinter (Publishers) Ltd, 25 Floral Street,
London WC2E 9DS England.   UK 1SBN 0-86187-652-0

Printed and bound in the United States of America

Contents

Tables

Preface

The editors and the sponsors of this book address a subject that needs much attention—national food policies as the setting for international food dependency. We regard this book primarily as a way in which scholars of public policy—in this case, political scientists—can offer their insights on this subject to an interested audience that includes those who make food policy.

The world food situation is a product of interdependent food systems. Countries with developing agriculture as well as those with highly developed systems depend upon food exports for income; and, increasingly, they also depend upon imports for adequate quantity and variety of food. Even in the development of domestic agriculture, nations have been, and still are, very much dependent upon others for capital, organizational energy, technology, and skills.

This interdependence is achieved within an environment of national public policies that are predictably oriented to national and subnational group interests. One could say that interdependence is achieved within a highly fragmented protectionist policy framework.

The intent of this book is to examine that paradox, keeping in mind that a better understanding of the relationship between public policy and interdependency will enhance our capacity to assure sufficient supplies of food for the world's expanding population. Both the editors and sponsors of this book are very much aware that decisions on food policy have been and are being made in many governments. Directions for food assistance are being debated everywhere. In 1985, for example, the U.S. Congress was confronted with the need to write a new farm bill. It also considered revisions of U.S. trade, diplomatic, fiscal, and monetary policies in ways that heavily impact upon the U.S. agricultural system. Confusion reigned. Domestic protectionism and international interdependence were sources of irreconcilable conflict. European policy debates have suffered similar consequences as national leaders have sought more information on international linkages.

To find our authors, we searched the scholarly literature, consulted leading experts, and examined the recent and future program agendas of academic conferences of political scientists, economists, sociologists, and historians as well as the interdisciplinary International Studies Association.

We are much indebted to sponsors who urged us to undertake this book and who provided the necessary support. Stuart Nagel, executive secretary of the Policy Studies Organization, advanced the book project vigorously from the beginning. Initial encouragement and excellent advice were offered by Kenneth Farrell, director of the National Center for Food and Agricultural Policy of Resources for the Future. The center provided the major financial support for the book. Farm Foundation also provided sponsorship and financial assistance; and, as in the past, we turned to its knowledgeable managing director, James Hildreth, for good advice and information. We are most grateful to these sponsors for their substantial support.

We do not wish to overlook the enormous support from our own academic institutions, Central Michigan University and Iowa State University, which provided the libraries, support facilities, and/or professional time.

We are also most grateful for the excellent assistance of our secretaries, Annette Van Cleave and Judy Neely, as well as the resources and assistance of Iowa State University's Agricultural Experiment Station.

William P. Browne
Don F. Hadwiger

1 Issues of World Food and Trade: Perspectives and Projections

William P. Browne

This book is about the public policies that make world food supplies available. Food is the product of a highly interdependent system. No nation stands alone in sustaining its own food needs. Nor can any nation shoulder the burden of providing the bulk of world food demands by itself. Supplying sufficient quantities of food depends on international food partnerships among nations.

The world has been exceedingly fortunate that food production has more than kept pace with population increases. Fears of inadequate food supplies have proven to be unfounded as member nations of those partnerships continually delivered greater food abundance in the mid- to late-twentieth century. This success, this volume demonstrates, is not just the result of intensive agricultural producer efforts. The agricultural policies of individual nations have been no less responsible for present and projected abilities to satisfy food demand. Without these public policy developments, the dire predictions of Thomas Malthus might now be a reality.

Understanding the many commentaries on world food sufficiency is largely a matter of sorting through the values that these various observers have attached to the topic. The complexities of food availability obscure many of the facts about its production, distribution, and consumption. As a result, observers of the international food scene focus on food from the perspective of their own particular interests in it. These perspectives, unfortunately for purposes of a common dialogue, vary dramatically and become more at odds with one another as facts are used selectively to confirm the orientations of those who hold them. A large percentage of the U.S. public, for instance, worries about food because all human nutrition needs are not being met. Data on scarcity and agricultural sustainability as well as continued reports of hunger and starvation capture their interest and become the basis for substantiating this world view. These public beliefs matter. Politicians, social planners, and activists from church and community food programs share origins with that public. More importantly, as widespread concerns these beliefs provide generalized support for government efforts to ensure a lasting and plentiful supply of food.

1

Another perspective on world food is shared by U.S. farmers who, like much of the public, aspire to the ideal of maximized production. Farm attitudes, however, are shaped mostly by the desire for increased personal prosperity and economic importance, and the facts of oversupply of food commodities are overwhelmingly evident to these producers. Consumers are oriented instead toward inexpensive food, a by-product of large supplies. Agricultural economists hold yet another perspective, one that places many of them at odds with farmers but is still focused on oversupply. From an economic viewpoint, high-priced world food supplies from export nations—especially the United States—presently exceed world demand despite much evidence of need. World prices simply outpace much of the world's capacity to buy what is available. Under these and present public policy conditions, increasing farm production is undesirable no matter how attractive it is to the public and to farmers. Consumer interests, farm interests, and economic interests expressed in marketplace decisions thus seem irreconcilably divided.

At the center of these disagreements and value differences lies the debate about appropriate public policy. For in a complex and multi-interested situation, public policies structure the production and supply of agricultural products as much as does water, weather, land quality, and climate. U.S. agriculture's structural character has been shaped by government price supports, loan programs, and the resulting incentives to increase both production and farm size. As a result, U.S. food prices have been stabilized to support U.S. farmers; but, as a secondary consequence, price stabilization has lowered worldwide demand. Import nations, plagued with their own economic problems, cannot afford to increase consumption and pay for U.S. farmers' abundant production. In short, accelerating standards of nutritional need cannot be met despite an oversupply of available food.

This controversy, despite widespread discontent with U.S. policy results, is made more difficult to resolve because U.S. agriculture occurs within the context of a global food system. It is not a U.S.-driven model. Each nation sets its own policies. Those of the European Economic Community (EEC), for example, compete with the United States for exports and assist their own producers to claim import markets. Other nations, such as Japan and the Soviet Union, have their own internal policies to encourage agricultural growth. Developing nations, with a potential for increasing imports, determine policies that impact on U.S. agriculture. Korea, for example, has been able to expand food imports as its own agriculture and industry increased. Many others have not been notably successful in development and have been forced both to subsidize consumer food prices and to establish restrictive policies that prohibit domestic dietary changes. Quite clearly, the perspectives from which forces within these various countries view food and food trade differ greatly.

The intent of this book is to provide a background for examining world food sufficiency holistically. The perspectives from which the conditions of agriculture are viewed must be brought together. The various forces at work in structuring the array of national public policies must be understood and must understand each other. There is no evidence that such awareness exists. This awareness is especially important for U.S. agriculture, the subject of our own interest, because U.S. public policies will only succeed if they are responsive to other world forces and events. Our immense productive capacity must be allowed to work; but, if U.S. agriculture is to have a viable future, producers must find a continuing use in the world while not exhausting their long-term resource base. Serious questions about each of these conditions exist.

U.S. farm policy, in the wake of the 1985 farm bill, is still being set through reforms in farm support, trade, taxation, and budget deficit reduction. Emergency proposals will no doubt be raised because of the U.S. farm crisis. This book, we hope, makes some contribution to the deliberations that surround the policy process. There are several issues that must be dealt with in these discussions, and they must be treated from a macropolitical and macroeconomic perspective. Given the general history of U.S. agricultural policymaking, and the specific example of the 1985 farm bill as it was played out in Congress, macroanalysis usually has not happened. The focus of the decisionmakers has been incrementally directed either by those who have a single interest or those who have unrealistic policy goals for U.S. agriculture.

In Chapter 2 the major conditions confronting U.S. agriculture and its place in the global food system are briefly summarized and related to one another. Later sections and chapters explain the interdependence of U.S. and world food policy, examine the policies and policy results of developed and developing nations, and evaluate the consequences of an interdependent food system. Several of the world's most knowledgeable agricultural policy scholars outline conditions in each of these areas. Two somewhat contradicting themes prevail throughout these chapters. On the one hand, the developed nations, as the authors note, are especially attracted to free trade and open markets that could provide them competitive advantages. On the other hand, the authors concerned with developing nations raise questions about the efficacy of free markets, high technology agricultural production, and cash crop policies for Third World countries. U.S. policymakers confronting a world food situation will, it seems, be faced with issues of both national food linkage and delinkage. These policymakers, in broadening their own perspectives to better understand this international dilemma, will be doing so in the context of the recurring conditions surrounding the issues of U.S. production problems, agricultural sustainability, export country needs, and import markets. These conditions are reviewed in the next section.

CURRENT U.S. DOMESTIC AGRICULTURAL ISSUES

No one can argue that U.S. farmers and farm policy have not provided a plentiful supply of relatively inexpensive food. Even under conditions of severe stress such as drought or freeze, U.S. consumers have seldom known crop shortages for desired commodities. Regardless of whether farm prices are at a high or low point, consumer costs for food—if expressed in percentages of income—tend to be among the lowest in the world. This occurs against a dietary backdrop that makes the U.S. population as well fed as any in the world and nutritionally far better off than that great majority of world inhabitants who still subsist largely on grains.

Despite such an appealing bottom line for the domestic recipients of U.S. food products, U.S. agriculture is as much burdened with problems as laden with successes. Many farmers are in economic trouble, the future direction of agriculture is questionable, agricultural programs no longer protect farmers from the effects of national and international monetary policies, and the costs of those policies has escalated to the point that many consider them overly burdensome and even misdirected. These conditions defined the issues relative to the traditional agenda items that were debated in the 1985 farm bill and will continue to be important for future legislation.

The Fading Farm Sector

Although 24 million U.S. workers are employed in farm-related industries, the number of farmers are in a steady decline. Compared to the early 1950s, less than 30 percent of the total number of producers still farm (Lin, Coffman, and Penn 1980). Continuing losses are projected for small and most especially middle-range farmers. In addition, the relationship between farmers and farm income continues to change. Sixty percent of net farmer income now comes from non-farm sources. Although the ratio of farm to nonfarm income varies considerably among farmers, the effect of this variance is that agriculture—in a given year—provided an inadequate livelihood for the largest percentage of its participants.

These changes in the farm ranks have widespread repercussions for the rural United States. Fewer farmers mean fewer farm communities, or at least economically less healthy ones. Many rural consumers are gone, and other consumer habits change as the remaining large farms move toward efficiency in purchasing, equipment use, and product sales. These changes, in particular, have altered the operations of such diverse industries as equipment manufacturers and meat-packing operations. The primary effect of these changes has been fewer agribusiness firms and fewer workers.

Rising Production Costs

Farmers were especially hard hit by both inflation and the massive hike in energy prices during the 1970s. Because production and distribution are so heavily capital-intensive with a dependency on both fuels and fertilizers, farm costs exceeded those of other sectors of the economy. But interest rates generally have been blamed for creating even more havoc than these other factors. In the best of times, farmers borrow heavily to plant and purchase livestock needs. As a result, agriculture ranks highest among U.S. commercial borrowers. During the 1970s, however, many U.S. farmers borrowed more heavily than usual. Some additional credit was necessary to meet other cost increases; but large amounts of credit were used to finance the purchase of additional land and equipment as farmers were encouraged to increase production under provisions of the 1973 farm legislation.

When interest rates rose so rapidly in the mid- to late-1970s, many producers were caught in unanticipated credit squeezes. Foreclosures have become commonplace events and have sparked numerous farm protests throughout the Midwest. The Farmers Home Administration (FHA) reports that these conditions have created a delinquency rate approaching one-third of its outstanding loans. Although many delinquencies must be attributed to FHA's liberal credit and collection policies, the figures are illustrative of generalized farm difficulties that have resulted from various public policies of the past decade.

An Oversupply of Goods and an Undersupply of Cooperation

Higher costs supported by higher commodity prices still would have produced favorable conditions for the U.S. farmer. However, net farm income declined and continues to do so. It dropped nearly 20 percent in 1982 alone. Major commodity prices, in particular, have not kept up with costs. Even the federal Payment in Kind (PIK) program and the drought of 1983, both of which reduced production, did not enhance prices. All this indicates, from everybody's perspective, that consumers are not willing to pay even present prices for what farmers produce. This unwillingness exists at a time when U.S. farmers and those from other developed agricultural nations are on a growth roll, developing their production at a 3 percent annual rate (ERS undated).

Farmers, however, do not find controlled production a feasible means of forcing prices up. Grain producers two decades ago rejected acreage allotments. To minimize financial returns and stay in business, many farmers now must plant as much as possible. Others simply recognize that there is no individual benefit in being the only producer to scale down. So, in response, they plant whatever they can in hopes that other farmers, somewhere, incur losses. This cycle produces two things for many major commodity producers: unrealistic hope and continued inadequate prices.

Inequality in Agriculture

Not everyone loses money in farming, though. Far from it. The economic and political turmoil in U.S. agriculture disguises the fact that while rising costs and low prices force certain producers out of the market, others prosper. For many who operate successfully, federal supports only add to, rather than make possible, economic gains. These beneficiaries are many of the nation's largest farmers, a group who can minimize financial risks through private investment strategies and the protection provided by an equity base.

In the late 1960s, 90 percent of farm supports went to approximately one-half of U.S. farmers (Lin, Johnson, and Calvin 1981). These figures appear to have changed very little. Among those who gained 1978 benefits, that 10 percent of eligible producers who are largest received 46 percent of the income. Quite clearly, public policies have not worked to preserve the wide range of farmers. At worst, such policies have created economic conditions in which large-scale farmers use their economic leverage and available capital to speed the out-migration of their smaller scale peers.

Costly Programs

Increasingly, as U.S. agriculture wrestles with its surpluses and continues to experience declining numbers of producers, the costs rather than the benefits of farm programs have become the focus of attention. After all, productivity has expanded in the face of that fading farm sector, and because of food's necessary demand, someone will continue to produce. The Office of Management and Budget, the Congressional Budget Office, and the General Accounting Office all have raised criticism at U.S. agricultural policy based on fiscal and monetary—as opposed to farm prosperity—concerns.

The complaints of these government agencies contain a certain logic. Farm programs have continued an annual and unchecked escalation. When policymakers moved to encourage production increases through incentives contained in the 1973 farm bill, they also succeeded in further increasing the costs of the programs themselves (Penn 1979). Not only that, the multibillion dollar expenditure on the 1983 PIK program can be traced to a need for eliminating the surplus products of the policy directions established in 1973.

The conditions of domestic agriculture and agriculture's place in the U.S. budget guaranteed that the concerns of the 1985 farm bill did not revolve around just ensuring continued supports for those who have previously found them useful. Although evidence exists that some farmers need help, there also is reason to believe that the health of U.S. agriculture does not require supporting those farmers who need financial assistance. It is from that position that policymakers and policy analysts will confront those farm and commodity interests who intend to preserve if not enhance present policies.

SUSTAINABILITY OF AGRICULTURAL PRODUCTION

Domestic agricultural issues are not all related to the relatively short-term conditions of production, prices, and program costs. Despite continued productivity increases and surpluses, the long-term ability of U.S. farmers to sustain their capacity to meet food demand is still in question. At least some of these issues, especially conservation, environmental, and genetic issues will affect policy deliberations. Others may be raised in policy debates.

Conservation Issues

The movement toward larger scale farming and the accompanying production growth of the last few decades have extracted a resource cost as well as a human one. Water use, in particular, has supported these trends with a sixfold increase during four decades and is in an ever increasingly precarious supply. Considerable numbers of wells for irrigation have gone dry in the plains regions, and aquifer levels continue to drop even as much of the irrigation supply is wasted in the process. Situations such as these raise questions as to whether federal farm supports should be tied in some way to conservation efforts because prior benefits have helped create the expansion that strains the resource.

Soil conservation is most frequently discussed as appropriately linked to support programs. Extensive farming operations, in efforts to use larger equipment and cover more territory, have removed many of the terraces and other conservation devices previously installed at federal expense. As a result, many midwestern farmers suffered severe field losses during the heavy rains of 1982. On a national level, per acre soil loss has increased significantly with specific regions experiencing major deterioration. However, larger farms have more readily accepted new soil-conserving technology, such as minimum tillage practices, that permits large yields with less resource expenditures. Land itself has became an issue that may demand policy attention. Urban and industrial forces converted 875,000 acres of potentially usable cropland to their purposes during the 1970s. This relatively small loss of 875,000 acres comes from a national inventory of nearly 540 million acres (Batie and Healy 1983).

Loss of actual farmland is only one facet of a concern with preservation. Water and soil loss might eventually take some significant percentage of cropland permanently from production. This conservation issue has taken on preservationist overtones as a result of two observable trends that have focused the fears of some observers. First, increased sales of cropland, although primarily to other farmers, have placed more and more land in the hands of absentee owners. Because tenancy is being associated with deteriorating soil conditions, the question is raised as to whether sustained and reliable long-term food production can be maintained under such ownership.

The second trend of concern is agriculture's reliance on chemical use and the associated soil depletion. The replacement of soil nutrients with agricultural chemicals may only be partial despite the fact that nitrates placed on the soil become a serious contaminant when leached off into ground and surface waters.

The effects of herbicides and pesticides on both farm conditions and food consumers also are challenged in terms of their potential consequences for farm conditions and food consumers. Preservation of farmland may need to be dealt with in the context of saving a resource that many are inclined to abuse because of the press of immediate economic conditions. U.S. agriculture's sustainability, therefore, is open to serious challenges—but only if there are no compensating mechanisms that can improve gains through some new technologies.

Technological Questions

Resource losses, although never desirable, may be more than offset by technological changes, however. The history of twentieth century agriculture, with its exponential rather than linear growth rates, supports the view that productivity can continue increasing. Indeed, those phenomena that have raised questions about long-term hazards—mechanization, irrigation equipment, fertilizers, and chemical control products—have allowed farmers to presently grow far more than past capabilities allowed.

Although these agricultural tools will continue to be improved, the promise of larger yields lies with technological advances. Biotechnology has made advancements in disease resistance and stronger genetic strains. Breakthroughs in many production areas are said to be on the threshold.

From a policy perspective, technology relies on more than just a scientific base. Who will experiment? How will advances be disseminated throughout the farm community? It may well be that federal support programs made it possible for large producers to secure and utilize risk capital in improving yields. It certainly has been true that federal support for land grant college research and extension services was responsible for both innovations and their promulgation within farm ranks. Whether these institutions are prepared to best support future advances is unclear. It may well be, in terms of both their capability and their ability to finance technological programs, that large agribusiness firms will emerge as a better source or at least a partner in this endeavor. At any rate, the present agricultural research establishment is now as much housed within agribusiness as it is the public sector, and as a result, sustainability is dependent on a maturing partnership arrangement.

The danger is not that the importance of long-term sustainability will not be recognized. Rather the question is whether sustainability will be defined as important enough to merit a comprehensive policy. Farm interests exhibit a strong preference for separating these issues from the basic farm support measures of a major farm bill. Their present values dictate an emphasis on production support rather than restrictive and confining measures that offer no immediate returns. It should be clear that any policy changes that attempt to expand farm markets and therefore alleviate oversupply problems must be based on a predictable future supply of food products. If the agriculture resource base fails, however, or if its deterioration is not offset by a supportive technology, any such excursions into a world market will do little to really help the U.S. farmer or world food needs.

THE PROBLEMS OF EXPORT NATIONS

U.S. agriculture is increasingly dependent on a world market. The domestic consumer market has little chance of expanding to meet the increasing productivity of agriculture. Expanding production is dependent on farmers and agribusinesses who wish to sell more of their products, policymakers who want to support U.S. agriculture and reduce the national trade deficit, and consumers who want to continue the economic benefits of a prolific and low-cost agriculture. All back expanded trade as if it were an easy escape route from existing farm and policy problems. Export expansion requires a move from the United States' previous high level of the world food trade market to a figure approaching 50 percent. The hope that this market change can come to pass seems to assume that such changes occur through national will, as if the United States alone controls the world supply of food. This most certainly is not the case. Nor is it true that international forces wish to invite the United States to feed the world.

Competition Among Developed Nations

Developed nations throughout the world—most notably the European Economic Community, Canada, Australia, and Argentina—have become efficient food producers and exporters. Their yields have increased because of the same technology and production incentives responsible for increased yields in the United States. These countries have produced abundant exportable supplies of basic commodities as well. These products compete in the world market with those of the United States. The result is an institutionalized set of suppliers who compete with each other for export sales and who, collectively, keep world prices low while attempting to keep their own domestic prices above costs of production. Other countries, Brazil with soybeans for example, have begun to copy production practices of developed agricultural nations when possible for the specific purpose of recovering from their own trade deficits. As technology increases the likelihood of such imitation among countries with a strong incentive to trade, more competition and greater pressure on prices will result.

Protective Domestic Policies

Strong domestic forces exist within producer nations to support their agriculture. As a result, EEC sets prices above the world market to keep farm incomes from dropping. Other countries use similar inducements to keep agriculture active. The results are two-sided. Farmers within each country produce even more to gain available financial benefits. Thus, the exporter nations are under even more political and economic pressure to sell on the international market for whatever price they can get, even if subsidies are required. Of course this causes increased national expenditures.

Disincentives for Cooperation

In the face of such costly competition, several strategies for cooperation have been proposed. These range from strong cartel agreements among export nations that would arrange prices all the way to simple cooperative agreements for facilitating an exchange of information useful in domestic planning. However, international agricultural cooperation is even less easy to bring about than domestic farm unity. All countries are interested in maximizing foreign sales and want, at least, to maintain their own previous highest levels of exports per commodity. Unfortunately, when allocated by country, this expectation always exceeds 100 percent of total demand. Instead of cooperation, U.S. farm interests espouse an orderly approach where the marketplace generally determines prices. Although their belief in the innate competitive advantage of U.S. agriculture seems reasonable, the corresponding hope that other export nations will eliminate policy supports and subsidies in deference to the United States seems entirely misplaced. However, competing nations should not count upon the United States as the principal exporter to continue in its position as stabilizer of world markets.

Economic Factors

One important fact of life that also serves to undermine international exporter cooperation is the secondary role that agricultural policy plays to economic policy in determining food trade. Nations cannot pay for things they cannot afford. From the U.S. perspective, cooperation would be unnecessary if, for instance, EEC efforts collapsed in the face of the community's immense subsidy costs. Recent conflict within the EEC about farm policy and support levels encouraged this attitude.

Economic conditions, however, are a two-edged sword internationally and provide hope for other than U.S. interests. Competitors have taken solace in the strength of the U.S. dollar on foreign markets and have been encouraged by the discouraging effect that strength has on U.S. sales. Their belief, and one shared by U.S. observers as well, is that a continued strong dollar will drive the world price of U.S. food increasingly higher. This eventually may allow competitor nations to claim more of the world market at higher prices while lowering their own subsidy costs.

These conditions make clear the interrelationships that exist among an expanding number of countries whose interests are tied to gaining a larger share of the agricultural export market. Developmental policies are only partially geared toward the need to balance trade deficits. In large part, for the United States and traditional export nations, agricultural development is the result of efforts to maintain their own domestic farm incomes while ensuring their abilities to provide food products for a more extended period. Cooperative efforts to stabilize this chaotic and costly situation, although attractive, are viewed as both politically unacceptable and, perhaps, economically unnecessary. Policymakers, it seems, can produce excess hope and excess food products as well as can their farmer constituents.

THE PROBLEMS OF IMPORT NATIONS

Though most nations export food, the global food system is still primarily directed toward home-grown consumption. Approximately 85 percent of the world's food is used in the country of origin. Although the percentage of imports continues to grow, the incentives to produce domestically and the public policy conditions that provide those incentives determine much about the availability of markets to exporters. Gaining access is not simply a matter of discovering a basic food need or creating new consumption habits.

Who Imports?

The answer is both simple and complex. At its simplest level, nearly every nation imports food. However, both the rate of and reasons for importation vary dramatically. Developed agricultural nations import food for purposes of variety and because some products are less expensive than similar ones raised at home.

The large-market import nations purchase food primarily for reasons of scarcity and to satisfy domestic dietary changes. Wheat to Africa and feed grains to the Soviet Union are prime examples. These importers include Eastern Europe and especially the Soviet Union, Japan, and the developing nations. China can be considered an emerging import nation although its status is still largely in a state of flux. Trade with any of these countries is far from easy as their own economies and politics impose limits on domestic consumption.

Protectionism

For each of the countries listed above, imports are limited in order to protect a nation's agriculture just as they are limited for reasons of inadequate financial resources or because of occasional political conflicts between exporters and importers. In general, the more developed a nation's agriculture, the more restrictive will be its protectionist policies. EEC is the best example among the large-scale export nations; Japan exercises the greatest restrictions among the large importers. Both have established agricultural interests with long-standing political influence. Due to development concerns, and because of varying domestic pressures to restrict agricultural imports, the public policy positions of most nations foreclose any hope that a free market world agriculture will emerge.

Need or Demand?

World food trade is no more a hunger-driven model than it is a U.S. one. The number of hungry people and the prescribed levels for their adequate nutrition may set targets for meeting human needs, but these do not reflect actual market demand. Projections for increased trade opportunities must be determined on the basis of what dollar amount individual countries and other purchasing sources will make available. This reality is rooted in the need for farmers to sell their products rather than give them away and in the ability of individual countries to adopt policies that restrict diets.

Not only has food demand been outstripped by supply, increases in demand also lag. Compared with the total 2.7 percent annual increase in food production, worldwide demand has been growing at only 2 percent (ERS undated). This implies that markets will not be available unless additional factors trigger increased consumption.

Development

Almost no one is content with a world where abundant food supplies and malnutrition coexist. One component of U.S. agricultural programs, as an expression of this discontent, has emphasized food assistance programs. These programs, however, have had as much foreign policy as food policy content. This tendency will no doubt remain strong.

Agricultural problems, nonetheless, can move to some solution through food assistance even though unlimited supplies of food cannot be given away indefinitely. When food assistance—through both product and technology transfer—enhances national development for the importer, development has created both dietary change and a better export market. One of the primary tasks for U.S. international policy is to target developing nations and potentially successful national leaders who can use food aid for transformation purposes. This type of support is intended not only to alleviate nutritional problems but also to create stable economic and political conditions. In situations such as these, new development policies can be formulated that will, in the long run, enhance mutually profitable food trade.

The development of markets, the recognition of those political and economic conditions that foster protectionism and subsidized exports, and the acceptance of competitors and their permanent place in the export market are all critical to identifying the policies and support necessary to maintain U.S. agriculture. The global food system is no more an untapped deposit of consumers then it is a panacea for all that troubles the U.S. farmer and farm policy. However, it does have a critical place in the farm economy if U.S. policymakers can assess that system realistically, provide an inexpensive supply of food to the greatest number of potential users, and give these consumers confidence in the stability of their food supply. In this sense, food trade is part of a broader set of solutions for the United States rather than any sort of cudgel that can be used against the rest of the world.

REFERENCES

Batie, Sandra S., and Robert G. Healy, "The Future of American Agriculture." *Scientific American* (February 1983):45–53.

Economic Research Service, U.S. Department of Agriculture. "The Global Food System and the Future of the U.S. Food and Fiber System." Washington, D.C.: unpublished and undated manuscript.

Lin, William, George Coffman, and J. B. Penn, *U.S. Farm Numbers, Sizes, and Related Structural Dimensions: Projections to Year 2000*. Washington, D.C.: Economics, Statistics and Cooperatives Service, U.S. Department of Agriculture, July 1980.

Lin, William, James Johnson, and Linda Calvin. *Farm Commodity Programs: Who Participates and Who Benefits*. Washington, D.C.: Economic Research Service, U.S. Department of Agriculture, September 1981.

Penn, J. B. "The Structure of Agriculture: An Overview of the Issue." In *Structure Issues of American Agriculture*. Washington, D.C.: Economics, Statistics and Cooperatives Service, U.S. Department of Agriculture, November 1979, pp. 2–23.

Part 1
U.S. Agriculture in a Global Food System

Those holding diverse perspectives on the subject of world food sufficiency need to understand the development of agriculture from macropolitical and macroeconomic positions. Only this sort of viewpoint can
bring an understanding of how interdependent U.S. agriculture is with
the rest of the world. The United States is neither in charge of the global
food system nor entirely dominated by it.

Leo V. Mayer and G. Edward Schuh address specifics of U.S. agriculture's place in that global system. Mayer, in Chapter 2, examines the
growth and meaning of interdependence for the United States. Much of
his emphasis is on the instability of a gigantic world market for trade and
its potential for disruption of U.S. domestic policy. Schuh, in Chapter 3,
discusses how the United States can maximize the potential benefits of
interdependence as both an export and an import nation. He offers policy
criticisms and makes suggestions for enhancing the flexibility of U.S. responses. At the heart of his suggestions is the recognition that U.S.
policies cannot effectively take charge of forces beyond U.S. boundaries.

2 Farm Exports and the Farm Economy: Economic and Political Interdependence

Leo V. Mayer

Agricultural exports have become big business for U.S. farmers. At peak export levels, forty percent of all crop production and 5 percent of all livestock output goes overseas to foreign buyers. The interdependence between the U.S. farm economy and overseas markets reached a high in 1981 when farm exports totaled $43.8 billion. Net farm income that year was $25.1 billion. In 1982, exports slipped to $39.1 billion, and net farm income declined to $20.2 billion, illustrating the vulnerability of the farm economy to a softening of export markets. Exports continued to decline from 1983 through 1985.

Declining exports touched not only farmers, for whom lower commodity prices caused economic distress, but also a wide range of agribusinesses that sold items to farmers or bought products from them. In fact, the whole agricultural and food system in the United States was influenced in one way or another by the drop in exports. This meant that some 24 million workers were affected. This statistic—which comprises the number of workers in agribusiness firms, on farms, and in the retail food system—helps explain why economic conditions in the food and agricultural system receive so much public attention. Declining exports also help explain the congressional preoccupation with international agricultural concerns.

ECONOMIC INTERDEPENDENCE

The farm economy was not always so sensitive to changes in international markets. As recently as three decades ago, exports absorbed a much smaller share of U.S. farm production, taking for example, only 25 percent of wheat, 5 percent of corn, and 10 percent of soybean production. When exports varied in the 1950s, the impact was smaller on both the upside when export expanded and on the downside when overseas sales retrenched.

In those earlier years, federal farm programs were also more protective. High price supports and government-operated storage programs insulated the farm economy during periods of overproduction or declining exports. With farm income protected, farm families went on purchasing consumer goods and farm inputs from Main Street. The surplus production was absorbed by federal storage programs that accumulated large stockpiles of farm commodities and required large outlays for farm price and income support programs.

All of this began to change after wheat growers voted down acreage quotas in a producer referendum in 1963 (Hadwiger and Talbot 1965).[1] Farm legislation that maintained high price supports and imposed farm programs was redirected toward lower price supports and voluntary supply reduction programs, a shift that was difficult politically. But supporters of more traditional support programs faced a new reality: Two-thirds of all producers would no longer vote for mandatory production control programs—programs that were necessary if farm output was to match quantities that could be marketed at the high support prices.

Support for mandatory programs had waned as more efficient growers saw lower price supports as a means of expanding exports and larger exports as a source of more income. Although traditionalists questioned the rationale behind the low support–larger export thesis, experience with wheat soon illustrated that it would work. In the decade after support prices were lowered in 1964, wheat exports climbed sharply, and the U.S. share of world markets increased markedly (Table 2.1). This was a period when market opportunities existed and the support price for wheat was well below market prices. When the wheat support price was raised and market prices fell in 1982/83, this trend reversed. The support price once again became a floor for wheat prices, and U.S. overseas sales lagged.[2]

POLITICAL INTERDEPENDENCE

The downturn in the value of farm exports in 1981 after thirteen years of continuous growth brought deep recession to the rural economy. By early 1983, after a further drop in 1982 brought even lower farm prices and incomes, a

Table 2.1
U.S. Wheat Prices and World Market Share

MARKETING YEAR	U.S. PRICE SUPPORT	U.S. FARM PRICE	PRICE SUPPORT /FARM PRICE	WORLD MARKET SHARE
	(Dollars/Bushel)		(Percentage)	
1964–1973	1.25	1.66	75.6	39.3
1974–1980	2.04	3.34	61.1	43.9
1981/82	3.00	3.65	82.2	48.2
1982/83	3.55	3.40	104.4	41.5

Source: U.S. Department of Agriculture data

Table 2.2
U.S. Farm Exports, Imports, and Trade Surplus

MARKETING YEAR	EXPORT VALUE	IMPORT VALUE	TRADE SURPLUS	EXPORT VOLUME
	(Billion Dollars)			(Million Tons)
1975/76	22.8	10.5	12.3	114.1
1976/77	24.0	13.4	10.6	111.9
1977/78	27.3	13.9	13.4	131.9
1978/79	32.0	16.2	15.8	137.4
1979/80	40.5	17.3	23.2	163.9
1980/81	43.8	17.2	26.6	162.3
1981/82	39.1	15.4	23.7	158.1
1982/83	35.5	15.4	20.6	154.6

Source: U.S. Department of Agriculture data

prominent Democratic party figure, Robert Strauss, charged that "the agricultural Midwest is a basket case, still in 'free fall.' It is a very serious situation" (Risser 1983, 22).

The depressed rural conditions followed, by eighteen months, the January 4, 1980, embargo imposed on U.S. grain sales to the Soviet Union. As might have been expected, the Soviets sought out other suppliers to replace grain no longer available from U.S. sellers. Although tight supplies during the remainder of the 1980 marketing year limited Soviet possibilities for buying elsewhere, the full impact of the embargo became evident when favorable weather increased world grain production in 1981. The Soviets then increased purchases from other countries and decreased purchases from the United States.

As export sales dropped in late 1981 (Table 2.2), the rural economy faltered. Farm prices slipped month after month, passing critical levels for farmers who had recently purchased land or made other major investments. Interest payments alone often exceeded gross returns on acres recently purchased at inflated land prices and high interest rates.

For farmers with high debt loads, economic pressures multiplied in the final months of 1981 and throughout 1982. The dismal economic situation extended to agribusinesses where purchases of all types of farm inputs dropped. Main Street businesses in rural areas suffered. Despite adjustments, the only answer for many was to discontinue operations and look for other employment.

How depressed conditions were became clear in the 1982 congressional elections. In district after district where agricultural conditions were particularly acute, voters expressed their frustrations by electing new representatives. Especially hard hit were districts whose members had served on the House Agriculture Committee. Members from North Dakota, South Dakota, Minnesota, and Illinois were removed from the committee by the election.

The impact of the depressed farm economy extended to Virginia where the ranking minority member of the House Agriculture Committee lost his seat in

Congress. Even in Mississippi, where congressmen have a record of serving long tenures, a veteran member of the Agriculture Committee chose not to run again in what was diagnosed as a tough race. In Arkansas, a two-term member lost his seat in the House and on the Agriculture Committee, at least partly because of slumping commodity prices.

Added to other changes due to retirement, resignation, and one decision to run for a Senate seat, the House Agriculture Committee lost eleven of its forty-three members in the 1982 elections. Of the eleven losses, only three were clearly for reasons unrelated to the economic downturn in the farm belt. After reducing the committee size to forty-one in the 98th Congress, nine new members were added. States represented by new members on the committee included Illinois with three, and Minnesota, Missouri, Georgia, South Carolina, Virginia, and West Virginia with one each. Committee changes, although less dramatic in the face of an election that did little but reaffirm President Reagan's popularity, continued in 1984.

POLITICAL ASSESSMENT

The latest round of economic and political losses in farm states was not a new phenomenon. Economic downturns in U.S. agriculture and their heavy impact on the Midwest are legendary. There are also previous instances where elections held during the wrong phase of the farm cycle resulted in major changes in the national political structure. One relatively recent example was in 1968 when the Democratic candidate for president, who came from Minnesota, failed to carry the Midwest. Some analysts at the time connected the election outcome to the dismal farm situation.

In the mid-year election of 1982, the direct political impact of the farming situation was limited to Congress. But Congress-watchers saw an impact on the White House. In a Special Report published on November 3, 1982, the day after the fall election, *World Perspectives* (p. 1), a Washington-based newsletter, suggested that "in the Agriculture Committee, as it is likely to be generally in the House, the loss of Republican seats could make it more difficult for the Administration to win approval of controversial farm policies." Moreover, the report suggested, "the loss of several strong spokesmen on the Republican side could be a debilitating factor." This impact was certainly evident in deliberations about the 1985 farm bill—the House Committee thoroughly rejected administration proposals.

In part, the farm agenda of the 98th Congress was coopted by the Reagan administration when it announced on January 11, 1983, that it would administratively implement a Payment in Kind (PIK) program to reduce crop acreage and production. Still on the congressional agenda was the question of what to do about lagging farm exports, an issue addressed in the 1985 farm bill primarily through lowering loan rates for price-supported commodities.

THE FUTURE AND FARM EXPORTS

The emphasis on large supply control programs by the U.S. Department of Agriculture left many analysts in a state of uncertainty. Some remembered the forty-year period from 1933 to 1973 when surplus supplies of U.S. farm commodities dominated public discussions of agricultural policy. The focus of public farm programs during that period was primarily on how to control surpluses. The question now arises: Are we returning to those days? Was the emphasis on exports during the past decade only temporary?

These questions are especially important for farm states. Exports were the driving force behind the economic revival that occurred in the 1970s. Many persons, including those investing in farm land and related agribusinesses, thought the expansion associated with exports would never end. For some, it was wishful thinking, but others may have based their views on official publications that stressed, overly so it appears in retrospect, a growing world scarcity of food.[3]

One conclusion to be drawn from the experience of the past few years is that just as expanding exports can bring economic revival, declining exports can weaken growth trends and reduce farm profits. Given the economic and political costs of variation in exports, it seems fair to ask, "Will farm exports receive less priority in the remainder of this decade?" For various reasons, exports probably will play an even larger role in the coming years.

One very basic reason for the larger role of exports is that the world is going to need more food. World population growth continues. Although larger than expected downturns have occurred in population growth rates in some countries, an overall pattern of growth continues (Table 2.3). This growth will cause world food demand to grow. A recent report of the U.S. Department of Agriculture (1983, 3) for example, suggests that "over the next two decades, world demand for food and fiber is expected to increase by 50 percent." With appropriate domestic farm policies, this growth can lead to larger farm exports, especially in years of less favorable world weather.

A second reason that exports will increase is continuing technological improvements in agricultural production. These improvements are expanding the supply of farm commodities regularly. Unless there is an expansion in markets, farm prices will decline, and farm income will drop. Drawing back on exports would inflict severe economic damage on U.S. farmers, an outcome that ensures continuing political interest in export expansion.

A third reason for the continued importance of exports is the growing recognition by nations that trade is the key to improving standards of living. Even a period of world recession, like we have just been through, no longer brings a wholesale turn to protectionism as occurred during the years of the Great Depression. A December 1982 meeting of trade ministers in Geneva, Switzerland illustrated that nations support their international trade agreement despite intense political pressures from high unemployment and lagging economic

Table 2.3
Present and Projected World Population Growth

TYPE OF COUNTRY	1980 POPULATION	2000 POPULATION	STATIONARY POPULATION	
			SIZE	YEAR REACHED
(Millions of Persons)				
Low Income	2,161	3,090	5,405	2100
Middle Income	1,139	1,789	3,541	2085
High Income - Oil	14	23	55	2090
Industrialized	714	787	838	2025
Nonmarket	353	409	459	2060
World	4,381	6,098	10,298	2090

Source: World Bank. World Development Report 1982. Washington, D.C.: World
        Bank, 1982.

growth. Clearly, December 1982 was not an optimal time for removing obstacles to trade. But world leaders recognized the dangers posed to the free flow of trade between nations. Their lengthy efforts to find ways to keep the world trading system intact represented a victory over forces favoring protectionism.

A fourth reason is that not only trade ministers recognize the importance of trade. Singapore's ambassador to the United States, Punch Coomaraswamy, noted in a Washington news interview that "in the old days, an Ambassador's concern was politics and defense. Now it's commerce and trade policy" (*Washington Post* 1983, 21). Similarly, President A. W. Clausen of the World Bank recently observed that "one-quarter of everything produced in the world is now traded across national borders" (Clausen 1983, B6).

These same trends have also raised the importance of trade issues for U.S. farmers. In turn, agricultural leaders have developed a new interest in trade issues. Chairman of the Senate Agriculture Committee Jesse Helms, for example, was a major congressional spokesman on agricultural matters at the General Agreement on Trade and Tariffs (GATT) ministerial conference in Geneva in November 1982, the first time an Agricultural Committee chairman has taken on such a role. Following that involvement, he wrote an article for the *New York Times* stressing the growing role of exports for U.S. agriculture. He observed that unlike earlier years when U.S. agriculture supplied mainly domestic markets, "by the mid-70's, the situation had changed, and today our farmers [are] highly dependent on foreign customers." He then went on to note that "predatory trade practices" of the European Economic Community (EEC) were at least partly responsible for U.S. farmers "suffering through their third year of depressed commodity prices" (Helms 1982, 3).

As might be expected in this highly charged environment, hearings before the Senate Committee on Agriculture on March 2 and 3, 1983, illustrated a strong determination in the Congress to guarantee that U.S. farm products will be competitive in world markets, even if export subsidies are required. Broad concern was expressed in the hearings about the current state of the farm economy. There was also bipartisan support for measures to increase exports. This type of political recognition suggests efforts will continue to expand those exports in the future. It also makes more likely appropriate domestic farm legislation that will tend to keep U.S. farm products competitive in world markets.

EXPORT ISSUES

One can legitimately conclude that farm exports have become so economically important to the nation, and especially to farmers, that there is no turning back the political forces favoring export expansion. This public consensus, however, does not remove farm exports as a policy issue. There are, in fact, several issues surrounding farm exports that will continue to confront congressional and administration policymakers.

One issue is the appropriate composition of U.S. farm exports. This is currently known in Washington parlance as the value-added question. That is, should the United States try to focus more attention on exports of value-added farm products, like poultry, canned fruits and vegetables, raisins, dairy products, and other processed food items?

There are pros and cons to the issue. In support are statistics that show that processed food exports generate employment. Production of 1,000 tons of corn, for example, requires 3.1 worker-years of labor, and 500 tons of soybeans, 2.9 worker-years, or a total of 6 worker-years. This same grain and oilseeds exported in the form of 335 tons of poultry add another 5.6 worker-years of employment, or in the form of 250 tons of pork another 6.8 worker-years of employment, or in the form of 300 tons of packaged meats another 8.5 worker-years of employment (USDA 1982).

Similarly, export earnings increase as more processing is added. At 1982 prices, for example, 1,000 tons of corn were worth on the international market about $130,000 and 500 tons of soybeans about $120,000. As poultry, these commodities were worth about $825,000, as pork about $1,250,000, and as packaged meats about $1,750,000. Obviously, value-added exports would be helpful in solving the nation's balance-of-payments problem as well as creating more employment in rural areas.

There are several problems, however, in moving larger amounts of value-added farm products into export markets. One problem is that the policies of some nations restrict the import of processed food items. These restrictions frustrate U.S. exporters who would otherwise have growing sales of value-added products to these countries.

Another part of this same problem is that some exporting nations subsidize their exports of value-added items. These subsidies lower world market prices below costs of production in the United States even though we are often the most efficient producer, as for example, in broiler production. This prevents U.S. products from competing for third-country markets unless the U.S. government also subsidizes the sales price.

Both aspects of this issue were discussed at the GATT trade ministers conference in Geneva in November 1982, at the follow-up ministerial level meeting in Brussels later in December 1982, and during the March 1983 hearings before the Senate Agriculture Committee. From the Senate hearings, one could easily conclude that if other nations continue to insist on subsidizing value-added agricultural export, the United States will soon adopt similar policies.

A second issue, although its intensity has lessened in the past few months, is the resource-use question involved in expanded exports. How intensively should this nation use its cropland and other agricultural resources for the purpose of feeding the populations of other nations? This issue has particular importance to the farm states of the Midwest because a large part of the nation's most productive farmland is located in these states; the amount of federal assistance Congress provides for protecting that farmland is in part determined by the level of public concern.

From recent public discussion of this issue, it seems obvious there are several viewpoints. Some analysts argue that even the present level of resource use endangers the long-term productivity of U.S. agriculture. Others argue that annual increases in farm productivity are evidence that farmland resources are, on average, being conserved and used in an appropriate manner. The intention, here, is not to discuss this issue at length but to note that in another forum the issue was examined in some depth, and it was concluded that the evidence does not support the argument that farmland resources are generally being overutilized (Mayer 1982; USDA Soil Conservation Service 1985).

A third issue is even more complex. How, and to what degree, does the nation protect its farm interests against economic disruptions like those caused by the recent downturn in farm exports? Or, stated in different terms, how much of the risk inherent in selling on an unstable world market should the federal government share with U.S. farmers? In practical terms, the question is this: What is the appropriate type of domestic farm legislation necessary to assist an agricultural industry that now sells one-quarter of its output on world markets?

A simple answer is not obvious. What is evident is that U.S. agriculture today faces very different markets for its output than was true when the current structure of farm programs was established a half century ago. Then, U.S. farmers produced primarily for the domestic market. Today, U.S. farmers produce large and growing amounts for foreign markets. Yet the institutions that assist farmers in the orderly marketing of their products during periods of economic distress operate in much the same fashion.

Take, for example, one of the major agricultural institutions, the Commodity Credit Corporation (CCC). The original purpose of the CCC was to loan funds to farmers so they can hold commodities off the market at harvest time and hold prices up to some prespecified level. This type of action was appropriate when U.S. farmers primarily supplied only a domestic market and that market was protected from supplies of other countries by tariffs or import quotas.

Today, however, U.S. farmers must sell approximately one-third of their crop output on foreign markets. Foreign markets are not protected from the production of other countries. When U.S. price supports are too high, other supplying countries undercut U.S. prices and take over markets. This situation results in the loss of market share for U.S. commodities as wheat exports illustrated in the 1982/83 marketing year.

It may be useful to stress at this point the important role that domestic farm policies play in assisting or preventing global sales of U.S. farm products. It seems almost unnecessary but perhaps one must emphasize that government farm policies should facilitate the flow of commerce, not retard it. This was a major lesson learned in the aftermath of high price supports following World War II, from the experience of the depressed farm economy of the 1950s, and the improvement that occurred after the turn to more flexible farm policies following the failure of the wheat referendum in 1963.

In today's global markets, farm policies must provide an economic framework that allows U.S. farmers to compete with the farmers of other nations. Thus, the U.S. should examine the policies of competing export nations as well as our own in the process of establishing future U.S. farm programs. Setting price support levels for U.S. farm commodities, for example, based only on U.S. production costs, may not lead to midwestern farm prosperity if the United States is no longer competitive in world markets.

One final point on future farm programs: It must be remembered that expanding farm productivity must be matched with growing farm markets if farm prices and incomes are not to suffer. It should be kept in mind, however, that overseas markets tends to be more volatile than domestic markets. Thus, development of future farm policies will have to include the determination of what is equitable in terms of government sharing with farmers the increased risk of conducting business in a global environment. This issue is not simple, and final answers are not possible. Answers must be developed, however, to fit each time period and its set of conditions.

CONCLUSION

Our nation's farmers have recently gone through another economic downturn in world demand with its fluctuations in farm prices and incomes. The economic impact was not limited to farmers but extended well beyond agriculture to include the main streets of a thousand small towns and communities. Caution must be used, however, in drawing lessons from this experience. Each new economic cycle brings a new generation of analysts who have a tendency to believe that their inquiry is unique in terms of conditions and events. In the case of agricultural assessments, it must be kept in mind that there are underlying cycles that affect all results. President Harry Truman's observation that "the only thing really new is the history you haven't read" is especially applicable to analysis of agricultural cycles and the related government policies.

Although caution is necessary, there are some conclusions that can be drawn from the experience of 1980–1986. First, farmers and policymakers, for example, should be convinced that conditions in agriculture can change very rapidly. Those who engage in activities related to agriculture should be reminded that they must be prepared for rapid turnarounds. Good management must include developing individual farmer "insurance policies" to protect against sudden downturns in sales, prices, and incomes. Government policies can protect the rural economy only to a limited degree if agriculture is to retain its competitiveness on world markets. Given the current magnitude of dependence on foreign markets, a loss of international competitiveness can only prolong and deepen rural recession. The United States faces a delicate task in designing future farm policies to protect farm economies and maintain international markets.

Second, the past decade should have convinced all analysts that U.S. agriculture exists in a global economy. Today, items flow across national borders in massive quantities. Current standards of living depend on those flows. Further progress in improving living standards mandates further increases in trade flows. A lessened global orientation and environment may appeal to many. But turning policies toward protectionism or to a larger dependence on domestic markets will provide a future of limited opportunity for U.S. farmers.

Third, world trade in huge volumes is now a reality. Analysts should broaden their analytical frameworks to match this fact. Unless they do, these analysts will become as outmoded as the farm programs of a half century ago. Both analysis and policy must adapt to the evolving world. To do otherwise could easily sentence the United States to the type of stagnation that Europe has suffered from for most of the period since the end of World War II.

NOTES

1. A Capital Hill staffer recently told my U.S. Department of Agriculture Graduate School farm policy class that the 1963 wheat referendum was the most significant event of his twenty-five years with the House Agriculture Committee.

2. Recent work by the Foreign Agricultural Service's Grain Division suggests that of the drop in wheat exports of 13.1 million metric tons (MMT) in 1982/83, 7.0 MMT was due to lack of competitiveness, 4.2 MMT was due to higher subsidized exports by the European Economic Community, and 1.9 MMT was due to other factors.

3. In April 1981, a USDA analyst evaluated global prospects for agriculture and concluded "that agricultural policymakers of the early eighties face the difficult task of easing the transition from the abundant supplies of and excess capacity to produce farm products that characterized U.S. agriculture over the last several decades toward the gradually tightening supply/demand balance likely in the late eighties and nineties" (USDA 1981, 26).

REFERENCES

Clausen, A. W., "Editorial." *Washington Post,* February 27, 1983, p. B6.

Hadwiger, Don F., and Ross B. Talbot, *Pressures and Protests: The Kennedy Farm Programs and the Wheat Referendum of 1963.* San Francisco: Chandler Publishing, 1965.

Helms, Jesse. "The EEC Can't Plough Us Under." *New York Times,* December 5, 1982.

Mayer, Leo V. "Farm Exports and Soil Conservation." In Don F. Hadwiger and Ross B. Talbot, eds. *Farm Policy and Farm Programs.* New York: The Academy of Political Science, 1982.

Risser, James. "Farm Belt Is 'Basket Case,' Says Strauss." *The Des Moines Register,* February 11, 1983, p. 22.

U.S. Department of Agriculture, Economics and Statistics Service. *Agricultural-Food Policy Review: Perspectives for the 1980's,* AFPR-4, April 1981.

U.S. Department of Agriculture, Economic Research Service. "Trade in High Value Farm Products—An Opportunity for the 1980s." Mimeo, 1982.

U.S. Department of Agriculture. The Cooperative Extension Service. "Extension in the '80s." A report of a joint committee of the U.S. Department of Agriculture and the National Association of State Universities and Land-Grant Colleges. Washington, D.C.: USDA, February 28, 1983.

U.S. Department of Agriculture, Soil Conservation Service. "RCA Appraisal Task Force Report." Mimeo, September 1985.

Washington Post. "Ambassador from Where?" *Washington Post Magazine,* February 20, 1983, p. 21.

World Bank. *World Development Report 1982.* Washington, D.C.: World Bank, 1982.

World Perspectives Inc. "Ag Perspectives, Special Report." November 3, 1982.

3 Maximizing U.S. Benefits from Agricultural Interdependence

G. Edward Schuh

U.S. agriculture has truly become part of an interdependent international economy. Observers of that interdependence tend to focus on our trade with other countries and also tend to think of trade in terms of our exports alone. That is too narrow a view. Our interdependence involves a number of other dimensions. First, the United States is a major importer of agricultural products—in most years ranking second only to West Germany. Second, U.S. agriculture is related to the rest of the international economy in important ways through the international labor market. Immigrants from other countries provide an important source of labor to the sector.

Finally, U.S. agriculture is connected to the rest of the world through the international capital market. There are two important dimensions to this market involvement. The international economy can be an important source of investment funds. Perhaps equally as important, with a well-integrated international capital market and a system of flexible exchange rates, the capital market becomes an important vehicle through which U.S. monetary and fiscal policy affects agriculture's export performance (Schuh 1981).

This chapter focuses on these dimensions of agricultural interdependence. Policies that will help the United States improve its agricultural export strategy are reviewed first. This is followed by a section that suggests how the United States might maximize its benefits from the import of agricultural products, and then by a section on the international markets for labor and capital.

Before discussing the substance of these various policies, however, it is important to note that policy choices inevitably involve conflicts and tradeoffs. Almost any policy, or change in policy, admits losers and gainers. Some people will be made better off by the policy, and others will be worse off. The chal-

This chapter draws heavily from a paper prepared for the Trade Policy Task Force of the National Agricultural Forum. The author wishes to thank the forum for permission to adapt from that larger study and the other members of the task force who contributed to the original manuscript.

lenge for the politician or policymaker is to balance the gains and losses for the greater common good and, if possible, to find ways that the losers can be compensated by the gainers. In the interest of brevity these conflicts and tradeoffs will not receive a great deal of attention in this chapter. However, the reader should be sensitive to these issues.

The choice of proper policy also frequently involves a conflict between the individual and the larger collectivity of which he or she is a part. Hence, what is good for an individual may not be good for all individuals as a whole, and vice versa: What may be good for the collectivity as a whole may not be good for the individual.

MAXIMIZING THE BENEFITS FROM AGRICULTURAL EXPORTS

It is not easy to define an optimal export policy. Certainly it doesn't mean maximizing exports at all costs. Perhaps the best way to view the problem is to understand that a nation exports in order to be able to import. Presumably, what it imports will be something it does not produce in the domestic economy, or something it can acquire more efficiently by importing than by producing at home. In this sense, a country should export to that point at which it gives up no more in resource costs to produce the exports than the value of the inputs it imports. It is this economic criterion that should guide a nation's export policies.

This section reviews some of the critical actions that need be taken to improve trade performance and to maximize the benefits received from agricultural exports.

General Trade Liberalization

Promoting the general liberalization of trade both in this country and on the international scene, although time consuming, may be as important as anything the United States can do to improve the export performance of agriculture. Ultimately, further liberalization of trade will have to be a multilateral issue and will have to be pursued in multilateral forums. However, there are things the United States can do on a bilateral basis, and that is the perspective taken in this section.

First, the United States needs to recognize that it will not be a credible proponent of freer trade in agricultural products so long as it continues to be highly protective of its own agricultural sector. In particular, continued insistence on import quotas seriously weaken the U.S. case with the European Economic Community (EEC) as it attempts to induce the EEC to make changes in domestic and trade policies.

More general restraints on trade are also of significance in this context. For example, the proposal for domestic-content regulation is an example of a trade constraint that weakens our position in trade negotiations. Similarly, present cargo preference legislation that requires U.S. food aid to be shipped in U.S. bottoms also weakens the negotiating position.

The implication of expanded trade is increased specialization. That means the United States may need to shift resources from the production of commodities now protected to the production of other commodities either for export or for domestic consumption. The issue then becomes whether the resources now used for the production of protected commodities have alternative uses that don't require major reorganization in resource use or significantly lower returns. In some cases it should be recognized that very viable industries may well remain even after protection has been eliminated.

Second, the United States needs to recognize more generally that trade is a two-way street. In the case of the less-developed countries in particular, most will not be able to import agricultural products unless industrialized countries are more willing to accept their labor-intensive manufactured products. The same applies to China, a country with the potential to become a major importer of agricultural products. In both cases, the key to more rapid economic development is the opportunity for expanded markets.

Third, the United States needs to use a sounder strategy in attempting to negotiate trade liberalization. All too often the United States finds itself in the position of negotiating only on agricultural issues. In many cases that is a weak negotiating position because the United States already has the best of it and the other country has little to offer. With a broader negotiating posture, the potential for profitable tradeoffs will increase.

A case in point is negotiations with Japan. Japan is already the largest single market, with U.S. exports to that country in recent years running as much as $6 billion. Hence, when the United States negotiated agricultural issues alone, there was little leverage for U.S. attempts to gain greater access for high-quality beef and citrus. However, if the United States were to negotiate greater access for automobiles into the U.S. market in exchange for greater access to Japanese beef and citrus markets, the potential for tradeoffs might be quite great. Nevertheless, the United States has liberalized its quota on automobile imports from Japan apparently without extracting a single quid pro quo.

Similar negotiation strategies should be used with the less-developed countries. Providing greater access to U.S. markets for labor-intensive manufactured products should be given only in exchange for a reduction in high tariff barriers to industrial products or in exchange for greater access for U.S. agricultural products.

More Effective Adjustment Policies

The key to effective trade liberalization is to find more effective means of dealing with trade adjustment problems. The barriers to trade are placed by those who expect to find themselves disadvantaged by such trade. In an economic and political system like that of the United States, the potential for trade liberalization will be limited unless some means can be found to deal with this problem. Trade liberalization typically means that some people lose their jobs. The only effective way to have trade liberalization, therefore, is to have effective adjustment policies.

An important problem with international trade disputes is that these are typically articulated as a conflict between domestic producers and foreign producers. When the problem is stated in that way, the chance that the foreign producer is going to lose is quite great. In point of fact, consumers are generally the primary beneficiaries of freer trade. The benefits to consumers are generally widely dispersed in society, however, and there generally are few strong political representatives of consumer interests. In fact, the benefits to individual consumers of trade liberalization in a single product are generally so small that few consumers are going to give or withdraw political support on that basis alone.

The objective of adjustment policies is to provide the means whereby those harmed by freer trade are enabled to adjust to alternative, equally attractive employment alternatives. Presumably, the gains from freer trade will be sufficiently large that the losers can be relocated and/or compensated for the consequences of the trade and a surplus will still be left over, even though such compensation is seldom actually paid.

Adjustment programs may include technical assistance and retraining programs for alternative employment or alternative production activities in agriculture, support for geographical relocation, and subsidized credit or direct financial support to develop alternative production activities. Often, some combination of all of these programs are needed. Similarly, in some cases, only specialized programs to raise productivity in current activities are needed.

Improvements in the Marketing and Transportation Systems

An important aspect of the strong export system of U.S. agriculture is the very efficient marketing and transportation systems that service it. The transportation and communication systems that serve agriculture are without peer anywhere in the world.[1] The same applies to the marketing system that results from these efficient transportation and communication systems. Marketing institutions such as futures markets, cash markets, and mechanisms by which prices can be established in markets are unusually rich and effective. In fact, other countries depend heavily on U.S. central markets such as Chicago as the source of their market information; and they use Chicago and other U.S. marketing institutions as the means of pricing and marketing their own commodities.

Current efforts to deregulate the U.S. economy can only further strengthen that system. Deregulation of the credit and banking system promises to provide a wider range of financial instruments to facilitate trade. Deregulation of the railroad system may revitalize railroads as a factor in international trade. This deregulation has led to the abandonment of some spur lines, but it also has led to such innovations as unit trains. The potential for innovations in the communication system from the breakup of AT&T promises to be quite great.

An important feature of the U.S. infrastructure is the role private enterprise plays in it and the potential for rapid innovation and investment that grows from private enterprise involvement. Most of the investments in U.S. ports have been made by the grain exporting companies or other private companies. These investments keep the latest in new technology on line. The rapid adoption of unit trains is another example.

Two potential problems loom on the horizon. The first is the proposal to impose fees on inland waterways. The major portion of those fees will be borne by farmers. Although the imposition of user fees for inland waterways may be an economically efficient policy, this may not be an appropriate time to institute such a policy.

The second potential problem is with the highway system. Roads and bridges in many states are in a serious state of disrepair, as are some parts of the interstate highway system. The highway system does need to be strengthened and maintained.

It is important that the United States sustain and strengthen its marketing and transportation systems. Inefficient systems in countries such as Canada and Australia have given the United States an advantage in the past, but those countries now are taking steps to improve their systems.[2]

Increased Productivity in Agriculture

High productivity in agriculture is the basis of a strong export performance. In fact, it may be as important as any of the other factors mentioned in this chapter.

Observers of U.S. agriculture often comment how fortunate the United States has been in having such a rich endowment of agricultural resources. The implication is that much of the country's production potential is rooted in its soil resources and in the climate that goes with them.

The United States obviously is endowed with fertile soils, especially in the Corn Belt, and with a climate that so far has given it a strong comparative advantage in products such as corn and soybeans. But a major share of U.S. production potential is manmade, not God-given. The U.S. market system has promoted freedom of choice and innovation, the economic system has provided incentives to produce, and during the years, public investments in infrastructure and in education, science, and technology have made U.S. agriculture one of the most productive in the world. High productivity and sustained growth in productivity are important keys to capturing and sustaining foreign markets.

At one time the United States and other industrialized countries dominated

Table 3.1
Research Expenditures by Region, 1959–1980

	(000 Constant 1980 U.S. $)		
	1959	1971	1980
North America and Oceania	760,466	1,619,404	1,722,390
Western Europe	274,984	971,704	1,489,588
Eastern Europe and USSR	568,284	1,360,196	1,492,783
Latin America	79,556	237,088	462,631
Africa	12,740	55,615	75,156
Asia	261,114	1,339,769	1,734,535
Total	1,957,144	5,583,776	6,977,133

Source: Summary tables from Robert Emerson, Foreign Agriculture Service, U.S.
         Department of Agriculture

investments in agricultural research and development (Table 3.1). For that reason, among others, these countries, especially the United States, have tended to dominate agricultural exports. However, the predominance of U.S. investment in agricultural R&D is rapidly diminishing. The less-developed countries are rapidly developing their agricultural science and technology capability. Brazil, for example, in 1985 spent almost $400 million at the federal level on agricultural research. On a per capita basis, that is almost what the United States spent. India already has a well-developed agricultural research, teaching, and extension system and, as a result, recently shifted from being a large net importer of food grains to being an exporter.

In addition to what national governments are doing, the international community has established a system of twelve International Agricultural Research Centers. Expenditures on this system now amount to approximately $200 million per year. The objective of this system is to produce new technology for less-developed countries located in the tropical and semitropical regions of the world.

The positive aspects of these developments is that obtaining a sustained rise in agricultural productivity in those countries is the key to future U.S. markets. U.S. agriculture has a vital interest in the success of these programs; the growth of U.S. export markets depends on this success.

At the same time, the development of new production technology for those countries in tropical regions can alter comparative advantage and change trade flows. Hence, it will be important that the United States sustain and perhaps increase investments in agricultural research and development and that the United States be sensitive to possible shifts in its comparative advantage. These shifts may open important market opportunities for some producers, while creating the need for adjustments on the part of others.

Economic Development in the Third World

Conventional wisdom has it that population is the driving force behind the demand for food. Hence, some observers at the time of the export boom of the 1970s attributed the boom to an emerging Malthusian crisis associated with rapid population growth in the less-developed countries. In point of fact, however, export/import activity by the less-developed countries was driven largely by increases in per capita income.

Tables 3.2 and 3.3 present data that provide insight into this aspect of agricultural trade. The data in Table 3.2 show the changes in the value (in current dollars) of exports and imports of agricultural products during the 1970s for four groups of countries. Table 3.3 provides some general economic data on those same groups of countries.

Table 3.2
Value of Trade in Agricultural Products,[1]
by Major Groupings of Countries,
1969–1971 and 1977–1979

	DEVELOPING MARKET ECONOMIES			DEVELOPED MARKET ECONOMIES	CENTRALLY PLANNED ECONOMIES	WORLD TOTAL
	Low Income[2]	Middle Income[2]	All			
1969–71 (Billions of U.S. Dollars)						
Exports	4.0	13.3	17.3	30.8	4.6	52.7
Imports	2.3	7.2	9.5	40.6	6.1	55.8
Net Trade[3]	1.7	6.1	7.8	-9.4	-1.5	--
1977–79 (Billions of U.S. Dollars)						
Exports	10.5	43.6	54.1	107.7	12.0	173.8
Imports	6.2	32.1	38.3	127.6	25.2	191.2
Net Trade[3]	4.3	11.5	15.8	-19.9	-13.2	--

Notes: [1]Includes agricultural trade only; forestry and fisheries are excluded.

[2]Low income, less than $370 per capita in 1978; middle income, more than $370 per capita in 1978.

[3]Excess of value of exports over imports. A negative size indicates net imports.

Source: FAO, FAO Trade Yearbook, various issues

Table 3.3
Selected Characteristics of Major Regions

	DEVELOPING MARKET ECONOMIES			DEVELOPED MARKET ECONOMIES	CENTRALLY PLANNED ECONOMIES
	Low Income[1]	Middle Income[1]	All		
Population[2] (millions)	1,294	933	2,227	668	1,352
GNP/capita[3]	200	1,250	696	8,070	1,190
Agricultural Trade ($/capita, 1977-79)					
Exports	8.11	46.73	24.30	161.22	8.88
Imports	4.79	34.41	17.20	191.02	18.64
Growth Rates (percent)					
GNP/capita (1960-78)	1.6	3.7	--	3.7	4.0
Population (1970-78)	2.2	2.4	--	0.7	1.4
Agriculture (1970-78)	2.0	3.1	--	1.0	--

Notes: [1]Low income, less than $370 GNP per capita in 1978; middle income, more than $370 GNP per capita in 1978.

[2]Mid-1978

[3]1978

Sources: World Bank, World Development Report, Washington, D.C.: World Bank, 1980, pp. 110-14 and 142-43, and FAO, FAO Trade Yearbook, various issues.

These data show that the smallest increase in agricultural imports during the 1970s was in the low-income developing market economies. These economies had a quite rapid population growth of 2.2 percent (Table 3.3), but a slow growth in per capita income of 1.6 percent. The largest increase in imports was for the middle-income developing market economies, which had population growth rates that were only slightly above those for the low-income countries (2.4 percent), but high growth rates in per capita incomes (3.7 percent). The developed market economies had slow population growth, relatively rapid increases in per capita income, and a high growth rate for agricultural imports.

Two other aspects of these data are important. The countries with the highest growth in agricultural exports—such as the middle-income developing countries—were also the countries with the highest growth in agricultural imports. Moreover, a large production of agricultural exports per capita does not preclude large imports of agricultural products per capita (Table 3.3). Hence, agricultural progress in other countries does not necessarily mean that they are not considerable importers of agricultural products. That is because agricultural progress is often associated with increased specialization in production and with increases in per capita incomes. This is especially true of the less-developed countries.

These data point to the importance of general economic development as the basis for expansion of agricultural markets and diminish the number of people or the growth rates in population as a factor. The slow growth in agricultural imports by the low-income developing countries is almost certainly associated with the slow growth in their per capita incomes. Similarly, it is almost certain that if per capita incomes in these countries were to grow more rapidly, their imports of agricultural products also would grow.

The importance of accepting exports from the less-developed countries was underscored above. Every one of the newly industrialized countries, such as Taiwan, Hong Kong, Malaysia, Mexico, and Brazil, has experienced rapid rates of economic growth when each turned outward to develop foreign export markets.

Despite the importance of trade as the basis for economic development, however, there is still an important role for foreign assistance, especially to help developing nations increase their stock of human capital—education at all levels, improved nutrition, and a stronger scientific and technological capacity. All the evidence indicates that the social rates of return to such investments are quite high and that the social returns play a major role in promoting economic development.

More Flexible Support Levels for Export Crops

U.S. commodity programs for the major export crops were changed significantly with the 1973 Food and Agriculture Act to make them more compatible with the increased importance of exports as a source of income for U.S. farmers. The programs were further modified with the 1977 legislation. The essential feature of the programs that emerged was the movement away from a rigid support level with stocks held in government hands and the release back to the market whenever commodity prices started to rise, to a system in which prices were expected to be managed within a price corridor that would permit wider fluctuations. Limits to these fluctuations were expected to be provided by the loan level, which would provide a floor to prices, and the call level for loans on stocks held by farmers in the Farmer Owned Reserve. It was expected that stocks would be accumulated as market prices settled on the loan level and then be released back to the market as prices rise to the call level for the loans.

Not unexpectedly, those who designed that program did not envisage the large rise in the value of the dollar in the early 1980s, nor the unexpected embargo on sales to the Soviet Union in 1980, which caused the loan program originally designed for stabilization purposes to be used for price support purposes. The embargo also caused Congress to tinker with the program, raising loan levels as a means of compensating producers for the deleterious consequences of the embargo.

This combination of events caused the commodity programs to eventually become a means of pricing U.S. commodities out of international markets and of providing strong incentives to producers in other countries. This can perhaps best be illustrated by events in 1981 and 1982. During that period the loan level for our major export crops—corn, wheat, and soybeans—were virtually constant if corrected for inflation. However, during that same period the value of the dollar rose some 25 percent. That rise, in effect, translated U.S. prices to foreign buyers at levels that were on the average 25 percent higher than they would otherwise have been. That rise in export prices choked off demand from foreign importers and made the United States less competitive in relation to other exporters.

Longmire and Morey (1982) estimate that the rise in the value of the dollar alone in 1981 and 1982 reduced the value of U.S. agricultural exports by $3 billion and 16 million tons, 10 million tons of which were corn. Those numbers account for a major share of the decline in exports from their peak in 1981–1982. Under these circumstances, the loan levels of the present commodity programs price the United States out of international markets, and the surplus grain is then swept into the Farmer Owned Reserves. When stocks thus burgeon, costly programs such as PIK are conceived.

Unfortunately, the problem does not stop here. The higher prices being reflected to other countries encourage producers in those countries to expand their output. Hence, the United States is left in a situation in which its domestic commodity programs price it out of international markets, encourage production elsewhere, and provide a price umbrella for other countries to undersell U.S. products. Anyone would be hard pressed to design a better program to lose market share.

A solution to this problem is to introduce more price flexibility into the commodity programs so that prices can decline when the value of the dollar rises. This can be done in a number of ways. One way would be to index loan levels and target prices to the value of the dollar. Another way would be to take moving averages as the basis of both loan and target prices. The advantage of using a rule in a well-designed system, of course, is that policymakers do not have to make politically difficult decisions.

The challenge that policymakers and agricultural interests face today is that there is a direct connection between loan levels and export performance. As support levels go up, the risk of becoming less competitive in international markets increases. As these levels decline, of course, markets tend to become more competitive if other conditions are equal.

If the United States were to have flexibility in its support prices (loan levels), exports would tend to be more stable in the face of fluctuations in international demands. That would keep stocks from fluctuating so widely and would avoid large buildups that hang over the market. If, however, the support price (loan level) remains rigid, the United States can expect exports to fluctuate a great deal and with them the stocks carried either in government hands or under government control. Such stocks are costly to carry, of course, and they can become a burden on the market.

MAXIMIZING THE BENEFITS FROM AGRICULTURAL IMPORTS

The United States benefits greatly from its imports of agricultural products, many of which cannot be produced at home or cannot be produced in adequate quantities except at very high levels. Typical products of this variety, of course, are those produced in tropical lands—coffee, cocoa, tea, bananas, and related fruit.

For the most part, such products come into the country relatively free of duties and other restrictive measures. When value is added to these raw materials, however, by processing or some other form of manufacture, tariffs tend to escalate—as they do in most other countries. This is an example in which mutual tariff reduction might be in the interest of all parties.

The United States has been protective of certain sectors of agriculture where competition from abroad is perceived to be a threat to the domestic industry. Chief among these threats are sugar, dairy, and fresh fruits and vegetables from Mexico. These commodities merit special attention because in some cases the costs to U.S. consumers are quite large, and in other cases there are important foreign relations issues.

Sugar is a case in point. It has been estimated that protection of the U.S. sugar industry at recent levels has been costing U.S. consumers as much as $3 billion a year. At the same time sugar protection has important implications for foreign policy. Large components of President Reagan's Caribbean Basin initiative, for example, would not be required if it were not for our restrictive trade measures. Rather than requiring foreign assistance, these countries would be able to acquire foreign exchange by increasing their exports to the United States.

The other side of this coin, of course, is that supporting sugar prices above levels that would otherwise prevail is providing protection for the development of a significant synthetic or artificial sweetener industry. In the longer term, however, such industries will not be in the best interests of the sugar producers because demand for their products will eventually lower demand for sugar.

A similar thing is happening in the case of the dairy industry. The dairy industry is protected, in part, because of severe adjustment problems that would occur in places such as upstate New York and Wisconsin if trade in dairy products were to be liberalized. However, that same protection is providing strong incentives for the emergence of artificial cheeses—products that again might not be in the best long-run interest of the industry. A more proper policy would be to deal directly with the adjustment problem so that a vigorous industry would prevail.

INTERNATIONAL MARKETS

Political and adjustment problems aside, the United States would benefit in the longer term by more open capital and labor markets in the international arena. This openness has to be on both sides of the exchange, however, and not just on the U.S. side. This international exchange equation may provide the United States with an opportunity to negotiate more open markets.

Consider first the labor market side of it. Unlimited immigration, especially of unskilled workers, is feared because of the perceived loss of employment by present unskilled U.S. workers. Ironically, however, the extent to which jobs are actually lost is fairly limited, because the higher labor costs that result from the restriction on immigration cause a substitution of labor by capital. An unfortunate side effect is that plants are then bred for mechanization rather than for product quality, and the consumer loses both by having to pay a higher price for the product and, at the same time, by consuming an inferior product. This has been the case in tomatoes.

It is important to recognize that there are tradeoffs between trade in commodities and trade in labor and capital. At some point one becomes a substitute for the other. In the case of the immigrant worker, one can accept either the commodity that person would produce back home or accept the newly arrived worker. To preclude the entrance of both sacrifices consumer benefits.

CONCLUSION

The emergence of a well-integrated capital market and the shift to flexible exchange rates have significantly changed the economic relations among countries. Programs such as U.S. commodity programs have different impacts under present arrangements than they had in the past. Similarly, exports subsidies and tariffs also have very different effects today than they had twenty years ago. It is imperative that these changed conditions and their significance and benefits to trade policy all be understood.

NOTES

1. Cargo preference legislation causes us to forego some of the benefits from this system.

2. The Crows Rate subsidies to rail transportation in Canada have helped producers in the Canadian Great Plains be more competitive, but port congestions often offset this. The Crows Rate system is now being forced out.

REFERENCES

Longmire, Jim, and Art Morey. *Exchange Rates, U.S. Agricultural Exports, Prices, and U.S. Program Stocks*. Washington, D.C.: Economic Research Service, U.S. Department of Agriculture, November 1982.

Schuh, G. Edward. "Floating Exchange Rates, International Interdependence and Agricultural Policy." In Glenn Johnson and Allan Maunder, eds. *Rural Change: The Challenge for Agricultural Economics*. London: Farner Publishing Company, 1981, pp. 416–422.

World Bank. *World Development Report*. Washington, D.C.: 1980.

Part 2
Public Policies in Developed Agricultural Nations

Chapters 4 through 7 turn to the public policies of nations, such as the United States, that share technologically developed and expansive agricultures. These chapters focus on the content, politics, and consequences of these policies, the realities of which affect the ability of the United States to engage in world food trade and set trade goals.

The countries discussed in these articles were selected because of their prominence as producers and trade partners and also because their policies offer interesting insights. Appropriately, Chapter 4 addresses the European Economic Community (EEC) and its Common Agricultural Policy (CAP). Nicholas Butler and Fred Sanderson find that European agriculture, despite recent economic conflict about CAP, is entrenched in world food markets and now poised to be an even larger participant. These efforts will be enhanced by an emerging Common Export Policy (CEP) and continued resolution of intracommunity differences.

Hyam Gold and Ramesh Thakur examine two other export nations with close European ties and a joint agricultural trade agreement—Australia and New Zealand. They note that trade agreements between the two countries, with agricultural exports to third nations very much in mind, fostered both economies and their general development. Chapters 4 and 5 illustrate the importance of economic and fiscal problems and policies in determining the content of agricultural policy. Although established agricultural interests may be distressed by policy initiatives, the need to respond to issues of international economics and trade deficits will force action and bring some resolution or muting of conflicts.

Chapters 6 and 7 examine two developed nations who primarily are importers but whose experiences also show how agricultural policy is affected by larger forces. Anton Malish looks at the Soviet Union and its present Food Program. The USSR policy of development has changed in response to domestic consumer pressures that could no longer be ignored, changing diets, increasing reliance on imports, and the U.S. embargo of 1980. Japan's agricultural policies, David Balaam writes, are likewise changing with more emphasis on efficiency. Japanese agriculture produced vast oversupplies of rice while wheat and other items remained in short supply. Japanese policymakers have chosen to respond by moving from protectionist stances on several commodities and allowing imports. This change was accompanied by a recognition that self-sufficiency in food is not the most appropriate goal in a world where trade partners need be considered an important factor in determining overall economic policy.

4 The Common Agricultural Policy and World Food Trade

Nicholas Butler

To the casual U.S. observer, skimming the intermittent news of budget crises, deadlocked meetings, and demonstrating farmers, the Common Agricultural Policy (CAP) of the European Economic Community (EEC) must appear to be on the brink of self-destruction. As its costs have pushed the European budget closer and closer to the limits set by the resources available to the community under the terms of the Treaty of Rome, that destruction has come to seem inevitable: a matter of economic logic that the European farm lobby, however powerful, could do no more than delay.

For those actually involved in the U.S. farm sector, whether in the Farm Bureau or in the offices of the Department of Agriculture, the prospect of an imminent collapse of the CAP has long been attractive and enticing. To some the closeness of the moment of crisis, as the European budget spending reached first 95 percent and then 99 percent of the available funds, has been an excuse for inaction based on the hope that by allowing time and events to take their course instead of confronting the problems of trade relations, a rupture of wider political relationships could be avoided. Unfortunately, the collapse has acquired the characteristics of a mirage—a point on the receding horizon that the traveler never reaches.

Two decisions, one taken at the EEC's Brussel's summit on March 15, 1984, the other taken at a meeting of the agricultural ministers of the ten EEC nations on March 31, 1984, show that the CAP will continue and that, with only one exception, output of European agricultural products will continue to rise. (See "CAP Update" in this chapter for developments after mid-1984.)

On March 15, British Prime Minister Margaret Thatcher, the fiercest opponent of public profligacy and no instinctive supporter of the EEC, accepted that, as part of a complex deal on the future shape of European finances, the overall limit on community spending could be raised. The resources provided to the community are determined by the allocation to the EEC of a fixed percentage of the Value Added Tax (VAT) collected in each member state.[1] Since 1970 the limit of that levy has been set at the level of 1 percent, a level that the community barely avoided breaching in 1982 and 1983. Mrs. Thatcher's concession was that a level of contribution, up to a new limit of 1.4 percent of the VAT base, would be acceptable and that in the late 1980s even higher figures might be justified by the expansion of the community.

By mid-April, full agreement had not been reached because of the inability of the other EEC states to agree on a ceiling to individual national contributions in place of the present system that imposes a substantial annual membership fee on the United Kingdom and on West Germany.

Confirmation of the trend of events came with the meeting of the farm ministers on March 30. After months of careful negotiations led by French Farm Minister Michel Rocard, agreement was reached on a structure of price supports for the coming year. Under the terms of the final agreement, total EEC production of milk will be limited to 99.5 million tons in 1984 against a projected out-turn of 108 million tons. Quotas for each country will be imposed, with only Ireland exempt, from a restriction to 1981 output levels. Production above quotas will be penalized by "superlevies." Cereal prices will be reduced by 1 percent (as will prices of some other agricultural products) with durum wheat (used for pasta) and rye exempt.

Despite the organized protests of the farm sector the implications of the agreements are clear. Although an overall limit and quotas have been agreed to, the community has agreed to a system of milk-product management that anticipates a surplus of 12 million tons over and above projected demand of 87 million tons. Grain production, expanding by 2.3 percent per year on the basis of capital investment, technical advance, and rationalization will continue to grow. A 1 percent cut in prices for wheat and other grains represents more a stimulus to increase productivity than a discouragement to planting. The European Commission is already actively pursuing efforts to find new internal markets for surplus grain, concentrating on the exclusion of the grain substitutes now imported for animal feed.

Apart from the quotas for milk producers, nothing was agreed on that sets a limit to the amounts of produce that can be subsidized. There have been no major cuts in support prices for products that are in chronic surplus, and the wine lakes and beef mountains will remain part of the European landscape. Farm ministers will continue to set prices on their own, without the involvement of finance ministers, and no ceiling on the proportion of the EEC budget devoted to agriculture or on the growth of farm spending in total has been agreed on.

Underlying the pricing package is the assumption that money will be available to finance further agricultural growth. For the first time the farm ministers have agreed to proposals that take community agricultural spending above the limits set in the EEC budget and, indeed, above the limits of that budget itself. Unofficial estimates (which weather and world market conditions will modify) show that the package will cost an extra 1–3 billion ECU, over and above the 16.5 billion ECU ($14 billion) allocated under the 1984 budget. Taken together the agricultural ministers' agreement and the emerging consensus on the future financing of the community represent a stark and simple message for the world agricultural community: The apparent limit ("the sound barrier" in one commentator's words) thought to have been set by the limit on resources has been broken.

The CAP, shaken but unscathed, has survived and as the agreement to increase resources is finalized, will continue to develop and expand.

Farmers and policymakers in the United States and in every other farming nation must adjust to the realization that European agriculture is now not only entrenched for the foreseeable future but with domestic demand saturated, posed to play an even greater role as a participant in world markets.

CAP AND THE WORLD MARKET

Although numerous official and academic studies have been published during the last decade analyzing the development and the impact of the Common Agricultural Policy in Europe, few have given more than passing attention to the relationship between agricultural policy within the community and world market conditions. Countries that earn their livelihoods through the export of agricultural produce have long protested the limitations placed on their potential market in Europe by the mechanisms and workings of the CAP. But only in the last few years, as the dynamic effects of generous agricultural support have produced not only self-sufficiency but export surpluses in one commodity after another, have the international dimensions of the debate about agriculture in Europe become fully apparent.

Since its inception in the late 1950s and 1960s, the Common Agricultural Policy has had a dramatic impact on trade flows within Europe and between Europe and the rest of the world. A decade ago the community was a net importer, usually on a substantial scale, of all major agricultural products. The latest figures available from the community show that by the early 1980s the EEC had achieved 108 percent self-sufficiency in wheat, 97 percent in cereals as a whole, and 124 percent in sugar. Although the community in overall agricultural trade terms is still a net importer because of large imports of fruit and tropical products that it at present produces in only minimal quantities, the EEC has emerged during the 1980s as a net exporter of beef, for the first time, and as an exporter of wheat on a significant scale.

In less than a decade the EEC has established itself as a significant exporter of a number of commodities, taking as much as 12 percent of the world cereal market on a regular basis. Agricultural exports now account for 30 percent of all exports from the community, against only 9 percent in 1973.

These figures stand in sharp contrast to the situation twenty years ago when the community as a whole, measured on the basis of either the original six members or the nine members after the first enlargement, was a relatively secure market for other agricultural exporters. As recently as the mid-1970s, the community was regularly importing 20–30 million tons of grain net.

There are three key elements of the CAP that determine and have determined the shifting trade picture. The objective of security of supply contained within the Treaty of Rome has been interpreted to mean the security achieved through indigenous production, even though the goal of self-sufficiency is not itself explicitly mentioned in any of the clauses setting out the purposes of the CAP. Security has been taken to mean the elimination of unnecessary dependence on external suppliers.

Price guarantees, by providing an assured revenue for all production to all producers, have encouraged and sustained production and thereby import substitution without the constraint usually provided by market forces. Because of the Common Agricultural Policy the community's degree of self-sufficiency for many of the principal agricultural products has increased. But the CAP is now faced with the problem of "supporting farmers' incomes by means of guaranteed prices or direct product subsidies for unlimited quantities not necessarily geared to the needs of the market" (*Guidelines for European Agriculture* 10311/81).

Since the 1960s the EEC grain economy has been almost completely disconnected from the world market for grain. Prices are set by political decision and in practice vary between a target price—the price the European ministers would like to see prevail—and the lower intervention price. The community intervenes to keep prices up by buying all surplus grain at the intervention price. To prevent the European farmer from being damaged by foreign competition, imports are subject to levies that push the price of any imported grain up to the internal target price, thereby making import prices uncompetitive. Conversely, on the export side, farmers selling grain at the lower world market price are compensated by export restitutions that cover the difference between the guaranteed domestic intervention price and the world price.

These mechanisms, coupled with the explicit commitment of the CAP to improving productivity, have given added incentive to farmers seeking to mechanize and to introduce new technology and techniques, with the result that yields have shown considerable improvements. The improvement of yields achieved by the EEC has continued to outstrip average world yields. Table 4.1 shows the relationship between world and EEC price levels.

Price guarantees have kept land in production, and a combination of factors has produced a steady rise in output. The gearing of prices to marginal costs to protect the least efficient farmer has inevitably brought windfall returns to the larger and more efficient producers. Production overall has risen in volume terms by some 3 percent per year on average since 1973. Import levies and export restitutions determine the precise relationship between European agriculture and the world market. Export restitutions are not a net device invented to cope with surpluses, but they were established at the inception of the CAP to allow European exporters to compete on world markets. Since then they have

Table 4.1
Comparative Grain Prices

U.S. $/METRIC TON		WORLD MARKET PRICE	EEC THRESHOLD PRICE	NOMINAL RATE OF PROTECTION
Wheat	1968	63.10	115.17	0.83
	1977	110.19	205.38	0.86
	1979	164.90	274.37	0.66
Maize	1968	54.7	93.10	0.70
	1977	118.4	182.17	0.54
	1979	122.6	244.73	1.00
Barley	1968	58.4	92.83	0.59
	1977	125.8	181.46	0.44
	1979	113.0	244.05	1.16

Source: U.N. Economic Commission for Europe data

grown both in scope and in cost and in 1982 are estimated to have accounted for 46.4 percent of the community's agricultural budget expenditures.

The Common Agricultural Policy is characterized by its lack of any trade component. Trade, either in terms of imports or exports, is merely regarded as a residual consequence of the operations of the other elements of the policy. The commission and the member states of the community, with the exception of France, have only recently begun to think in terms of an explicit trade policy, defined particularly by the French as a policy for the promotion of exports.

In considering European agricultural trade policy it is important to recognize that CAP, and the agricultural sector in the community, is not a single entity and that consideration of aggregate community trends alone presents an incomplete picture. Agriculture holds a very different status in each of the national economies of the ten member states, with different patterns of production and industrial composition. The institutional structure of the CAP is such that each of the member states has been best able to pursue its own interests, particularly the interests of the farm sector, by conceding price increases for other products and other producers in return for price increases for its own output (Pearce 1982). This bargaining process between producers in which the consumer is essentially unrepresented has generated a further impetus through the price mechanism to increasing output. The operation of the budget mechanism is such that each country has a direct incentive to increase its agricultural output.

In each of the member states there has been a trend towards self-sufficiency in main products. Germany, therefore, at the outset considered a major net importer of food and a market for the agricultural produce of the rest of the community, particularly France, has become a significant producer, much more nearly self-sufficient in main crops and an exporter of some. In crops where incentives to production have been highest, output has increased dramatically, displacing in the process less well-rewarded crops.

Since the institution of the CAP, West German agricultural exports have grown at more than twelve times the rate of imports, and in recent years German exports have been rising much more rapidly than French exports. Germany is now the supplier of more than 10 percent of the wheat traded in Europe. Yet the German farm industry, with more than 60 percent of farmers working part-time (i.e., with another source of income outside agriculture), is very different from the French. Agriculture in France, by contrast, remains strongly labor-intensive with considerable scope for technological improvements and much larger output expansion. France has long been an exporter of a significant proportion of its farm output. The value of the principle of community preference, written in at the inception of the CAP for the benefit of the French, has declined as other member states have improved their own levels of national self-sufficiency. Enlargement too, with its challenge to French fruit and wine markets, is not altogether welcome and helps to explain the concentration of current French agricultural policy on the export, beyond the community, of cereals and to a lesser extent meat products. Exports, whether to the other members of the community or not, are of significant importance to the French balance of payments, "le pétrole vert" ("green petroleum") in Valéry Giscard d'Estaing's words, and for employment and regional policy in France, factors that explain the unity and persistence with which the French pursue their agricultural policy in the community. As Table 4.2 shows, French exports of wheat and other grains dominate the net trade figures, outweighing the net import positions of the other EEC member states.

The United Kingdom, traditionally a large-scale importer of food from the world market, is gradually finding the pressures and incentives of the CAP a force for change along the German path. Table 4.3 shows the trend in terms of

Table 4.2
Net Trade in Grains

EXPORTS + IMPORTS −	WHEAT AND WHEAT FLOUR (THOUSANDS OF TONS)			COARSE GRAINS (THOUSANDS OF TONS)		
	1979/80	1980/81	1981/82	1979/80	1980/81	1981/82
France	+9777	+12676	+11629	+6921	+6542	+5273
Other EEC members	−2992	− 3057	− 2931	−15782	−13978	−14444
EEC 10	+6785	+ 9619	+ 8698	− 8861	− 7436	− 9171

Source: U.N. Economic Commission for Europe data

Table 4.3
The Trend in UK Self-Sufficiency

| | AVERAGE (%) | | | | | |
	1971/3	1978	1979	1980	1981	1982
Wheat	53	71	75	88	88	109
Barley	94	121	106	116	141	127
Total Cereals	65	80	71	88	102	105
Sugar	36	40	47	47	50	57
Butter	20	40	47	57	56	63
All food consumed	50	53	54	60	62	62
All indigenous food consumed	62	67	69	75	76	77

Source: U.K. Ministry of Agriculture. Annual Review of Agriculture 1984.
Cmnd 9137. London: Ministry of Agriculture, 1985.

self-sufficiency for cereals and other agricultural products since Britain joined the community.

British producers whose efficiency was established under the precommunity system of agricultural support have been quick to take up the potential increase in output and income. According to the Ministry of Agriculture, since the early 1970s the average yields of wheat and barley have risen by 43 and 25 percent respectively. In 1982, for the first time since the repeal of the Corn Laws in the 1840s, Britain was a net exporter of wheat.

The Common Agricultural Policy, by inducing increased production across the community, has reduced the potential for intracommunity trade and has made those countries with particular surpluses look to export markets as a means of disposing of their continuing excess output in the absence of any clear, politically acceptable policy for restructuring the industry.

There is one further significant reason that coupled with the CAP goes a long way to explaining the trend in European aggregate trade. That is the relative stagnation in overall consumption of food products. While output, particularly of cereals, has continued to rise, consumption overall has barely increased and for some products has fallen. Per capita consumption of cereals in total has fallen during the last decade, and while consumption of meat has increased, demand for beef, veal, sugar, and some meat products has grown only marginally.

Three factors account for this trend. First, population growth in Western Europe is now slower than in any other region of the world at only 0.2 percent per annum. The impetus to demand, which causes major problems for the developing countries, is absent.

Second, economic growth has slowed, though this is of relatively minor significance given the fact that consumer spending has continued to increase at a faster rate than the increase in food consumption. Food prices alone cannot be blamed for the level of demand because in recent years agricultural price increases in the community have on average been below the rate of inflation. Substantial food price reductions to the consumer—for instance, the cut in prices after the introduction of a special subsidy in the mid-1970s—do not always generate matching increases in demand.[2]

The third and probably most important factor is the saturation of demand as socially adequate as well as nutritionally sufficient levels of consumption of food products have been reached. The plateauing of food demand suggests that demand patterns will change as a result of consumer preference and relative prices rather than as a result of any further rises in disposable income.

CONSEQUENCES OF EEC ACTION FOR THE WORLD MARKET

The net result of low demand growth and rising production has been a gradual decline in imports and a shift in the pattern of imports in favor of those products, in particular substitute animal feeds, that are not subject to the import levies of the community.

Although U.S. supplies of soybeans under this heading have compensated for the loss of previous and potential grain markets, other producers have found their market share squeezed and now, with the community emerging as an exporter, face the prospect of also losing third markets to subsidized European exports. The CAP, as a result, has had a number of effects on the pattern and the structure of the world market.

European efforts to achieve price stability within the community and security of supply through import levies and enhanced production have had the effect of passing any instability within Europe onto the world market as well as insulating the community from world market pressures. Europe has imported or exported according to its immediate needs, and because the system of controls prevents external circumstances influencing either prices or production levels in the community, the world market—a relatively small volume of supply compared to total world output and consumption—has been forced to absorb fluctuations. The community is, of course, not unique in regarding the world market as a residual supplier or absorber of fluctuations in the domestic market, but the scale of EEC output and requirements in relation to world trade enhances the EEC's significance.

Within the overall picture there have been both winners and losers. Tim Josling (1979), analyzing the effect of European agriculture on the developing world, has shown that although European surpluses set back the process of agricultural development in many Third World countries, the depression of world prices can only assist the net importers who, at present at any rate, are numerous and more populous.

The net effect of the CAP, by generating relatively cheap supplies for the world market and by reducing prices, has been to discourage production of certain "export crops" elsewhere. Exporters in particular are discouraged by the combination of subsidies and the EEC's significant marketing strength. This adds to the disadvantages of developing-country producers who seek to penetrate the European market itself and who are confronted not with a quota system but with the use of the price mechanism. The nearest approach to a quota system has been in the sugar market. There the community has been prepared to guarantee purchases of sugar from affiliated underdeveloped countries that have become linked to the community. The result has been that "a favored group of nations sell a sizable part of their sugar output to the EEC at a high and stable price while the Community still protects its own producers and its processing industry" (Josling 1979).

Although the CAP, by protecting European agriculture and subsidizing exports, clearly distorts the world market and represents a misallocation of resources, it is possible to define both beneficiaries and net losers within the overall picture, not all of whom would gain from an abandonment of the policy.[3]

Subsidized exports represent, on balance, a net transfer of resources to developing countries, although only accidentally, and then in a far from optimal manner. Food aid recipients have clearly benefited, although food aid is unreliable and reflects the community's wish to dispose of its surpluses rather than any objective assessment of need or any long-term policy. Recipients of the heavily subsidized exports of community surpluses, such as consumers of butter in the Soviet Union, have also benefited, though not on any regular basis. The most consistent loss has been felt by those exporters of agricultural products who have lost both their European markets and now see their markets in third countries threatened by European exports. Australia and one or two South American countries are the most obvious members of this category. For some, the operation of the CAP has created new markets. Grain substitute suppliers, particularly Thailand, have benefited from the high prices of European grain and the inducements to livestock production that have combined to create a valuable, if somewhat insecure, market for manioc and other substitute feeds that can replace European-grown grain. The United States, having lost a significant proportion of its grain market in the community, has found a compensating trade in soybeans and other substitutes that has sustained a continuing increase in the volume and value of Atlantic trade.

These gains and losses have been at the root of the tension in relations between the European Economic Community and other trading nations about the nature and future of the CAP. The EEC dispute with the United States about agricultural protection has persisted, since the mid-1960s, in a series of disagreements and threats and a general atmosphere of acrimony. Though the wider common interests of the two sides have set limits on the conflict, the dispute has done nothing to improve transatlantic relations. The nature of the dispute has changed gradually as conflicts about access to third markets have been added to the long-standing conflict about U.S. access to the European market itself. The increased reliance of the U.S. farm sector on exports has sharpened U.S. criticism of the operation of the CAP.[4]

The general criticism of subsidized exports is less than totally justified, given the proliferation of export subsidy schemes in so many countries, but the threat posed by the extension of the CAP and the possible development of an aggressive export policy are now provoking sustained political hostility from the United States, Australia, and a variety of other exporting countries.

The General Agreement on Tariffs and Trade (GATT), established after World War II as one of the Bretton Woods institutions with the authority to supervise the liberalization of trade, has been the focus for sharp criticism of the community. Complaints, particularly in relation to the marketing of beef and sugar, are based on the grounds that export restitutions were giving the community an inequitable share of world markets. GATT regulations, however, have had little impact on EEC policy. During the establishment of the CAP, minor concessions were granted under pressure from the United States to make the policy compatible with the general principles of the GATT. Since then, however, the community has claimed that the CAP constituted an internal policy beyond GATT jurisdiction. The Tokyo Round of trade negotiations included an unspecific EEC commitment not to extend its export markets, and although this commitment prevented a full-scale challenge to the CAP at the time, it was sufficiently vague to permit the debate on a formal and expansionary export policy to continue. Since the mid-1960s the community has absorbed GATT criticism of the CAP but has rarely responded by changing its policies. In this period, the EEC has probably been more responsible than any other country for the failure of GATT to make any significant process in liberalizing agricultural trade.

Although neither agricultural trade liberalization nor formal commodity agreements have won endorsement from the EEC, there has been a significant degree of support from the community for bilateral deals on agricultural trade. The special status accorded to a limited number of sugar producers, noted above, is illustrative of this attitude. The Lome Convention and various Mediterranean agreements have given privileged access to the community for particular producers whose output does not threaten European production itself. None of the agreements implies any commitment to production ceilings or limitations.

There is evidence that the pursuit of bilateral arrangements and negotiations with particular countries and groups of countries with particular common interests are still the preferred approach to the international market. The commission's *Guidelines for European Agriculture* (8/44/81) on the mandate of May 30, 1980, published in June 1981, refers explicitly to "better organized world markets" and "cooperation agreements with other major exporters," and it is clear that those who now favor the development of an explicit EEC export policy would wish to use such agreements to control either prices or market shares to the advantage of those producers involved.

CONCLUSION

The emerging European agreement in budget contributions and resources gives a new lease on life to the Common Agricultural Policy. Even if some product support prices are constrained, the structure of agricultural policy—the variable levies and the export restrictions—will remain in place. So, too, will the inducement to individual farmers and agribusinesses generally to invest in further technological advance.

The CAP has already changed trading relationships in each of the world commodity markets concerned. For the traditional producers of beef, sugar, dairy products, and grain—the United States, Australia, Argentina, and Canada—as well as the potential producers of these and other products discouraged by their inability to match the community's financial resources, the CAP has become a major influence on patterns of trade and on the prosperity of the farm sectors of these producers. In these countries the CAP conditions agricultural decisionmaking and public policy.

The thrust of the above comments is that the CAP influence is now set to grow. In the areas of cereal substitutes and wine the possibilities of control are already apparent and already are live issues of transatlantic debate. Contentious though cereal and wine control will be, the major source of conflict in the coming years may lie elsewhere, as the community negotiates the admission to membership of two more strongly agricultural economies—Spain and Portugal. Once the barrier of available resources has been lifted that negotiation can begin in earnest.

In a static analysis, based simply on the figures for a single year, the effect of Spanish and Portuguese entry could be calculated and accommodated. Spain and Portugal would absorb a substantial proportion of the community's current cereal surplus, but they would add to the surpluses for wine, fruit, olive oil, and vegetables. The latter effect has been the main bone of contention with the other countries with substantial production of Mediterranean products, particularly France. The deficit of Spain and Portugal in the cereals market could reduce substantially the cost of export restitution for cereals, currently running at some $1.1 billion per year. But the relief might only be of short-term value, and it is in the dynamic, rather than the static, situation created by accession that the real problems have been identified.

In part, any analysis depends on the extent to which the community supports the production of wine, where substantial surpluses are a prospect in a community of twelve. Beyond that is the broader question of the development of consumption and production. If Spain and Portugal provide extensive new markets for existing output the saving would be considerable. The strong possibility, however, is that price incentives would induce a growth in output far beyond the likely consumption increase, thereby adding to European surpluses and European costs.

Under present arrangements, the Mediterranean products receive only a fraction of the total amount spent under the terms of the CAP. Only some 4 percent of guarantee payments go to producers of olive oil, 4 percent to fruit and vegetable producers, and 2 and 1 percent respectively to tobacco and wine. Spanish and Portuguese entry will bring into the community hundreds of thousands of small producers seeking to improve their present meager incomes through guaranteed prices and at the same time carrying with them the potential of modernization and consequent major increases in output.

Spain, with some 15 percent of its population directly employed in agriculture, and Portugal with 25 percent, would add two-thirds to the agricultural populations of the EEC. The desire for common facilities and support would be strong, although the ability of the Spanish and the Portuguese, with Gross National Product (GNP) both in absolute and per capita terms well below the European average, to contribute through the current financial structure to common funding would be very limited.

The willingness of the two potential new members to accept an unchanged CAP, and therefore no new extension of EEC provisions for Mediterranean producers, is made less likely by the fact that without change the Mediterranean countries will be major net losers. Both Spain and Portugal would suffer in resource and welfare terms from a system that required them to pay more for their imports (i.e., to pay community level rather than world level prices). The current bias in the CAP toward Northern European products such as cereals would result, if it were left unchanged, in both Spain and Portugal emerging as net contributors to the European budget, regardless of their relative poverty.

Accession may still be some years off, but the continuing process of negotiation faces the community with pressure for decisions on its future scale and shape. An extension of current common price regimes to the Spanish and Portuguese might well have the effect of stimulating production to the extent that short-term savings created by current deficiencies would become still greater costs as a result of new surpluses. Spanish agriculture is weak in both technological application and structure, but its potential is considerable.

A decision to establish a full-scale regime for Mediterranean products would add to costs because the community is already a net exporter and would be a substantial net exporter if Spain and Portugal were taken into account. A new regime designed to assist Spanish producers would cut across existing agreements with the associates of the community around the Mediterranean whose exports to the EEC would be badly hit by a common EEC policy and the variable levies, export restitutions, and other devices that might accompany it. Other third-country producers would also be adversely affected.

The record of the last twenty years shows that agricultural policymakers in the United States and elsewhere have failed to anticipate the effects of Europe's

Common Agricultural Policy and have found themselves unable to do more than respond after the event. Now, with the CAP on the verge of spawning a Common Export Policy (CEP), and with a major enlargement of the community's agricultural base imminent, the development of an anticipatory strategy based not on rhetoric but on analysis and the lessons of the past has never been more urgently required.

NOTES

1. Revenues are gathered from a number of customs duties and levies that together provide an average 40 percent of total income, with the balance made up by the VAT contribution.

2. Williamson (1981) concludes that because both population and demand are static, the community must place its emphasis for the future on a commercial export policy.

3. In his recent study, Koester (1982) estimated the welfare gains of a liberalization of the community's grain policy. The figures show clearly that the gains would accrue to the United States, Canada, and Australia with almost all the other countries in the world suffering a net loss of welfare as a result of increased prices and reduced food aid availabilities. On the first order effects (i.e., without taking into account the effect on other commodities) Koester estimates a net welfare loss of 0.4 percent of GNP for the developing countries.

4. See Butler (1983) for a full discussion of the Atlantic trade dispute.

REFERENCES

Butler, Nicholas. "The Ploughshares War." *Foreign Affairs* 62, no. 1 (Fall 1983): 105–122.

Commission of the European Communities. *Guidelines for European Agriculture*. Com (81) 300: 8144/81.

Commission of the European Communities. *Guidelines for European Agriculture*. Com: 10311/81.

Josling, Timothy. "The European Community's Agricultural Policy and the Interests of Developing Countries." *ODI Review* (1979).

Koester, Ulrich. *Policy Options for the Grain Economy of the European Community*. London: International Food Policy Research Institute, 1982.

Pearce, Joan. *The Common Agricultural Policy: Prospects for Change*. London: Royal Institute of International Affairs, 1982.

U.K. Ministry of Agriculture. *Annual Review of Agriculture 1984*. London: Ministry of Agriculture, 1985.

Williamson, David. "The Future Direction of the CAP." Paper presented to the Agricultural Economics Conference, 1981.

CAP UPDATE   *Fred H. Sanderson*

The trends described by Nicholas Butler have continued in the two years since he wrote. The European Economic Community's net grain surplus rose from 4 million metric tons in 1981/82 to a record 31 million tons in 1984/85. Weather conditions in that year were unusually favorable, but the U.S. Department of Agriculture estimate for 1985 still indicates a surplus of production over consumption of 19 million tons.

Sugar production declined from its 1981/82 peak but seems to be on the rise again; the surplus of production over consumption is running at about 2–3 million tons. Milk production rose from 96 million tons in 1981 to a record 104 million tons in 1983 and then declined slightly to a little more than 100 million tons, leaving a surplus over consumption of more than 15 million tons. Beef has been in surplus since 1980. The annual cost of managing, storing, and disposing of these surpluses has now reached 21 billion ECUs, of which about 8 billion is for export subsidies. Projections by the European Commission indicate further growth in the grain surplus to 32 million tons by 1990/91 and surpluses of sugar, milk, and beef continuing at approximately present levels.

Moreover, the costs of disposing of these surpluses will increase if world prices fall as a result of the lower dollar, lower market support prices, and increased export subsidies in the United States. The relief brought by the decision in March 1984 to increase the budget ceiling to customs receipts plus 1.4 percent of the value-added tax base has proved to be short-lived; the 1986 budget is already close to the new limit. As Butler points out, the accession of Spain and Portugal is more likely to increase than to reduce the drain of agricultural expenditures on the community's budget.

It would be wrong to conclude, however, that there are no limits to the growth of subsidized production. Although the Common Agricultural Policy is not likely to collapse—if that ever was the expectation of any well-informed person in the U.S. farm sector—it seems headed for major adaptations. The reasons are obvious. Although the community was a net importer of agricultural products, open-ended price supports did not involve large budgetary expenditures. The cost was borne by the European consumer in the form of higher prices and by the community's foreign suppliers. Now that the EEC has become the number two agricultural exporter in the world, and surplus disposal costs are soaring, the community has come to share some of the problems of number one, the United States. There is virtual agreement within the community that the costs of subsidizing surplus production must be restrained.

As in the United States, the debate is on how this is to be accomplished. One approach is to place a ceiling on total expenditures as well as on agricultural expenditures. The community has a statutory requirement that its budget must be balanced within the limits of the agreed contributions. New financial guidelines provide that the rate of growth in agricultural expenditures must be less than the rate of growth of budget receipts. As the March 1984 decision has shown, these rules will not prevent further substantial growth in agricultural expenditures.

The second approach is restraints on support prices. Although restraints have been popular with farmers and farm politicians, the community has, for some time, tried to follow a "prudent" price policy. Grain support prices have been allowed to fall, in real terms, by about 2 percent a year since 1977, following increases averaging 2.5 percent during the 1972–1977 boom. For all agricultural products, the rate of decline since 1975 has been 1.8 percent. Because of the continuing increase in agricultural productivity, these cuts have not been sufficient to slow down the growth of output. Economists have estimated that it would take a cut in real grain prices of 3–4 percent during a number of years and a total cut of 12–18 percent in milk support prices to stabilize production at approximately present levels.

As in the United States, farm groups and farm politicians have strongly resisted meaningful cuts in price supports. This has led a reluctant commission to pursue alternative approaches to limiting the budget exposure. One approach, involving assessments on producers for part of the cost of surplus disposal, has been in effect for some years in the dairy sector. It is now being proposed for grains as well, to replace the formula linking support prices to a "production threshold," which would have suggested an 18 percent price cut in 1986. As it turned out, the Council of Ministers of Agriculture ignored the formula, and the German minister even refused to agree to a 1.8 percent cut that was acceptable to his colleagues.

Production assessments may be more effective in producing marginal budget savings than price cuts of an equal magnitude, but they, too, are resisted by producers. The modest co-responsibility levies on milk producers did not result in a measurable slowdown of surplus production or budget outlays.

Direct controls on production were never viewed with favor by the European Commission. Production quotas are not only difficult to administer, they also seem incompatible with the concept of a common market in which the economically efficient have a chance to expand their production.

Until 1984, the only commodity subject to a quota system in the EEC was sugar. The sugar regime, in effect since 1968, combines quotas and assessments. It provides for an "A" quota, with high price supports, that approximates domestic demand, and a "B" quota, which is subject to a producer levy to finance export subsidies. Any excess is paid for at the world price. In principle, producers receive the export price, at the margin, and production should, therefore, be no different than it would be under a free market. However, substantial excess production has occurred because of the way the scheme has been administered. In some member countries, EEC sugar growers receive a blend price from the factory and thus do not see, and respond to, the marginal price received in the world market. Because production quotas are not freely negotiable (the purpose being to keep high-cost producers and their factories in business), there are low-cost producers whose marginal costs are less than world prices. Quotas may stimulate production above what it would have been without the quota system because of producers' desire to protect their quota against the risk that it will be reduced if not fulfilled every year (Sturgess 1984). Although the sugar policy has not required major net budget outlays, its cost to consumers has averaged 2.4 billion (1982) ECUs per year from 1975/76 to 1983/84 (Bureau of Agricultural Economics 1985).

Faced with a continuing growth of surplus milk production, the EEC introduced milk delivery quotas in March 1984. The total community quota was set at just under 100 million metric tons, which corresponds to 120 percent of domestic consumption but represents a 4 percent cut from the 1983 record. A penalty equal to 75 percent of the support price effectively prohibits deliveries in excess of the quotas.

The new system has been effective, thus far, in arresting the upward trend of milk deliveries to creameries. However, some milk is being diverted to processing on the farm and thus escapes control at the creamery. Widespread dissatisfaction among small producers as well as large, efficient producers caused numerous exceptions to be granted. As in the case of sugar, there is a tendency to leave the implementation to individual member countries. This may blunt the effectiveness of the policy.

Does the adoption of a quota system for milk mean that the European Economic Community is abandoning price policy as its principal tool and is turning to a general policy of production controls? It is too early to tell. The Commission of the European Communities has described the new milk marketing order as a temporary expedient. Its "green paper" calls for "diversification of the instruments of the CAP," but the emphasis is on special assistance to backward regions, structural improvements, conservation, selective income aids for marginal producers, and the creation of supplementary income and employment opportunities. The commission notes that quotas are often perceived as a "lesser evil" as compared with cuts in support prices but stresses the disadvantages: difficulties of negotiation and management; the freezing of production patterns, which inhibits productivity growth and regional specialization; the conferring of a "right to produce"; the adverse effects on domestic demand; and the risk of encouraging substitutes. It concludes that "quotas cannot be more than a palliative. The only sound approach in the medium and long term is to give market prices a greater role in guiding supply and demand" (Commission of the European Communities 1985, 23).

For cereals, the commission reaffirms its position that support prices should be reduced more sharply than in the past and should take account of productivity growth. Efficient producers could survive such cuts; marginal producers should be assisted by selective income supplements. If a co-responsibility levy is introduced to help finance surplus disposal, it should be differentiated according to size of farm. (The commission's subsequent proposal to the Council of Ministers would exempt small farmers.) Quotas and land diversion payments are not ruled out but considered undesirable and of questionable efficacy.

The "green paper" clearly favors greater market orientation. Its recommendation to shift the emphasis from price supports to other, less market-distorting, more precisely targeted, and less expensive forms of assistance to farmers reflects a growing consensus among European economists and others concerned about the economic as well as the budget costs of the CAP. The need to conserve resources for the new members in Southern Europe strengthens the case for revamping the system. These countries, which derive little benefit from present price policies favoring already prosperous farmers in Northwestern Europe, will undoubtedly press for structural assistance to increase their agricultural productivity and to facilitate adjustment.

Strong resistance to CAP reform was to be expected from beneficiaries of high price supports and their political leaders. Recognizing that the budget costs of the CAP must be brought under control, they are searching for ways of accomplishing this without reducing price supports. From their point of view, production controls and producer levies may seem preferable, especially if there is hope of transferring the costs to the European consumer. Attempts will be made to shift some of the costs of farm support to another account—for example, by diverting surplus grain and sugar beets to fuel alcohol, which is then subsidized by an exemption from gasoline taxes. The U.S. reader will have no trouble finding similarities with the situation in the United States.

Resistance to cuts in price supports has been successful in the case of milk and grains. In both cases, the commission has suffered setbacks in its drive for greater market orientation. Whether these setbacks will prove to be temporary or will prove to be harbingers of a wholesale conversion to supply management remains to be seen.

REFERENCES

Bureau of Agricultural Economics. *Agricultural Policies in the European Community*. Canberra, Australia: BAE, 1985.

Commission of the European Communities. *Perspectives for the Common Agricultural Policy*. Brussels: CEC, July 15, 1985.

Sturgess, Ian M. "The Common Agricultural Policy for Sugar: Possible Improvements and Lessons." In K. J. Thompson and R. M. Warren, eds. *Price and Market Policies in European Agriculture*. Newcastle: University of Newcastle upon Tyne, 1984.

5 Australia and New Zealand: The Role of Agriculture in a Closer Economic Relationship

Hyam Gold and Ramesh Thakur

Australia and New Zealand both have relied considerably on overseas trade for national development and prosperity. Yet despite shared isolation, attributes, and experiences, the two countries have not been close trading partners for most of this century. Their trade and economic ties are to be given a boost, however, as a result of a Closer Economic Relations agreement (CER) signed on March 28, 1983, designed to establish a comprehensive trans-Tasman free trade area by the mid-1990s.

Agriculture has occupied a central place in the overseas trade of Australia and New Zealand historically and continues to do so today. In 1980/81, food items alone made up 32 percent of Australia's total exports, particularly wheat, beef, and sugar, and 47 percent of New Zealand's exports, most notably dairy products, sheepmeats, and beef[1] (*Year Book Australia 1982*, 638–650; Department of Statistics, Wellington 1983, 29–30). But little of this agricultural trade flowed across the Tasman, despite the absence for the most part of any significant barriers to agricultural trade. In this period only 4 percent of New Zealand food exports went to Australia, generating 2 percent of New Zealand's total export returns, while a miniscule 1.5 percent of Australia's food exports went to New Zealand, bringing in less than .5 percent of Australia's total export income. Consequently, although the Australia–New Zealand free-trade CER agreement does have direct relevance for some specific areas of bilateral agricultural trade, its major significance for Australian and New Zealand agriculture lies in its prospects for enhancing cooperation in third-country markets.

This chapter is accordingly divided into two main parts. In the first section we sketch the background and nature of the CER agreement, and in the second section we address the particular role of agricultural policies in the context of CER.

THE ROAD TO CER

CER is in fact the second attempt in recent decades to introduce a broad free-

63

trade zone between the two countries. In the early 1960s, New Zealand proposed a free-trade arrangement in forest products with a view to securing market access in Australia for its burgeoning timber output. The Australian response was to suggest a broader trading deal, both to satisfy General Agreement on Trade and Tariffs (GATT) requirements and to widen export opportunities for Australian manufacturers in New Zealand. Agreement was reached in 1965 on a New Zealand Australia Free Trade Agreement (NAFTA). The central element of NAFTA was Schedule A, which provided for the elimination of duties on all goods listed in the schedule, many of which in fact were already being traded free of duty. NAFTA also contained a number of other arrangements intended to promote reciprocal trade. During the 1966–1982 NAFTA years there was a substantial increase in two-way trade. At the time of NAFTA's signing, Australia ranked third in New Zealand's external trade. Today, Australia is New Zealand's most important trading partner. Between 1964/65 and 1981/82, New Zealand exports to Australia increased from (NZ)$34 million to $1,029 million, and imports from Australia rose from $128 million to $1,365 million.

The extent to which NAFTA deserves credit for this increased trade flow is, however, debatable. Exchange rate fluctuations and unilateral tariff reductions by Australia have probably influenced these figures as much or more than trade concessions won under NAFTA. Moreover, NAFTA was from the start a partial, not a comprehensive, free-trade agreement. Its rules and procedures, and the domestic interests favored and protected by them, worked very effectively to prevent significant liberalization of trade. Consequently, NAFTA rapidly reached a plateau in furthering the development of bilateral trade. It became encumbered by excessive government involvement in the trading relationship; it proved unable to tackle nontariff barriers to trade such as export incentives; and it produced increasing resentment in Australia of New Zealand's continuing import licensing restrictions. By the 1970s, the painfully slow rate of progress in extending the range of duty-free goods coverage and in removing nonmarket trade inequities—e.g., quota controls, export incentives, and government purchasing preferences—was producing frustration in official circles on both sides and in business circles in Australia. The accumulating dissatisfactions with NAFTA gave rise to negotiations culminating in CER, and they help to explain the differences between the two. CER is designed to be more comprehensive in coverage; its procedures are meant to be automatic, gradual, and progressive. It tackles the question of direct controls on imports, e.g., licensing and tariff quotas, and it addresses itself to the indirect obstacles to trade liberalization.

The roots of CER negotiations stretch back at least to September 1977 when New Zealand Foreign Minister Brian Talboys bluntly stated that the time had come for New Zealand "to recognise that our relationship with Australia is more important to us than our links with any other country in the world" (*New Zealand Foreign Affairs Review* 1977, 28). Concerned that NAFTA squabbles might spill over and damage the broader bilateral relationship, Talboys undertook an unprecedented three-week tour of Australia in March–April 1978, visiting all the state capitals as well as Canberra. The highlight of the tour was a joint statement with Prime Minister Malcolm Fraser on March 19, the so-called Nareen Declaration, where the two agreed on the desirability of the further opening of bilateral trade.

The declaration was followed by a prolonged gestation period during which Australian manufacturers became ever more insistent in demanding opportunities for reciprocal market penetration. Increasing Australian industry murmurings of dissatisfaction were paralleled by misgivings voiced by Australia's senior politicians at the April 1979 NAFTA ministerial meeting in Wellington. Fraser's deputy, Doug Anthony, was very unhappy with the interminable NAFTA wrangles about petty issues, such as peas and beans, and he was concerned to combine and enhance the two countries' negotiating strength vis-à-vis the rest of the world. Preliminary studies were accordingly initiated in both countries to explore possible means of bringing about closer economic association, culminating in a meeting between Fraser and Prime Minister Robert Muldoon in Wellington on March 20–21, 1980.

At their Wellington meeting, the two prime ministers reviewed the full range of the bilateral relationship and noted that a habit of cooperation already existed with a common language, shared political beliefs, free movement of peoples, and closely linked financial, commercial, and service sectors. Nevertheless, Muldoon and Fraser believed that NAFTA "in its present form did not seem to be providing sufficient impetus to the kind of cooperation which would best serve the interests of the two countries in the changing international economic environment." The time was considered ripe to take the special relationship a step further. The joint communiqué accordingly included an annex setting out the framework for further detailed exploration and examination of possible arrangements for CER (*New Zealand Foreign Affairs Review* 1980, 15–18).

However, the progress of negotiations between the prime ministers at their meeting in 1980 and the eventual signing of the CER accords were not smooth. One troublesome task was to isolate discussions about CER from growing irritations in other aspects of the bilateral relationship. In this respect, 1981 proved a particularly difficult time as relations grew strained regarding a whole range of items, from the unilateral Australian decision to impose passport controls across the Tasman to public bickering between the two prime ministers at the Commonwealth Heads of Government Meeting in Melbourne. A second vital task was to keep the CER proposals well away from the arena of electoral politics and party competition. A major effort was therefore undertaken by both governments to win bipartisan support for CER goals, by such means as high-level official briefings for opposition spokesmen (a very unusual departure from previous practice in New Zealand), sponsorship of joint party parliamentary study tour groups, and extensive lobbying of legislators by diplomatic delegations in the respective capitals. Even so, the final consummation of the CER negotiations was considerably delayed by the approach of national elections in New Zealand in late 1981 and on-again, off-again anticipations of early federal elections in Australia from late 1982 until their eventual proclamation in February 1983. Both sets of elections inevitably imposed a temporary freeze on further development of all potentially controversial political initiatives, including CER. The efforts of officials to mobilize bipartisan support for CER, however, and their concern to remove the issue from the electoral arena were amply vindicated when the new Labor cabinet in Australia agreed to the draft CER treaty at its very first meeting in March 1983.

In its essentials, the agreement calls for a progressive and automatic elimination of bilateral tariffs, quantitative import restrictions, and export subsidies and incentives. Goods with tariffs up to 5 percent became duty-free from January 1, 1983; graduated annual tariff cuts will be made on other goods to produce duty-free treatment within one to five years. Quantitative import restrictions in New Zealand are to be eliminated through exclusive Australian licenses. For most goods an initial access level of (NZ) $400,000 will increase at 15 percent yearly in real terms up to $1 million, and at 10 percent thereafter until 1995 when all remaining restrictions will be removed. Performance-based export incentives were removed in 1983 in Australia and will be eliminated between 1985 and 1987 in New Zealand. Some products, e.g., wine and carpets, are subject to a modified timetable for liberalization, and final arrangements for other products, e.g., motor vehicles and steel, are still to be determined. There are also procedures for a general review of the agreement in 1988; for antidumping or countervailing action in the case of material injury inflicted by dumped or subsidized imports; and for other safeguards against severe material injury during the transition period.

The central purpose of the new agreement is thus the establishment of a full free-trade area linking the two countries according to an agreed timetable, on a mutually beneficial basis. The liberalization of trade in turn is designed to generate new trading opportunities, enhance economies of scale, and assist moves toward a more rational and efficient use of resources in both countries. Realization of the objective of free trade is predicated on four major principles. First, the new agreement is comprehensive in scope: It applies to all agricultural and industrial goods. Second, the process of introducing free trade will be gradual and progressive in order to give industries time to adjust to the new regime. The third principle is that of automaticity. Deferments from the liberalization process are listed in the agreement, but these are industry-specific, time-bound, and limited; no new item can be added to the list. The emphasis is not on long and complicated exemptions, but on establishing a trading relationship characterized by predictability in tariff reduction and access-generating mechanisms, with administrative management and review procedures kept to a minimum. Finally, the CER agreement endorses the principle of fair competition between the two countries, but it suggests that many of their current differences in areas such as wages and fiscal measures may balance out in total effect and therefore not need deliberate harmonization in the foreseeable future.

MOTIVES FOR AND OBSTACLES TO CER

The impetus for CER in both Australia and New Zealand came from critically placed groups and individuals who pressed during the late 1970s for liberalization of regional trade. In New Zealand these groups comprised a few leading politicians, high-ranking bureaucrats, and certain business elements; all were motivated largely by their shared desire to redirect the ailing domestic economy from import-substitution to export-led economic growth. Protective tariffs and license controls have proven useful in shielding New Zealand industry through infancy and youth, but were regarded increasingly as an inappropriate defense against senescence. On the Australian side, manufacturers had long called for greater access to New Zealand markets to match the trade concessions New Zealand exporters enjoyed under NAFTA, and at the governmental level Deputy Prime Minister John Douglas Anthony publicly emphasized the need for the two countries to combine economically in the face of a bloc-oriented external world. By itself, however, this latter consideration does not explain why Australia chose to tie itself to New Zealand, rather than, for example, to the larger and more dynamic Association of Southeast Asian Nations (ASEAN) economies to its immediate north. Other considerations that appear to have been important include the perceived need to deal comprehensively with problems of economic interdependence that had developed with increased trade, capital, and labor flows under NAFTA; joint security interests with New Zealand that might be better pursued were the two countries more closely linked economically; and considerations of cultural and political affinity.

Underlying the increased commitment of groups in both countries to further closer economic ties were some significant changes in the objective bases for the relationship itself. First, the complementarity of the two economies appears to have increased in recent years, while their direct competitiveness has lessened somewhat. High wage rates in Australia in the late 1970s led manufacturers to emphasize more capital-intensive forms of production; labor-intensive products were increasingly discarded or made offshore in lower wage countries like New Zealand. Although economic logic rationalization is desired because of competition, from a political point of view complementarities make a free-trade agreement more feasible. The growing disparity in income levels of the two societies since the mid-1970s has also led their policymakers to give careful attention to the bilateral relationship and its impact on New Zealand's economic performance, both in order to bolster New Zealand's ability to contribute effectively to joint security concerns in the South Pacific and to stem large labor flows across the Tasman. The post-Vietnam reduction of U.S. forces in the Pacific encouraged greater concentration on how the two societies could best order their relations so as to promote their shared security interests in the region. Trans-Tasman migration, in the meantime, became a political problem in both countries. In the three years from 1978 to 1981, the net outflow of people from New Zealand to Australia averaged almost 30,000 annually. Although Australians made up only 32 percent of immigrants to New Zealand in this period, 56 per cent of New Zealand emigrants went to Australia. The Australian government came under some pressure to impose restrictions on the right of free entry, and the New Zealand government was attacked in the 1981 elections for a record of mismanagement that had seen thousands of people lose hope in their country's future and seek their fortunes across the sea.

Leadership motivations and parametric changes in the Australia-New Zealand relationship were essential elements in overcoming the substantial sectional and institutional hurdles that stood in the way of a bilateral free-trade agreement. Previous attempts to broaden the NAFTA trading regime had failed repeatedly in the face of opposition from domestic economic interests threatened by trade liberalization. The key to the success of the more radical CER proposals lies both in the care and speed with which the respective governments moved to head off or weaken opposition from (dis)affected sectors and in redoubled determination to stand firm in the end against remaining obdurate opponents of trade expansion. Government success in disarming sectional opposition was particularly important in New Zealand. For with its smaller, weaker and more vulnerable economy, New Zealand has many more manufacturers, labor unions, and even some primary producers apprehensive about the effects of bilateral trade expansion. They are fearful of what they see as New Zealand's competitive disadvantages resulting from its smaller size and higher infrastructural costs in areas such as fuel, freight, and taxation. In courting these groups the New Zealand government adopted a wide range of tactics, ranging from coopting opposition leaders into the policymaking process to undermining their unity of opposition by playing on existing group divisions or by creating new ones (e.g., by sponsoring pro-CER business groups within the manufacturing sector). The government also made much of the gradualism of the CER proposals, with full free trade being postponed a decade or more into the future (well beyond the time horizon of many of its opponents), and the government successfully bought off further opposition by offering existing commercial interests special privileges during the transition phase. In Australia, too, there was vocal opposition to CER from certain business, labor, and farming interests, but with the very significant exception of certain farming interests, sectional opposition to CER in Australia was distinctly less ferocious than that encountered in New Zealand.

The negotiating partners had to surmount important institutional obstacles as well as tackle domestic economic interests opposed to a more open trading relationship. In Australia's federal system the states retain many powers to regulate agriculture, industry, and commerce within their borders. Bringing the state governments into line with CER added greatly to the complexity of the negotiations and involved extensive intergovernmental consultations, particularly between the federal and state governments in Australia but also between the latter and New Zealand. It would appear that state government cooperation with the CER exercise has largely been secured, at least in principle.

A second institutional obstacle has been the existing trade preference agreements that both Australia and New Zealand have negotiated with neighboring island-states in the South Pacific. Australia has a bilateral trade agreement with Papua–New Guinea; both New Zealand and Australia, since 1980, grant broad trade preferences to South Pacific island exporters; and New Zealand also allows the Cook Islands and Niue a special place in the domestic market under earlier arrangements. Both Australia and New Zealand were anxious that in introducing mutual free trade they should not be seen as cutting across the vital trading lifelines of these Pacific island-countries. Special consultations were held with the governments of these island-states to allay their suspicions and to deal with the criticisms they have of the CER proposals. Three years after the actual commencement of CER, its eventual economic and political spillover effects in Oceania remain uncertain.

POLITICAL IMPLICATIONS OF CER

The importance of the CER free-trade agreement for the two countries is self-evident. With goods being traded freely as well as the already existing free movement of capital and labor, Australia and New Zealand are to become a single unified market of 18 million people. Moreover, as the negotiating partners have recognized, CER will provide considerable impetus for additional measures of bilateral economic integration and policy coordination in the near future. These will impose further constraints on national autonomy in regulating such areas as transport, company law, foreign investment, and external tariff structures. The eventual need for at least shared common judicial institutions to oversee joint regulation of these areas is foreseen already by some leading politicians, although the CER agreement itself contains no provisions of this kind.

CER may also have significant effects on domestic political relations, especially on center/periphery and federal/state ties. In New Zealand, inter-island integrative ties could be undermined by increased east/west economic links across the Tasman. Thus, in a speech to the South Island Promotion Association in Christchurch, Minister of Trade and Industry Hugh Templeton acknowledged that CER confronted southern industry with a challenge. If its Auckland–North Island market was undercut by Australian industry under CER, then southern industry too would have to move aggressively into the larger and more profitable Australian market. The theme was picked up by other speakers at the conference (*Otago Daily Times* 1983). Within Australia, the political effects of CER may be felt in federal/state relations, particularly in the way CER may impinge on the powers of the states to regulate agriculture, commerce, and industry within their borders.

CER is a bilateral trade agreement. But political and economic reality is rarely bilateral, and CER, too, will have consequences for countries other than the two signatories. Major questions arise concerning the implications of CER for the island-states of the South Pacific. One possible development, given the threat CER poses to their existing trade patterns and privileges, is that the island-states may jointly wish to develop some kind of common associate membership or special form of trade arrangement with the evolving trans-Tasman economic unit. Moreover, CER will affect not just how Australia and New Zealand stand with the South Pacific states, but also their relations with countries and trading blocs elsewhere.

THE AGRICULTURAL DIMENSIONS OF CER

As noted above, only very small proportions of Australia's and New Zealand's agricultural exports are traded across the Tasman, even though trade in manufactured goods has expanded dramatically. This has not always been the case. In the very early days of European colonization, New Zealand's infant farming industry exported basic food items like potatoes, grain, butter, and cheese to the Australian market. With the development of the wool trade, however, Britain became New Zealand's principal export market, absorbing 70 percent of New Zealand's exports by 1860. The introduction of refrigerated ships in 1882 made it possible to diversify exports of farm products, but also underwrote the development of New Zealand's economy as a complement to Britain's. Initial

Table 5.1
New Zealand's External Trade, 1920–1982

YEAR	EXPORTS (%)				IMPORTS (%)			
	Britain	Australia	Japan	USA	Britain	Australia	Japan	USA
1920	74	5	..	16	48	17	..	18
1930	80	3	..	5	47	8	..	18
1940	88	3	..	4	47	16	..	12
1950	66	3	..	10	60	12	..	21
1960	53	4	..	13	43	18	..	29
(June year)								
1970	36	8	10	16	30	21	8	13
1975	22	12	12	12	19	20	14	13
1980	14	12	13	14	15	19	13	14
1981	13	14	13	13	11	19	15	18
1982	14	15	13	14	9	20	17	16

Source: New Zealand Official Yearbook 1983, 597

rapid expansion took place in exports of frozen mutton and lamb, with dairy produce export expanding greatly only in the twentieth century. Although dependence on the British market continued in the post-1945 years, there has been a conscious effort at market diversification since the 1960s, an effort that was given a special boost with Britain's membership in the European Economic Community (EEC) in 1973 (Table 5.1). The range of diversification is reflected in the growth of beef exports to the United States, cheese and forest products to Japan, lamb exports to the Middle East, Canada and the United States, and wool exports to the USSR. Special terms of access to the European Economic Community were negotiated for New Zealand lamb and butter. With the introduction of a common EEC marketing regime for sheepmeats in 1980, New Zealand entered into a voluntary restraint agreement whereby sheepmeat exports to the EEC were limited to an annual quota in return for a reduction in the community's import tariff. A special arrangement for butter marked an acknowledgment of New Zealand's dependence on access to the British market. The quota of New Zealand butter permitted for supply to the British market has nevertheless been slowly but steadily reduced, from 94,000 tons in 1981 to 87,000 tons in 1983.

The strategy by which New Zealand has negotiated its annual quotas with the EEC has been one of quiet diplomacy, a marked contrast to the tougher public postures of Australian politicians. In a sense New Zealand has carefully avoided compromising its case by aligning itself with its stronger economic neighbor, and has reaped the rewards of an image of "reasonableness" in appealing as a small, weak state to the "powerful" community (Lodge 1982, 217–218; Ross 1981, 88). In consequence, however, New Zealand faces a dilemma. Diversification requires a pursuit of reliable alternative markets. Success in the pursuit, however, would divert exports from a safe outlet to less dependable ones and reduce the case for special treatment, thereby lowering the threshold of safety for New Zealand agricultural exports.

For Australia as well as New Zealand, the problem is not one of shortages in agricultural production for domestic consumption. Rather, both countries are confronted with the need to find overseas markets for surplus dairy and meat products or face severe disruptions to their national economies. The central thrust of the CER negotiations therefore involved the manufacturing sectors, not agriculture. CER was of primary interest to agriculturists in its potential for helping to rationalize third-country marketing of meat, wool, and dairy products without mutually detrimental price-cutting competition. The farmer organizations on both sides were much keener to explore the export potential of the large and expanding Asian, Pacific, and Middle Eastern markets than to invade each other's relatively small domestic market. Beyond this, the two agricultural communities recognized a common interest in dismantling protective barriers in the manufacturing sector that imposed significant additional costs on farming.

Agricultural input into the CER negotiations was shaped by six additional considerations. First, most trans-Tasman trade in agricultural commodities was already free of restrictions. Relatively few sectors, most notably dairy and vegetable producers in Australia and wine, wheat, and tomato growers in New Zealand, would be directly affected by freer trade. If necessary, special arrangements could be negotiated to ease liberalization of trade in these areas. Second, the very fact that Australia and New Zealand produce many similar products for sale on third markets gives them scope for mutually advantageous cooperation in these markets, particularly when dealing with large national buying organizations. Third, the production, pricing, processing, transport, and marketing of primary commodities such as meat, wool, and dairy produce are controlled, or at least strongly influenced, in both countries by statutory producer boards organized very largely along parallel lines. These provide the mechanisms for domestic stabilization and a significant measure of export control and could therefore be used in a new agreement for harmonizing and aligning international policies. Fourth, gains from freer bilateral trade in agriculture promised not to be one-sided. Extra opportunities for Australian wheat and fruit growers would be counterbalanced by greater access to Australia for New Zealand vegetable and horticulture producers. Fifth, even in these areas many of the concerns of competitive producers in both countries were very similar, most particularly the desire to include safeguards against dumping in any wider trading agreement and to eliminate unfair advantages arising from government subsidies across the Tasman. Finally, in the actual conduct of the CER negotiations, the Australian officials differed from their New Zealand counterparts in two important respects: They lacked the same close working relationship with industry leaders, and they were constrained by the federal division of powers.

Bearing these factors in mind, representatives of the two farming communities held formal meetings with each other to work out a strategy vis-à-vis the CER discussions. They argued for structures for promoting consultation, cooperation, and coordination in third markets, a reasonable time span to allow disruption-free adjustment to freer bilateral trading arrangements, protections against fluctuations in production patterns, and elimination of advantages accruing from government assistance schemes. Their aims were in striking contrast with those of EEC agriculturists in that the representatives sought a maximization of unsubsidized farm exports to world markets as well as reasonable prices for domestic consumers.

As regards expanding bilateral trade, the most sensitive primary commodities for the two countries were the export of New Zealand dairy products and processed vegetables to Australia and the export of Australian wheat, wine, fruit, and tomatoes to New Zealand. In particular, the National Farmers' Federation in Australia sought to ensure that New Zealand did not exercise its potential to disrupt Australia's dairy marketing arrangements (Whitelaw 1981, 83). Australians feared that if New Zealand were to lose European access for its dairy produce, then either the Australian market would be flooded or else pressure would be put on common third markets. The president of the Federated

Farmers of New Zealand replied that significant quantities of butter would continue to be sold to Europe, that reduction in sales to Europe would not place any excess on the Australian market, but that New Zealand was interested in producer boards' agreements providing mutual access to shares in any market growth from current levels of consumption (Wright 1981, 78).

The final CER agreement reflects the outward-looking perspectives of both agricultural sectors. Article 10(4) explicitly calls for cooperation between the two countries' marketing authorities in regard to trade in third-country markets. Although the CER agreement envisages free trade in all commodities eventually, most of its specific references to agriculture are incorporated in the form of special provisions, partial exemptions, or temporary modications designed to deal with the sensitive commodities identified above.

Tariff reduction and quantitative access formulas for increasing trans-Tasman trade are contained in Articles 4 and 5 of the agreement. But Articles 6 and 10(1) restrict their scope in certain agricultural goods by attaching qualifications in various annexes to the agreement. Thus, Annex C Part II endorses a modified agreement, concluded by the two wine industries themselves in 1982, to postpone the onset of CER tariff reductions on wine imports from 1983 to mid-1986, and to limit New Zealand imports of cheaper grade Australian wine well into the 1990s. At the same time, the agreement also incorporates general CER goals in aiming to increase wine consumption in both countries, maximize shares in each other's market, and rationalize production on the basis of comparative advantage. Similarly, clause 8 of Annex E takes note of a memorandum of understanding between the two dairy industries signed on April 13, 1982, and included as Attachment II of the annex. In this memorandum, the dairy industries agreed to form a Joint Dairy Industry Consultative Committee (JICC), with government officials invited as observers, to review production and trade trends, to protect established price structures in each other's domestic markets, and so sustain the confidence of the industries in both countries. Additionally, the two industries agreed to abolish existing limits on Australian imports of New Zealand cheddar cheese and to relate future sales of New Zealand cheese to overall growth trends in the Australian market, but to prohibit trade in the critical areas of fluid milk and cream without prior consultation in the JICC.

Annex E also contains significant provisions regarding access to the New Zealand market for Australian wheat, grapes, citrus, and tropical fruits. Clause 1 obligates the New Zealand Wheat Board to regard Australia as the preferred source for importing wheat to meet domestic shortfalls, thereby formalizing established practice. Under clauses 3 and 4, New Zealand agrees to treat Australian citrus fruits and fresh grapes on a par with domestic production and not to discriminate in the future against imports of Australian pineapples and bananas. Australia in turn recognizes New Zealand's existing commitments in these areas to South Pacific island-states.

In addition to these tariff reductions and quantitative access modifications, Australia and New Zealand also agreed to further variations in their CER agreement to placate the grievances of particular agricultural sectors. For example, although Article 9 requires the two to phase out government export subsidies and tax incentives on trans-Tasman trade by 1987, the New Zealand government agreed, in the context of the CER negotiations, to accelerate their removal before that date on processed corn and potatoes, peas and beans, and joint-venture-caught fish. Similarly, the New Zealand government in 1982 also announced the removal of special concessional loans and grants to dairying and vegetable processors.

Finally, on a few sore agricultural issues, interindustry or intergovernmental agreements could not be reached by the time the CER trade agreement was signed in March 1983. The two governments did commit themselves, however, to further discussions to settle future trade in tobacco and canned fruits and the liberalization of imports of Australian tomatoes and wheat flour to New Zealand. Progress on most of these matters has now been made.

Beyond these special arrangements and exceptions, trade in agricultural commodities between Australia and New Zealand is subject to the standard CER tariff phasing and access formulas. It remains to be seen whether the logic of closer economic cooperation will generate calls for the standardization of agricultural support and price and income stabilization schemes in Australia and New Zealand.

CONCLUSION

This study is primarily an account of the development of government policies aimed at reforming and consolidating the economic relationship between Australia and New Zealand, with particular reference to the agricultural dimension of that relationship. The two countries began the twentieth century as competing suppliers to Britain with similar, protectionist economies that offered little incentive for bilateral trade. As trans-Tasman trade increased in due course, New Zealand became anxious at the pronounced trade imbalance in Australia's favor. The NAFTA agreement of 1965 oversaw both an expansion of bilateral trade and a reduction of the imbalance in Australia's favor from 4:1 in 1965–1966 to 1.3:1 in 1982.

When NAFTA was seen as having exhausted its potential, however, moves to replace it with a more open economic framework were begun. NAFTA created both negative and positive forces pushing the two countries toward CER. On the negative side, difficulties inherent in NAFTA produced sufficient dissatisfaction to make the parties want a change in the existing state of affairs. On the positive side, the NAFTA experience was fruitful enough to convince key politicians, officials, and business leaders on both sides that still closer trading and economic ties would be in their sectional or national interests—hence, the pressures that developed for the replacement of NAFTA by CER. Yet the substantial political and institutional obstacles that stood in the path of the CER negotiations and the means by which they were overcome should not be overlooked. The timing of events also proved important, with the current global recession taking full hold in Australia only in the second half of 1982 when tentative agreement on all but a few details of CER had already been achieved.

The main features of CER—comprehensive scope, automatic procedures, and elimination of direct controls and indirect obstacles to free trade—cannot be understood other than in the light of NAFTA's history. CER aims to decentralize trade decisions to nonpolitical levels, to cleanse them of political interference, and to free channels of bilateral communication for other purposes. Thus, CER provides the framework for a full free-trade area—the responsibility for actual implementation is left to the private sector. CER's primary promise for Australian and New Zealand farmers may indeed be the impetus it affords for cooperation in world markets. Even so, its direct implications for trans-Tasman agricultural trade are not negligible, particularly for certain sensitive commodities, and require careful and prolonged attention in the successful conclusion of this far-reaching free-trade agreement.

NOTES

1. Including wool and other textile fibers, agricultural, pastoral, and marine products together accounted for 44 percent of Australia's exports and 65 percent of New Zealand's exports in 1980/81.

REFERENCES

Department of Statistics, Wellington. *Report and Analysis of External Trade Year Ended June 1981*. Wellington, New Zealand: Department of Statistics, 1983.

Lodge, J. *The European Community and New Zealand*. London: Frances Pinter, 1982.

New Zealand Foreign Affairs Review (July-September 1977).

New Zealand Foreign Affairs Review (January-March 1980).

Otago Daily Times, May 2, 1983.

Ross, B. J. "Agriculture's Role in a Closer Australia–New Zealand Economic Relationship." In R. Burnett and A. A. Burnett, eds. *Australia–New Zealand Economic Relations: Issues for the 1980s*. Canberra, Australia: ANU Press, 1981, pp. 85–91.

Whitelaw, J. "Agricultural Trade Relations." In Burnett and Burnett, *Australia–New Zealand Economic Relations*, pp. 80–84.

Wright, A. F. "Agriculture's Role in the Australia–New Zealand Relationship." In Burnett and Burnett, *Australia–New Zealand Economic Relations*, pp. 75–79.

Bureau of Statistics, *Year Book Australia 1982*. Canberra, Australia: Australian Bureau of Statistics, 1983.

6 Soviet Agricultural Policy in the 1980s

Anton F. Malish

The past thirty years have seen the USSR shift from its position as a modest grain exporter of some 5 or so million tons per year to a position, in the early 1980s, as an importer of some 30–45 million tons of grain.[1] First Secretary Nikita Khrushchev in addressing a Soviet Communist party congress once promised that the Soviets would "occupy such a position in the international grain market that the imperialist gentlemen will feel how our agriculture is expanding" and that they would produce 16 million tons of meat by 1965. Instead, Soviet agriculture followed a different course, and the famed 16-million-ton meat goal was not met until 1983.

During the early 1960s, the Soviet leadership decided that crop failures could no longer be met by drastic rationing. Thus, in 1963, the USSR first resorted to massive imports of food grains, primarily from capitalist countries. Although the leadership averted a crisis at food stores and bakeries, they sacrificed some 40 percent of their hog inventories. By then, Khrushchev's agricultural policies were in such disrepute that they formed the basis for his departure in 1964.

During the early 1960s, the USSR was, in fact, just entering its present stage where the pent-up forces for a higher standard of living could no longer be ignored. These forces show themselves in a demand for improved diets, particularly for higher quality food items such as animal products, vegetables, and fruits. In the 1960s, the leadership of the USSR was, in effect, challenged by its own "revolution of rising expectations" in which it could not "run an industrial society on a diet of pickled cucumbers and black bread" (Laird and Crowley 1965, 122).

The validity of this dictum was evident in the events following Khrushchev's 1962 increase in retail prices of meat and butter of some 25–30 percent. This, coupled with an increase in factory production norms, led to a demonstration in the city of Novocherkassk, which went so far that Red Army troops were called out, and seventy to eighty people were killed (Gidwitz 1982). Since then, no Soviet leader has risked a direct price increase on meat or butter in state stores.

The March 1965 Plenum of the Communist party set the basic principles for agricultural policy during the Brezhnev era. Although General Secretary Leonid Brezhnev's speech steered clear of consumption issues, it stressed strengthening grain production as a "very important condition" to developing a successful livestock sector. Record grain imports—the Western countries are the only sources of grain in the quantities needed—were still related to poor harvests as in 1972, 1975, and 1981, but the long-term goal of increasing meat consumption, and the realization that such a goal could never be met if animal inventories were periodically liquidated, raised Soviet demand for feed grains. By the mid-1970s, the Soviets came to rely increasingly on the world grain market, and particularly on the United States. Indeed, the United States became the guarantor of Soviet livestock herds in the 1975 Long-term (Grain) Agreement (LTA) whose requirements were considered so mutually beneficial that the original agreement was in effect for seven years before being replaced by an even stronger commitment to supply wheat and corn to the Soviets through 1988. Nonetheless, the smoldering consumer discontent about food supplies and the reliance on imported grain were weaknesses with strategic implications. In Eastern Europe, for example, worker discontent and food issues were often closely related, and in Poland the Solidarity trade union owed its start to a poorly disguised attempt to raise meat prices by transferring additional products to "commercial stores" where they would be sold for more than the prices prevailing in regular stores.

In January 1980, the United States tried to exploit this weakness with a partial embargo on agricultural commodities (except for the 8 million tons of wheat and corn specified in the LTA) destined for the Soviet feed/livestock economy. The Soviets reacted by searching the world for alternative supplies of grain, securing these supplies with long-term agreements, and increasing meat imports. Domestically, they began to formulate a Food Program to reduce their vulnerability. To be in effect through the remainder of the decade, the Food Program forms the basis of today's Soviet agricultural policy.

The Food Program is intended to reduce Soviet dependence on imported agricultural commodities from the West by increasing the efficiency of Soviet agriculture. To some extent, that objective will almost certainly involve increased imports of agricultural technology, an area where the United States is frequently considered the world leader. These countercurrents, already in evidence, could become major issues in U.S.-USSR relations. Will the Soviets risk an increased dependence on the United States for agricultural technology, and will the United States become the guarantor of Soviet agricultural technology imports as it was with respect to imports of wheat and corn?

THE SOVIET FOOD PROGRAM

The Food Program was first introduced under that rubric at the October 1980

Plenum of the Central Committee of the Communist party. Although often thought of as a Brezhnev policy, succeeding leaders have attached themselves to it in dramatically public ways. It was cited in General Secretary Yuri Andropov's speech celebrating the sixtieth anniversary of the USSR, and General Secretary Konstantin Chernenko opened a March 1984 national conference on the agro-industrial complex by stating:

> The Food Program drafted by the party is being implemented stage by stage. But this is only the beginning. . . . Today we are faced with the task of attaining higher levels in production of grain and industrial crops, and in supplying food products to the people, first and foremost meat, milk, fruit, and vegetables.

Unless the leadership were committed to the program's success, it is hard to believe that they would continue to lavish such public attention on the program.

New Organizations for Old Ideas

On May 24, 1982, after a year and a half in the discussion and planning stage, the Central Committee of the Communist party approved a Food Program to be in place until 1990. Its aim is to significantly increase per capita consumption of most high-quality food products, although even in 1990, supplies of meat, dairy, and fruits would still fall short of the consumption norms established by the Soviet Institute of Nutrition (Table 6.1).

Table 6.1
USSR: Rational Consumption Norms for and per Capita
Consumption of Basic Food Products, 1982 and 1990

ITEM	RATIONAL PER CAPITA CONSUMPTION NORMS ISSUED IN 1981[1]	PER CAPITA CONSUMPTION IN 1982[2]	PLANNED CONSUMPTION PER CAPITA IN 1990[3]
	(kilograms)		
Meat and meat products	78	57	70
Fish products	18.2	18.4	19
Milk and milk products	405	295	330–340
Eggs (in units)	292	249	260–266
Sugar	40	44.5	45.5
Vegetable oils	9.1	9.3	13.2
Vegetables and melons	130	101	126–135
Fruits and berries	91	42	66–70
Potatoes	110	110	110
Bread products	115	137	135

[1] Planovoye khozyaistvo, No. 10 (1981):17.

[2] SSSR v tsifrakh (USSR in Figures), 1982:197.

[3] Pravda, May 27, 1982:1.

In many ways an evolution of General Secretary Brezhnev's 1965 statements on the agricultural sector, the Food Program envisages an integrated agro-industrial complex that coordinates the planning, financing, and management of the agricultural sector, those industries serving it, and the downstream production and marketing facilities. Primarily related to improving management techniques and "intensifying agriculture" rather than earmarking significant new investment for it, the program views the agricultural solution as a vertical one, embracing all activities from farm to store.

At the highest level of the USSR government, the Soviets created a Commission for the Agro-Industrial Complex. The creation of a high-level commission is a typically Soviet measure to highlight a program and ensure top management attention. Thus, it became one of seven such commissions, headed by deputy chairmen of the Council of Ministers, with responsibilities for overseeing the Soviet government's highest priority projects. Similar commissions oversee the development of Siberian gas and oil and deal with foreign economic questions. Among the commission's more successful companions, it seems at least superficially similar to the Military-Industrial Commission that coordinates the defense and civilian economies in fulfillment of the USSR's defense plan.

During 1983, Soviet press reports indicated the Commission for the Agro-Industrial Complex met frequently, often at two-week intervals. The commission considered a variety of questions plaguing Soviet agriculture, including the problems associated with utilization and maintenance of farm equipment, agricultural organization, the expansion of collective contract teams, and what would appear to be relatively minor matters at rayon and oblast levels. Other matters under the commission's concern pointed up its strategic position in agro-industrial organization. Two of its sessions included reports on the increasing output of feed protein via microbiological synthesis, and two others involved the use of automated control systems (including microprocessor technology) in the agro-industrial complex.

At lower levels, the Soviets have been creating oblast and republic agro-industrial associations to overcome the bureaucratic barriers that compartmentalize agricultural management. Some 3,000 similar associations, called RAPOs in the Russian acronym, have been created at the rayon (i.e., county) level. Recent commentary has shifted away from addressing the creation of the RAPOs to defining their responsibility for arranging intersectoral ties as well as enumerating on their rights and opportunities in undertaking new management initiatives. Apparently, some RAPOs have been more cautious—an understandable trait in the USSR—than the central planners would have liked.

On the state and collective farms themselves, the Soviets are establishing "collective contracting teams," groups of workers who would be assigned tracts of land, equipment, inputs, and so on, with wages paid in the form of an advance against the harvest. Formerly, workers were paid on a piece rate basis—a tractor operator on the basis of area plowed, for example—so that few individuals had any financial interest in the final outcome. Some 53,000 such teams, perhaps one-third of the total, have been set up in animal husbandry, a sector that recorded numerous successes in Soviet agriculture in 1983. But, overall, the expansion of the team concept may be expanding more slowly than anticipated. An *Izvestiya* article on November 19, 1983, showed only 6 percent of all state and collective farm workers under the contract system.

As in the past when food supplies became short, the Food Program emphasizes the private plots and subsidiary holdings of enterprises as a quick way to increase production. Although private plots represent only 1.4 percent of all Soviet farming lands, they produce about 30 percent of the meat, milk, and eggs, 60 percent of the potatoes, and more than 50 percent of the fruits and berries consumed domestically. Whereas individuals formerly risked stiff penalties for keeping excess livestock, a decree issued in January 1981 imposes no limitations on the number of livestock belonging to private plotholders so long as the animals are raised under contract with state and collective farms. These farms, in turn, can sell this privately produced output to the state procurement agencies and count it against their own plan fulfillment goals.

Other elements of the Food Program include revisions in the state procurement prices. Although bonuses were once paid for above-plan sales, based on price reforms undertaken in 1981, bonuses are now paid when sales exceed the average annual level obtained in the Tenth Five Year Plan. This way, bonuses correspond to increased output; they don't necessarily flow to those who negotiate an easily reached plan target. Finally, procurement prices were raised on January 1, 1983, for cattle, pigs, sheep, milk, grain, sugar beets, potatoes, vegetables, and some other products. Additional payments will go to low-profit farms, and farm debts can be forgiven or rescheduled, all in hopes of providing more incentive and making agriculture more productive. Interestingly, state and collective farm profits for 1983 totalled 23.3 billion rubles, about the same as the total for the procurement price increases, 16 billion, plus another 5 billion rubles in funds transferred to farms to offset the loss of farm-price subsidies on inputs such as gasoline, spare parts, and agrochemicals. Mikhail Gorbachev, then the Politburo member with responsibility for agriculture, put important emphasis on improving the use of economic levers—wages, prices, and profitability—in agricultural management.

The Food Program's connection to the partial U.S. embargo of 1980 is also evident. Although understandably not anxious to reveal the full extent of difficulties associated with the embargo, General Secretary Brezhnev was quite frank in citing the program as a necessary countermeasure to efforts by "some countries" to pressure Soviet foreign policy through grain sales. At the June 1983 Central Committee Plenum, General Secretary Andropov noted that the Food Program's objective was to secure the population with quality foodstuffs "without any interruptions" and with the "greatest possible self-sufficiency." Whether the embargo proved more costly to the United States than to the USSR is a matter of debate, but the Soviets reacted in ways that indicated they considered it a serious threat.

A Mid-1980s Assessment

In the years that have passed since the Food Program was first unveiled, it seems to have become better integrated with the rest of the economy than it initially appeared. For example, although the program promotes individual incentive by more closely linking money wages to performance, the lack of consumer goods in the USSR suggested the incentive effect of higher money wages would be minimized if there was little to spend it on. But a government decree on May 7, 1983, announced increased output of consumer goods in 1983–1985. The consumer goods target for 1983 was apparently increased by 2.8 billion rubles. The Soviet press has linked the Food Program with the planned increase in consumer goods, calling the two "the pivot of the social program" ratified by the 26th Party Congress. Finally, the Politburo has directed planning to begin on a "comprehensive program" to more fully meet the demand for consumer goods and services during the 1986–1990 Five Year Plan.

The private plot initiative is more difficult to analyze. The USSR faces a strong outward migration from rural areas, and the accompanying fundamental changes in life style are not easily countered by the opportunity to invest more of one's free time in, for example, animal husbandry. Then, too, Soviet data show major declines in private sector sales of livestock products since the 1981 decree. The decreases are of such a scale, however, that they probably reflect not an actual decrease in private plot activity, but a change in on-farm accounting. The private sector livestock sales under the contract system may now be recorded as part of the output of the state and collective farms. Overall, of course, government purchases of meat and milk from all sources were up about 9 percent in 1983 and both meat and milk production set records (USDA 1984, 6).

Soviet ideology, and its historical experience, tends to run against the decentralizing theme of the Food Program. For example, *Selskayazhizn* (September 14, 1983), reported that the aforementioned Commission for the Agro-Industrial Complex—a fifteen-member body headed by the deputy chairman of the USSR Council of Ministers and composed of the highest ranking members of the national ministries and industries engaged in the production, planning, and marketing of food—approved work done by "amateur rabbit and fur-breeders' societies" at a local (oblast, interrayon) level. In a program designed to bolster local initiative, this may represent the unwillingness of central planners in Moscow to delegate any significant authority.

Of course, nothing in the Food Program suggests an upheaval in the basic tenets of the Soviet system. There is no hint that the collectivized nature of agriculture, central planning, or a price system that responds to the wishes of the central planners rather than market forces would be abandoned.

Soviet commentary on the Food Program has directed attention toward intensifying agriculture, improving the efficiency in the agro-industrial complex (state and collective farms, interfarm enterprises, and the industries serving agriculture such as the farm machinery, fertilizers, and processing industries), and reducing waste and losses. At least during the remainder of the Eleventh (1981–1985) Five Year plan, this kind of attention and direction are needed because Soviet capital investment plans do not seem to call for a larger commitment of resources to those industries that would be at the forefront of improved efficiency. The most recent data show that although investment in the agricultural sector will be up about 12 percent, investment in the industries serving agriculture will be about the same in the Eleventh Five Year Plan as it was in the tenth. In 1983, despite overplan investment in the agro-industrial complex as a whole, new capital investment in the industries serving agriculture seemingly fell short of target by some 16 percent. In a program designed to increase productivity, one would expect investment in such areas as fertilizer production, farm machinery facilities, and food processing and packaging to increase (Table 6.2).

These puzzling trends may reflect Soviet difficulties with managing the diverse claims on investments. The agro-industrial complex as a whole already

Table 6.2
Capital Investment in Agro-industrial Complex,
1976–1985

PERIOD	TOTAL COMPLEX	AGRICULTURAL SECTOR[1]	RELATED INDUSTRIES[2]
	(Billion rubles)		
1976–80 actual	213.0[3]	171.0	42.0
1981–85 plan	233.0	190.0	43.0
1981–85 plan (annual average)	46.6	38.0	8.6
1981 actual	45.8	37.2	8.6
1982 actual	45.6	38.3	7.3
1983 plan	47.0	37.7	9.3
1983 actual[4]	48.0	40.0	8.0
1984 plan	49.4	38.0	11.4

[1]Includes state and collective farms and interfarm enterprises.

[2]Includes input industries such as farm machinery, fertilizers, pesticides, and preliminary processing industries such as sugar refining, cotton ginning, and wheat milling.

[3]1976–80 data per notes on p. 51 and p. 342 of Narodnoe khozyaistvo v 1982.

[4]Plan fulfillment report Moscow News, No. 5 (1984).

Source: Compiled from official Soviet statistics.

accounts for some one-third of all capital investment in the USSR economy, and agriculture alone accounts for about 27 percent of investment. Most likely, the USSR is already devoting such a significant proportion of new investment to the agro-industrial complex that Soviet leaders are finding it difficult to meet commitments for defense, other investment, and consumption needs.

But although Soviet agricultural investment policy leaves many questions unanswered, Soviet data showed industries serving agriculture as among the fastest growers in 1983. These industries may have responded better to a series of decrees than to contradictory budgetary signals.

On April 10, 1983, *Pravda* reported a Council of Ministers decree that addressed the wellworn complaints about the poor reliability and short service life of Soviet agricultural machinery. It directed those ministries that, because of their overlap with the military, typically enjoy the highest claims on Soviet resources—the ministries of the Aviation Industry, Ferrous Metallurgy, Electronics, Instrument Making, and others—to ensure that better quality materials and subassemblies be delivered to the Ministry of Tractor and Agricultural Machine Building during 1984–1990. The decree called the reequipping of agriculture a "priority task of great economic and political significance."

On July 22, 1983, *Pravda* published still another decree that specifically established the actual increase in agricultural production on state and collective farms as one of the main indicators of performance for enterprises and organizations serving agriculture. Failures to fulfill contracts between the production ministries, the service enterprises, and the state and collective farms are to result in various financial penalties and fines.

Is the Program Showing Results?

If 1982 and 1983 were devoted to putting the Food Program in effect, it would not be unreasonable to see a response in production beginning in 1984. But 1983's performance was good enough that the Soviet leadership was willing to attribute that showing to the Food Program.

In speeches associated with Agricultural Workers' Day, USSR Minister of Agriculture V. K. Mesyats noted the rapid expansion of the collective contract wage system. Between March 1983 and the end of the year, the number of collective contract teams apparently doubled, though their share of arable land covered (about 18 percent) was higher than their coverage of farm workers. The better coordination between farms and supply agencies—the reason for the creation of the RAPOs—was also cited as having a good effect on 1983's results.

More concrete indicators—Soviet statistics of inputs and outputs—displayed significantly improved performance. Production in the mineral fertilizer industry, for example, was 10 percent above 1982; in tractors and agricultural machinery, 5 percent above; in machinery for livestock and feed production, 8 percent; and in pesticide production, 4 percent. Output statistics for key commodities were also up (Table 6.3).

Table 6.3
USSR Production Trends,
Selected Commodities, 1978-1983

ITEM	1978	1979	1980	1981	1982	1983
Gross agricultural output (billions of 1973 rubles)	128.3	124.3	122.0	120.7	126.0	133.8
Grains (MMT)	237	179	189	158[1]	185[2]	195[3]
Meat and fat (MMT)	15.5	15.3	15.1	15.2	15.4	16.0
Sugarbeets (MMT)	93.5	76.2	81.0	60.8	71.5	82.0
Oilseeds (MMT)	11.0	10.6	10.4	10.6	11.2	11.1

[1] Unofficial USSR sources.

[2] Author's estimate.

[3] USDA estimate.

Source: Adapted from USSR Outlook and Situation Report, USDA, from official USSR sources. 1983 partly estimated.

The Soviets also ended the year with substantially more forage, record livestock numbers on state and collective farms, and improved livestock productivity. Mikhail Gorbachev reported that all Soviet republics met procurement plans for the most important livestock products "for the first time in nine years." In such an all-encompassing reform mechanism as embodied in the Food Program, some positive results would almost have to ensue; overall, Soviet statistics for gross agricultural output surpassed the record of 1978 for the first time.

TRADE SHIFTS AND POLICY IMPLICATIONS

The Food Program appears to be a two-staged effort. In this first stage, the USSR appears to be laying down an ideologically acceptable institutional framework that would have to be in place before further investment in the agro-industrial complex could be effective. Thus, the reforms to date seem premised on an expansion of individual initiative *and* the maintenance of central direction and control. In the history of Soviet reforms, conflicts between central direction and individual initiative are but slowly and grudgingly resolved.

The second stage will more likely be characterized by the investment decisions that should accompany a program aimed at curbing waste and losses. Brezhnev's May 1982 speech seemed to imply as much when he noted that the resources available for further expansion were "far from limitless" and especially hard to redirect "in the middle of a five year plan." A further indication of a second and more heavily funded aspect to the Food Program might be deduced from the Politburo's May 1984 endorsement of planning work being done toward a 1986–1990 construction project for the on-site storage of fruits and vegetables in prefabricated metal shelters.

But what is a realistic assessment of the USSR's ability to redirect further investment toward an already high cost and low productivity sector of the economy? In fact, future investment is not as good as the Soviets would like it to be. The Office of Soviet Analysis within the Central Intelligence Agency (CIA 1983), for example, projects very slow long-term growth for the Soviet Union's economy at a rate of about 2 percent per year. Not merely anti-Soviet musing, the forecast is grounded in well-known unfavorable trends in USSR population and labor force, in increasingly expensive access to raw materials, in an ideology that works against substantial economic reform, and in a major resource commitment to military spending. This latter point, of course, implies a major reserve of resources that could be reallocated, but such changes would have been immeasurably easier to undertake had the Soviets achieved the freeze on military budgets that was called for at the June 1983 Warsaw Pact summit meeting, or had they obtained their other arms control objectives. Even so, however, the CIA revised downward its projections of the rate of increase in future Soviet military spending—it grew at an average annual rate of 4–5 percent (constant rubles) during 1966–1976—which implies a greater availability of resources for other uses.

A Shift Toward Technology Imports in 1986–1990

Basic documentation for the Food Program puts the burden of developing a modern technological base for Soviet agriculture on the USSR's domestic ministries and industries (*Kommunist* 1982). This would be consistent with an agricultural production policy that is essentially inward looking, and with the USSR's agricultural machine–building industry, which is primarily domestically oriented and is the largest in the world. Yet, as the USSR's deputy trade minister noted: "Foreign trade is to play a significant role in fulfilling the tasks for consolidating the material and technical base of the agro-industrial complex" (Sushkov 1983).

Though the resort to foreign trade to improve the "material and technical base" might seem at odds with a program designed for greater self-sufficiency, it is in keeping with the USSR's long history of selective imports of agricultural technology. For example, U.S. firms designed the first Soviet tractor plants, and Soviet imports of Western plant and equipment made important contributions to the Soviet's mineral fertilizer industry. Seen in this light, the minister's statement is no more than a recognition of the USSR's long-standing difficulties in equipping a modern agricultural sector with high quality inputs.

Agricultural technology—the term is used here in its broadest sense, including the machinery, equipment, chemicals, and other inputs needed for a modern food sector and also the techniques and know-how used in their manufacture and application—is widely diffused among countries. USSR imports of agricultural technology, in fact, have been steadily growing. Recent work in USDA from Soviet statistics shows these imports to have nearly tripled between 1975 and 1982 from $970 million to $2.7 billion.[2] Moreover, these figures probably represent no more than a *minimum estimate* of the value of embodied technology and unembodied technology (such as design assistance or production licenses) actually reaching the Soviet Union.

To reduce the threat of disruption, take advantage of coordinated production plans, and reduce hard currency outlays, the USSR would probably prefer to acquire its agricultural technology from its Eastern European partners in the Council for Mutual Economic Assistance (CMEA). In fact, CMEA countries were virtually the exclusive suppliers of Soviet imports of agricultural machinery. In 1981, the CMEA countries supplied about three-quarters (by weight) of the pesticides and herbicides and about the same percentage (by value) of equipment for the food processing industry.

Nonetheless, the Western countries, and particularly the United States, are generally the leaders in developing new methods of food production and distribution. The Soviets have recognized this, and in a speech in November 1982, USSR Foreign Trade Minister N. S. Patolichev virtually invited U.S. firms to participate in the agricultural technology aspects of the Food Program.

The Soviets have indicated interest in numerous areas of U.S. agricultural technology. They are interested in U.S. know-how for the production of grain harvesters and specialized equipment such as mechanized potato diggers, beet thinners, and fruit harvesters. They have purchased the technology for the production of liquid fertilizers using superphosphoric acid as raw material, have imported a number of Western pesticides and herbicides (often compounds developed by U.S. companies), and need more. They are interested in application techniques for both fertilizers and pesticides. The October 1983 Agribusiness-USA trade show in Moscow revealed interest in U.S. food processing machinery, especially equipment for modern slaughterhouses and dairies, for using soybean meal in animal rations, for using protein isolates in direct food applications, in veterinary supplies, in grain and vegetable storage techniques, and in irrigation and land improvement devices. Soviet statements suggest the Soviets are interested in breeding stock and new seed varieties. Under the U.S.-USSR 1973 agreement for cooperation in the field of agriculture—an agreement virtually dormant since 1980 but still in force—the Soviets have been interested in U.S. research in genetic engineering, remote sensing, swine hybrids, poultry breeding, and soil mechanics. Their interests in these fields probably still persist.

Implications for U.S. Trade

Trend analysis in the USDA's Economic Research Service shows Soviet grain production approaching 235 million tons by 1990, and, with only "very minor" increases in feeding efficiency, 1991 meat production at 20 million tons—as opposed to 16 million tons in 1983 (USDA 1984, 18). These trends suggest gradually diminishing grain imports, which, of course, are the major item in U.S.-USSR trade. A successful Food Program could diminish Soviet grain import requirements further.

Since April 24, 1981, U.S. policy with respect to agricultural commodities has been one of "full participation in the Soviet market" (Amstutz 1984). With our allies, the United States has argued that grain represents a renewable resource whose importation by the Soviet Union taps off foreign exchange that could otherwise be used for more dangerous acquisitions. Bilaterally with the USSR, the United States has pledged, in a second Long-term Grain Agreement, not to interfere with annual U.S. sales to the Soviet Union of up to 12 million tons of wheat and corn through 1988. Domestically, the embargo protection provisions of the Agriculture and Food Act of 1981, a presidential commitment (March 22, 1982), and control sanctity provisions of the Futures Trading Act of 1982 provide strong safeguards against the possibility of future selective embargoes of agricultural commodities.

But these safeguards do not cover noncommodity agricultural technology, an area of likely U.S.-USSR trade expansion. Indeed, some of the constituencies that have been most outspoken in favor of U.S.-USSR trade are likely to view expanded trade in agricultural technology as counter to their commodity interests. Probably for that reason, statements by USDA policymakers on this topic are most supportive when the technology is embodied in high protein feeds and foodstuffs, seeds, or breeding stock, but otherwise they are, at best, neutral.[3] The secretary of commerce's statement that "American and Soviet interests are well matched in agribusiness, and the technology involved is generally of a nonsensitive nature" is among the most positive responses, but it is a far cry from the president's unmistakable opposition to agricultural embargoes (Secretary of Commerce 1983, 7).

This more favorable security for U.S. agricultural exports to the USSR has led some to argue for similar but broader contract-sanctity provisions in a renewed Export Administration Act (Verity 1983). Another proposal suggests the need for a Long-term Comprehensive Agreement (LTCA) that would "give the U.S. a position in the Soviet agricultural technology market that is comparable with its position in the Soviet grain market" (Hardt 1983, 2). The rationale for such an LTCA is that U.S. agricultural technology represents the same kind of comparative advantage that we enjoy in grains, and with reliability of supply assured, the United States could benefit "in terms of hard currency income and increased farm and industrial income with limited concern about national security" (Hardt 1983, 3).

It seems clear that both the United States and the USSR have mutual foreign policy and economic objectives with regard to expanded trade in agricultural technology. Few countries find food interdependence more complementary for each partner. As noted, agricultural technology is widely available, and in many instances—poultry processing lines, for example—Soviet needs are such that even second-best alternatives from U.S. competitors could still make a contribution. Without question, the United States needs those markets and can easily serve them. As a result, the access of U.S. agricultural technology firms to foreign markets, including the USSR, could be an important consideration in framing U.S. domestic agricultural policies, and of course, sales of agricultural technology would seem just as effective in siphoning Soviet hard currency as grain sales. Thus, whether or not any further assurance of U.S. reliability is needed, U.S. policy restraints on U.S.-Soviet trade in agricultural technology would almost certainly be limited to those instances where a military potential "dual use" existed. Aside from more general controls on, for example, computer technology, those instances would seem rare.

NOTES

1. This paper draws on the author's statement before the Committee on Agriculture, Nutrition, and Forestry, U.S. Senate, on November 15, 1983, and the author's views on the U.S. foreign policy implications of the Soviet Food Program, which appeared in the *Foreign Service Journal* in November 1983. The views in this paper are those of the author and not necessarily those of the USDA.

2. In 1983, the USSR's total imports were valued (at official exchange rates) at about $83 billion, of which about $18 billion represented agricultural commodities. During the period used for the comparison, USSR imports of agricultural commodities more than doubled, being valued at about $9.1 billion in 1975 and about $19.3 billion in 1982.

3. In remarks by now Secretary of Agriculture Richard E. Lyng at the eighth annual meeting of the U.S.-USSR Trade and Economic Council, May 23, 1984, the closest the secretary came to supporting noncommodity agricultural technology trade was in advocating "increased cooperation in the production for mutual gains by both countries. The development of more ties in agriculture could lead to a broadened and strengthened commercial relationship."

REFERENCES

Amstutz, Daniel G. Under Secretary for International Affairs and Commodity Programs, USDA, before the Russian Research Center, Harvard University, February 6, 1984.

Central Intelligence Agency, Office of Soviet Analysis. *Joint Economic Committee Briefing Paper, USSR: Economic Trends and Policy Developments.* September 14, 1983.

Commerce, Secretary of. Letter to the U.S. cochairman of the U.S.-USSR Trade and Economic Council. *Journal of the U.S.-USSR Trade and Economic Council* (1983).

Gidwitz, B. "Labor Unrest in the Soviet Union." *Problems of Communism* (November-

December 1982).

Hardt, John. "Long-term Agreement (LTA): Some Considerations for Agricultural Trade." Paper originally prepared for a conference on East-West Trade, Technology Transfer, and U.S. Export Control Policy. Institute of International Studies, University of South Carolina, March 1–3, 1983.

Kommunist. "USSR Food Program for the Period Through 1990." (June 1982): 58.

Laird, Roy, and Edward Crowley, eds., *Soviet Agriculture: The Permanent Crisis.* New York: Praeger, 1965.

Selskayazhizn, September 14, 1983.

Sushkov, Vladimir. "Foreign Trade for the Agro-Industrial Complex." *Foreign Trade* (1983).

U.S. Department of Agriculture. *USSR Outlook and Situation Report.* May 1984.

Verity, Jr. C. William. "U.S.-USSR Trade: A Vital Need?" *Journal of the U.S.-USSR Trade and Economic Council* (1983).

7 Self-Sufficiency in Japanese Agriculture: Telescoping and Reconciling the Food Security– Efficiency Dilemma

David N. Balaam

Ensuring an adequate food supply for the Japanese people has frequently been a concern of Japanese officials. Today, the problem is not growing enough staple crops, such as rice, but rather meeting the demand for foods the Japanese prefer in relation to rising per capita incomes. Changes in self-sufficiency levels have been conditioned by a number of structural factors and decisions about food and agriculture policy made in three distinct postwar periods: 1945–1960, 1961–1977, and from 1978 to the present.[1]

By 1960, Japan had achieved a 90 percent average self-sufficiency rate (Table 7.1) and was completely self-sufficient in a number of items that made up the traditional Japanese diet: rice, eggs, meat, and fruit. Yet, during the past twenty years, self-sufficiency levels have declined to the point where, in 1980, Japan was only 72 percent self-sufficient. In the case of some items such as rice, diminished production was an intentional government response to a significant decline in the demand for rice. In the case of other items such as wheat, soybeans, and feedgrains, self-sufficiency levels were low to begin with and have fallen off dramatically.

The cumulative effect of these trends is to make Japan dependent on imports of foodstuffs to meet as much as 50 percent of its demand for food. In the 1970s, this situation bothered many officials and groups who supported self-sufficiency measures and who interpreted food dependency as a threat to Japan's national security. However, others viewed low self-sufficiency levels for imported items as a cost savings to Japan for products outside the traditional diet.

This analysis contends that until 1978 the issue of self-sufficiency in Japan was cast largely in terms of food security (enough food produced locally to meet demand) versus efficiency (some food produced locally but excess demand met by importing cheaper foodstuffs). This situation was based on farm support by the Liberal Democratic party (LDP), Japan's dominant political party, and on farmer influence on the annual rice price-setting process. In the 1980s, despite concern for Japan's dependency on others, the government is less willing to

91

Table 7.1
Self-Sufficiency Rate

	1960(%)	1970(%)	1980(%)
Food Total	90	78	72
Grains	82	45	33
Rice	102	106	87
Wheat	39	9	9
Soybeans	28	4	4
Fruits	100	84	81
Meat	91	89	81
Milk and Milk Fats	89	89	86
Eggs	101	97	98
Dairy Products	89	89	86

Source: OECD 1983

support food production inefficiencies or to protect its agricultural products from foreign competition. This development reflects a political strategy by government leaders to redefine Japan's agriculture problem so as to blur the distinction between and make more complementary to each other the agricultural and nonagricultural sectors. This strategy intends to maximize social and economic benefits for those employed and residing in all sectors of the economy while minimizing political costs to the LDP.

PROBLEMS OF SELF-SUFFICIENCY BEFORE WORLD WAR II

Efficiency has played an important role in helping Japan cope with the natural limitations that constrain its agricultural production. Until 1900, Japan was relatively self-sufficient. At the beginning of the Meiji period (1868–1911) a concerted effort was made to develop and implement an appropriate technology for an agriculture system based on small landholdings and crude farming methods. After a failure to adapt the land-extensive production techniques of Britain and the United States to Japan, success at increasing production to meet a growing population was gained by combining new technologies featuring "agriculture chemistry and soil science of the German tradition" with the practical farming experience of the *rōnō*, or veteran farmer (Ruttan and Hayami 1984). The Meiji government funded National Agriculture Stations that conducted field experiments to improve the land and to develop location-specific seed varieties and new animal husbandry techniques. Land productivity increased immensely and was further assisted by the use of new implements, fertilizers, and the development of fertilizer-responsive seed varieties. Rice grew well under a new intensive type of production based on small landholdings and heavy fertilizer use.

Production declined in the 1910s when maximum return per resource potential was reached. During World War I, inflationary conditions contributed to high food prices and unemployment. In 1918, rice riots swept through Japan's major cities, and large-scale rice imports from Taiwan and Korea met demand but reduced farm incomes and acted as a disincentive for Japanese rice farmers. New hybrid rice varieties were developed in the 1920s, but restrictions on fertilizers and other imports kept production levels down. An important point to make, however, is that until the 1930s, the efficiency of Japan's agricultural production process propelled the development of the economy. Agriculture demanded fewer resources than did industry, and the flow of most resources moved out of agriculture and into the industrial sector (Moore 1969; Johnston and Kilby 1975).

AGRICULTURAL POLICY FROM 1945 TO 1960

Agriculture continued to underwrite the industrialization of Japan after the war until the early 1960s. In an effort to deal with war damage and widespread hunger, Allied Occupation Headquarters and government officials adopted agricultural self-sufficiency as an objective and implemented four measures to stimulate production.[2] First, a series of land reform laws in 1946 and in 1952 redistributed land to tenants, paid compensation to former landlords, and imposed a three hectare restriction on land ownership in all prefectures except Hokkaido.[3] These measures modified the tenancy system significantly, resulting in a transfer of 61 percent of formerly tenanted land areas to new owner-cultivators. These laws intended to bring an element of democracy to rural society; they also led to an improvement in farm family living standards, and they socially stabilized rural communities. Second, the government supported agriculture by guaranteeing minimum delivery quotas to its Food Agency, which, since 1942, was the sole purchasing, pricing, and distribution agent of domestically produced and imported food.

Third, by way of subsidies and credits the government supported "basic improvement" production techniques and new scientific technologies. The recovery of fertilizer output and its use, along with improved flood control and irrigation facilities, land-infrastructure improvement projects, chemical pesticide and insecticide use, and the rapid spread of tillers and small mechanical reapers, produced bumper crops in 1955, 1959, and 1960. Finally, recovery efforts were enhanced by the Agricultural Cooperative Law, which reorganized the agricultural cooperative associations that assisted farmers with marketing and credit.

Although agriculture recovery was achieved by the mid-1950s, by the early 1960s, industrial recovery imposed a new structure of consumer demands for agricultural commodities. Rice demand was met rather easily and surpluses began to accumulate, driving down farm prices. After 1955, rising per capita incomes, population growth rates, and changing tastes increased the demand for commodities Japan had to import—namely, fruits, meat, soybeans, and wheat as well as feed grains for (as yet) small livestock industries. Given fixed-farm sizes, many farmers improved the self-sufficiency levels of small livestock, dairy, and fruit industries by implementing new basic improvement technologies that were appropriate to land-intensive production. It was also at this time that a shift of the labor force out of rural and into urban sectors gained momentum. Farmers who remained tended to be older and ideologically conservative. All farmers, though, were caught in a squeeze between declining prices for rice and increasing input costs. Many sought off-farm employment to supplement their incomes, generating a division of farmer classes between full-time and part-time farmers.[4]

By 1955, low farm income was of serious consequence to the LDP, which controlled the prime ministership and whose power base was in the countryside. As many as 80 percent of LDP Dietmen came from rural districts, and, despite the migration out of agriculture, the LDP resisted legislative district reapportionment. The LDP could be counted on to support any program that would relieve farmers of income problems, and it was also instrumental in erecting comparatively high tariff rates on foreign agriculture commodities competitive with major Japanese farm products.

In sum, the 1945–1960 period was one in which a political consensus developed for the goal of food security via achievement of high self-sufficiency rates in a number of traditional foods. Government-supported efforts that developed new production technologies enhanced production efficiency and the self-sufficiency of a variety of land-intensive products. As in the previous period, economic surpluses were again transferred from farmers to urban workers. Agriculture served Japan's recovery efforts. Because of a growing threat to its political base toward the end of this period, the LDP turned its attention to the economic and political side effects industrialization had upon agriculture.

AGRICULTURAL PROGRAMS: 1961–1977

Given the deteriorating economic situation for farmers, in 1961 the Diet passed the Basic Agricultural Law, which represented a fundamental shift in Japan's economic strategy. It was decided that more labor and land would not be absorbed by the growing industrial sector of the economy without compensation to farmers. Therefore, the Basic Agricultural Law had three main objectives, the first of which seemed to contradict the other two: (1) to close the income gap between the farm and nonfarm sectors; (2) to promote self-sufficiency by selective production of a number of commodities, including livestock, wheat, soybeans, and feed grains; and (3) to modernize the agricultural sector and improve production efficiency (Fukui 1975; Kihl 1982).

By 1970, farm income had improved significantly as a result of both increased productivity and government price support measures, adopted mainly for rice. Farmers used more fertilizer, chemicals, pesticides, and new seed varieties to farm their small acreages more intensively. Rice production leveled off, but surpluses accumulated in the 1960s as demand for rice slackened and the government subsidized the producer's price. Rice-related expenditures grew to 40 percent of the government's budget for agriculture and fisheries, pushing the price of Japanese rice to three times the world market price. What accounted most for improved incomes was the expansion of nonfarm employment opportunities. However, increasing numbers of part-time farmers continued to grow government-subsidized rice on small plots of land, the value of which had skyrocketed.[5]

The agricultural programs adopted and implemented in this period reflect a reconciliation of different actors' interests. Along with structural conditions, two particular aspects of Japan's political arena contributed to the government's attitude about farm support measures. The first was the character of the food policymaking process. The price of rice was set by the Rice Council, which is attached to the Food Agency, which is part of the Ministry of Agriculture, Forestry, and Fisheries (MOAFF). The MOAFF minister negotiated the support price with the Ministry of Finance (MOF) and others, including the prime minister. The Rice Council usually consisted of influential people including LDP Dietmen and other party representatives.

In the 1950s, "the final rice price was always determined by LDP politicians in their role as cabinet ministers or members of a ruling party firmly anchored in rural areas" (Donnelly 1977, 159). But in the early 1960s, farmers, who had decreased significantly in numbers, and their Diet supporters managed to enlarge the political arena in which the rice price-setting issue had its forum. The Food Agency gradually ceased to set price support levels. Prices were then set in accordance with a policymaking process that became more pluralistic and involved more groups sympathetic with farmers, including the press, who tried to influence policy outcomes (Donnelly 1977). Thus, until 1968, rice prices were set more often according to what was fair for a greater number of groups that had an interest in the price-setting process. Ironically, disagreement among these groups left the door open for the LDP, which had the most at stake, to decide what was fair.

Second, farmers also influenced price support levels and the structure of agricultural programs through their membership in the National Association of Agriculture Cooperatives (Kōkyō). This body performed the function of a grass-roots farm organization and represented almost all farmers at one time. The National horizontally unified three economic federations, a bank, and a Central Union of Agriculture Cooperatives (a lobby group) and vertically unified agricultural organizations at the national, prefectural, and village levels

(Fukui 1975). More importantly, the National was the political backbone of the LDP, which already played a major role in determining the outcome of rice support measures.

Because of accumulating rice surpluses and increasing government expenditures for agricultural programs after 1968, finance ministers and other officials were able to regain some measure of control over budget expenditures for agricultural programs. The government then cut back on rice subsidies and began a series of rice surplus disposal and land diversion programs to deal with the rice problem. The first disposal program was implemented from 1969 to 1974 and combined export subsidies, feeding rice to livestock, and using rice for industrial purposes (i.e., in processed foods such as sake and rice cake) to cut stock levels by 3.1 million tons at a cost of $3 billion.[6] Government costs and public resistance to the livestock feeding program ended it in 1973. Subsidized exports were more politically acceptable, given the needs of developing nations and of black-market conditions.

Beginning in 1969, the government initiated several diversion programs to achieve income support and to improve the self-sufficiency levels of some commodities. Two one-year provisional programs were initiated in 1969 and 1970 to support a variety of commodities or to idle rice cropland. Then, from 1971 to 1975, the Rice Production Control and Diversion Program set nationwide targets for rice at the prefectural, producing region, and even individual farmer levels. Incentive payments were made for the diversion of riceland into perennial and feedgrain production. Idling cropland was discontinued in 1974 due to the world grain shortage. Finally, in 1976, a Comprehensive Paddy Field Utilization Program was implemented for two of the three years for which it was planned. Rice targets were again scaled down and payments made for planting soybeans, feedgrains, vegetables, barley, wheat, and nonfood crops. This program was aborted because many part-time farmers did not participate in it and rice production exceeded targets (Coyle 1981).

However, these diversion programs did result in a significant decrease in the use of land—especially paddy areas—for rice production (Table 7.2). Between 1969 and 1977, 0.5 million hectares, or 15.6 percent, of areas planted in rice were diverted to other crops. Food Agency purchases at price support levels decreased from 49 percent of total rice production in 1969 to 42 percent in 1979. Even so, areas planted in soybeans declined by as much as 23.3 percent, and wheat areas declined by 70 percent between 1969 and 1977.

These figures point to two serious problems. First, efforts to improve self-sufficiency of nonstaple products through land diversion programs did not provide enough incentive to shift a majority of farmers out of rice production. Low subsidies on wheat, soybeans, and other land-intensive crops partially account for declining self-sufficiency levels of these crops. Farmers used new scientific developments and technologies such as mechanical rice planters to overproduce rice and fruits. Second, without serious government efforts to concentrate landholdings, part-time farmers, in particular, could not be induced to divert to

Table 7.2
Area Planted

	1969	1970	1971	1972	1973	1974	1975	1976	1977	1978	1979	1980
	(millions of hectares)											
Rice	3.2	2.9	2.6	2.6	2.6	2.7	2.7	2.7	2.7	2.5	2.4	2.3
	(1,000 hectares)											
Soybeans	103	96	101	89	88	93	87	83	79	127	130	142
Feed Crops (Pasture: others)	682	717	734	757	803	826	840	853	876	948	969	N/A
Wheat	287	229	166	114	75	83	90	89	86	112	149	191
Barley	283	225	163	121	80	78	78	80	78	92	116	122
Oats	34	27	30	25	20	17	13	10	8	11	6	6
Sugar Beets	59	54	54	58	62	48	48	42	49	58	64	N/A
Fruits and Nuts	413	416	422	428	431	435	430	423	415	412	N/A	N/A
Mulberry	162	163	166	164	162	158	151	143	136	130	N/A	N/A
Vegetables	682	688	689	676	652	642	632	626	630	641	N/A	N/A
Tobacco	76	71	66	62	59	56	59	63	64	64	63	61
Rapeseed	30	19	14	11	8	5	4	4	3	3	3	2

N/A = not available

Source: Ministry of Agriculture, Forestry, and Fisheries, Statistical Yearbook, Annual Issues

land-extensive commodity production. Measures that were adopted then paled in comparison to those necessary to increase production of nonessential items and to improve production efficiency.

International political-economic development also accounted for lower levels of self-sufficiency. Beginning with the U.S.-Soviet Wheat Deal and U.S. dollar devaluations in 1973, the United States became an aggressive food trader. Cheaper U.S. soybeans, wheat, and barley further undercut Japan's efforts to achieve self-sufficiency of these crops. After the Organization of Petroleum Exporting Countries (OPEC) oil price hikes of the late 1970s, Japan began to feel the impact of its dependency on others for natural resources and raw materials needed to run its industrial combines (Vernon 1983) and for food supplies to maintain a quality of life consumers had come to expect. Of serious concern to Japan was the world food crisis of 1972–1974 that drove up food prices to record levels precisely at a time when Japan imported more costly foods. Also, the United States, Japan's major food supplier, unilaterally embargoed sales of soybeans to Japan in 1975 in response to U.S. consumer complaints about high food costs (Gilmore 1982).

Paradoxically, given the magnitude of the external shocks Japan experienced and the degree of vulnerability it felt in the mid-1970s, the government did not make a substantial commitment to diversion programs to increase self-sufficiency levels of nontraditional commodities until 1978. Despite a genuine threat to food security, officials risked dependency on imports that were high in demand for a number of reasons. Imports satisfied consumers and in the short run delayed the issue of modernizing the agricultural sector, a modernization many farmers perceived as a threat to their livelihood and way of life. Cutting imports might have also jeopardized Japan's industrialization strategy, which was heavily dependent on high rates of citizen savings and capital investments.

Thus, the government struck a balance between urban consumers and farmers by continuing to import large quantities of food, supporting rice at high price levels, and using trade barriers to protect items Japan produced in abundance. The LDP's majority position was secure until 1976, and Dietmen justified price support of traditional products on the basis of improving Japan's food security.

In sum, structural conditions of this period were marked by continued rice surpluses and mounting government program costs despite efforts to dispose of surpluses. Additional problems were production inefficiencies, declining levels of self-sufficiency in both traditional and new crops, and increasing dependency on food imports from at least one major unreliable supplier. In the political arena surrounding agriculture and food policy, government officials and the LDP walked a fine line between supporting production efficiency and succumbing to political and social realities. Weak agricultural programs placated farmers while imports met consumer demands for the protein-enriched foods of the Western diet.

CHANGES IN AGRICULTURE FROM 1978 TO THE PRESENT

Since 1978, Japan's agricultural sector has undergone significant changes conditioned in part by achievement of long-term economic objectives that now make Japan the world's second largest economic power and third most active trader. Because farm income is now generally equal to or greater than income in urban areas (including part-time farm income), a more concerted effort has been made recently to increase levels of self-sufficiency and to modernize agriculture. This effort is not conditioned as much by vulnerability as is often suggested, which would imply that external forces condition Japan's policy decisions more than domestic considerations. Instead, Japan is in the process of selecting for itself a new course of action to deal with its agricultural problems.

A new ten-year program, the Paddy Field Utilization Reorientation Program, was initiated in 1978, and more crops became eligible for diversion from rice production. Incentive payments for diversion to wheat, barley, and oats have been raised to equal those of soybeans. Officials justified these measures by contending they would decrease Japan's dependency on major grain suppliers. The program also encourages afforestation, aquaculture, greenhouse construction, and paddy improvement in the offseason. Part-time farmers are encouraged to divert their land to a local cooperative to be leased to full-time farmers who agree not to produce rice. In 1979, the government also began a new rice disposal program in an effort to cut reserves by another 6.5 million tons. This program again includes livestock feeding provisions, industrial use for rice, and export subsidies, and adds domestic price regulation to its measures.

Politics still dominate the rice price-setting arena, and the government has again increased price supports in the early 1980s. But the percentage of the agriculture budget spent on both price support and total food programs has declined (Table 7.3). Success for the LDP–National Cooperative–farmer coalition in the 1960s generated political costs to these actors in the 1970s and 1980s. The National has been forced to broaden its attention to include part-time farmers whose interests do not differ as sharply from urban workers as they do from those of full-time farmers. This gradual diffusion of attention has weakened the role of the National in deciding policy outcomes. According to one report, farmers' associations have made the unprecedented move of recommending lower increases of commodity support prices than in the past. This reflects an effort to "opt for a more realistic price level and wide-ranging agricultural improvement program in a bid to enlist public support" (*JEI Report* 1983).

At the same time, the LDP's ability to determine policy outcomes has gradually eroded. In the 1960s and 1970s, the LDP gradually lost its solid majority in the Diet in conjunction with the steady migration of farmers out of agriculture.[7] The LDP's majority decreased from 296 of 511 seats in 1960 to 249 in 1976, the first year the LDP did not win a clear majority. Since then the LDP has failed to win a majority by itself and has had to recruit conservative

Table 7.3
Japan's Agriculture Budget, FY 1975–1983

FISCAL YEAR	TOTAL EXPENDITURES FOR AGRICULTURE (IN BILLIONS OF YEN)	PERCENT OF AGRICULTURE BUDGET SPENT ON PRICE SUPPORT PROGRAMS (%)	PERCENT OF AGRICULTURE BUDGET SPENT ON TOTAL FOOD PROGRAMS (%)
1975	2,176	34.6	41.7
1976	2,413	31.9	37.7
1977	2,640	26.4	31.4
1978	3,057	19.7	27.6
1979	3,463	18.3	25.9
1980	3,584	17.0	26.7
1981	3,693	15.4	26.9
1982	3,701	13.5	26.8
1983[*]	3,607	11.3	25.3

[*]Projected

Source: Ministry of Finance data, 1985

independents to maintain its control of the Diet (*Japan Times Weekly* 1983). In part, this explains a change in the character of agricultural support programs as elements of these programs more clearly reflect nonagricultural interests. Consumers have also become increasingly dissatisfied about government expenditures and high food costs. The result has been that in many cases the prime minister has had to accede to the demands of other parties. Interagency conflicts about program costs have increased, and the Diet has done some redistricting.

Although farmers still desire price support, they have devoted more attention to modernization efforts, including expansion of land under cultivation as a means to improve efficiency and funds for research and development of high productivity technology and plant breeding. Farmers seem less threatened by efficiency measures than they were in the past. Full-time farmers have pressured the government for land aggregation measures to support land-extensive commodities, especially grains. Part-timers have sought to increase production through land aggregation and/or the use of more efficient production techniques.

Although there is a good deal of counterpressure to continue more traditional forms of agricultural support, pressure to further rationalize agriculture and promote production efficiency is no longer divided along farm sector–nonfarm sector lines. In the past, farmers, the LDP, the MOAFF, and environmentalists were most likely to support rice subsidies, while urban consumers, the

MOF, the Ministry of International Trade and Industry (MITI), and financial experts were most likely to oppose them. Modernization and efficiency took a back seat to food security efforts that masked a disproportionate amount of political influence by farmers and LDP Dietmen who defined food security in terms of high self-sufficiency levels of traditional food items. Today, however, sectoral distinctions in Japan are breaking down rather rapidly. Where two distinct economies existed earlier, they have become more interdependent and integrated (Nakamura 1981). This blurs group and political actor interests and has generated a new agricultural policy agenda.

Because of slowed economic growth beginning in the 1970s and Japan's increasing interdependence with its trading partners, many Japanese officials believe that agriculture must now play a role more equal to the nonfarm sector. Urban areas have become congested, and rural areas are more often viewed as attractive places to live. The problem for policymakers is to design a strategy that supports an agricultural-rural structure that includes full-time farmers, part-time farmers, and nonfarmers alike. Officials are aware that this strategy must reflect the interdependent role that agriculture plays in the economy—one that is not disproportionately more or less important than other sectors (OECD 1983). Likewise, it is clear that any new strategy designed by the LDP must attempt to widen the LDP's base of support in urban areas if the party wants to maintain its majority party status.

Thus, contrary to the view that modernization threatens agriculture, many officials and groups now support rationalization and modernization efforts on the basis that production inefficiencies threaten all of Japanese agriculture and contribute to unnecessary food import dependency. Many believe that full- and part-time farmers can coexist and together further both self-sufficiency (i.e., food security) and modernization efforts. With this new goal in mind, the government has made an effort recently to ensure that full-time "core" farmers receive the lion's share of benefits of new research done on integrated operation systems for larger machinery, crop rotation systems, and direct sowing techniques.[8] Core farmers are also expected to become the basis of highly productive producer groups. The government hopes to implement new biotechnology developments in order to further improve production. Work is also being done on land, roads, water control facilities, and technical extension and information networks (OECD 1983).

As yet, there are substantial barriers to further change of Japan's agricultural system. Total cultivated land area is still about 14 percent of the total area, which is declining due to urban encroachment. More than 60 percent of all farmers cultivate rice, and farmers still resist selling their land. Further rationalization of agriculture could enhance the self-sufficiency of some products, namely land-extensive crops such as wheat and feedgrains. But structural reform is difficult to realize because of political and social pressure to preserve the structure of agriculture as it is. Thus, despite new land diversion programs, the government will continue to rely on imports to meet demand for land-extensive commodities that outrun domestic self-sufficiency efforts.

It is in this context that one can understand the latest U.S.-Japanese bilateral agricultural trade agreement. Japan has agreed to double its imports of U.S. beef and citrus during the next five years (*San Francisco Chronicle* 1984). It seems ironic that Japan would reduce import tariffs on beef and citrus precisely at a time when it is again promoting the self-sufficiency of nonessential items and increased consumption of domestic food production.

Diversion programs that emphasize self-sufficiency for wheat, feedgrains, and some fruits have been a sore point in trade relations between the Japanese and the United States as well as in Japanese relations with the European Economic Community (EEC). Japan is often portrayed as a "closed" society that forces high food prices on its consumers in order to support inefficient agricultural industries.[9] In 1980, Japan agreed to limit subsidized rice exports and has cooperated with the United States since then by adopting several voluntary export control measures on nonagricultural products. Still, the United States complains rather loudly and often about diversion programs that limit U.S. wheat imports (Coyle 1981) and has filed complaints with the General Agreement on Trade and Tariffs (GATT) about Japan's unwillingness to decontrol some thirteen farm and fishing commodities.

Japan feels that the United States is too aggressive about agricultural trade because of its own trade and balance-of-payments problems and that the United States fails to understand Japan's trade dilemma. To the extent that Japan is self-sufficient in traditional commodities, it must protect its agricultural industries. The promotion of self-sufficiency of nonessential crops limits dependency and improves overall levels of food security. Japan also points out that it has already liberalized its trade practices on 475 agricultural products since World War II and that only 25 remain to be agreed upon (Schlossstein 1984).

The new trade agreement undoubtedly will be regarded by many U.S. officials as a victory that signals Japanese acquiescence to U.S. pressure to liberalize trade. But the agreement is actually another in a long line that reflects purposeful choices on the part of Japanese officials. Their strategy is to rationalize agriculture and promote self-sufficiency by withdrawing protection from some inefficient producers and opening them up to competition. In conjunction with an economic plan devised to maintain economic growth in the 1980s, the trade agreement complements a domestic strategy to deal with farmer resistance to change, but at a slow rate and reconciled with other objectives.

Prime Minister Yasuhiro Nakasone is also in the process of demonstrating his commitment to trade liberalization and Japan's willingness to be a responsible actor on the international scene, as a means to further industrial economic interests. In essence, "Nakasone's policies protend a decisive tilt toward the liberal-realist vision of Japan's rule" (Pyle 1984). Japan is now, more than any time since World War II, determining for itself a new and more active role in world affairs. Because Japan is a major actor in the world political arena, trade liberalization, more so than protectionism, has come to be a preferable policy for sustaining economic growth. Therefore, Japan will attempt to limit external constraints on its domestic policy by consciously playing a more cooperative role with its major trading partners. The United States can also expect subtle pressure from Japan to reciprocate in some manner on any number of trade issues.

Japan's willingness to import more U.S. beef and citrus and to risk vulnerability to major food suppliers by importing almost half of its food does not signal an end to the goal of self-sufficiency adopted almost thirty years ago. Declining economic growth rates, a deteriorating base of support for the LDP, and external pressures on Japan to import more food, among other things, have resulted in a redefinition of the agriculture problem. Food security and efficiency are no longer considered incompatible with one another. What remains of Japan's agricultural sector is not threatened with complete extinction. Instead, Japan's now more integrated and interdependent economic sectors face common threats, including production inefficiencies and food import dependence.

CONCLUSION

Economics and politics have combined to influence levels of self-sufficiency in Japan. Until 1955, Japanese agriculture was characterized by two economic forces working in opposition to one another. Japan faced natural constraints that limited food production but achieved high rates of self-sufficiency in staple crops—especially rice. Local ingenuity was combined with appropriate Western technology to maximize both food production and production efficiency. Until that time, the goal of food security in traditional food crops was compatible with the goals of improving production efficiency and achieving economic recovery.

The accomplishment of those goals to a great extent transformed the agricultural sector and politicized agricultural issues in the 1960s and 1970s. Paradoxically, food self-sufficiency in traditional crops worked against Japan becoming completely food secure. Demand for nonessential commodities, brought on by income and population growth, divided interest groups and political actors on the issue of farm support. Some groups supported production efficiency and the import of cheaper foodstuffs to meet demand. However, rural groups supported relatively high self-sufficiency levels of traditional crops as a means both to protect farmers from the transformation process and later to solve the food security issue. Self-sufficiency levels and agricultural programs were the outcomes of a policymaking process that reconciled a variety of groups' interests. Officials tried to slow the structural transformation process so that rural and urban concerns were balanced.

In the 1980s, self-sufficiency is an issue about which the Japanese are less divided. A new strategy is emerging that attempts to reconcile food security with efficiency concerns based on the common interests of all Japanese groups and political actors. The strategy is a culmination of changes that began in the domestic political arena in the 1960s and international political economic conditions that shaped agricultural policy decisions in the 1970s. The success of this strategy depends on Japan's ability to sustain economic growth, which is the objective of newer, more liberal agricultural trade policies. If this strategy works in the 1980s, all economic sectors will have to rely on one another to absorb shocks related to high levels of self-sufficiency for all agricultural commodities achieved by more efficient production techniques.

Japan has had to face the consequences of a self-sufficiency policy much sooner than many of the other industrialized nations. Their food production processes are not yet as inefficient as Japan's, nor are import dependency issues as pressing. Japan caught up with the West with the help of the industrializing West. Now, perhaps, the West should study Japan's agriculture problems to gain insight into the political and economic tradeoffs that will condition the issue of self-sufficiency in highly industrialized nations.

NOTES

1. The analysis used here for this public policy issue is based on the work of Michael Donnelly who has studied in great detail rice price-setting policy in Japan. According to Donnelly, the boundaries of political arenas are fixed by underlying structural conditions or in accordance with the success or failure of past policies. Structural conditions include food production and population growth rates, industrial output levels, land tenure systems, cultural norms, and the like. They limit the range of options available to policymakers and must be reconciled with features of the political arena, namely, the decision and policymaking structure and process (Donnelly 1977).

2. Fred Sanderson reports that despite shipments of food to Japan, per capita daily consumption fell below 2,000 calories (Sanderson 1978).

3. Land reform laws passed in 1946 were the Amended Agricultural Land Adjustment Law and the Owner Farmer Establishment Special Measure Law. In 1952, the Agricultural Land Act was also passed.

4. Part-time farmers are divided between Class I farmers who earn more than 50 percent of their income from farm-related activities; Class II farmers earn less than 50 percent from farm activity.

5. In 1960, part-time farmers made up 65.7 percent of farm households, and by 1980 that percentage had increased to 86.6 percent. The Organization for Economic Cooperation and Development also reports that during that same period, Class II farmers increased from 37.1 percent to 65.1 percent of all farmers (OECD 1976, 201).

6. Rice was found to be a suitable substitute for corn in chicken and pig feed and could constitute 10–20 percent of compound feed (Coyle 1981).

7. Between 1960 and 1972, the rate of decline in the farm population increased from 4.6 percent to 8.4 percent yearly. Whereas there were 11.8 million farmers in 1960, by 1980 there were 4.1 million who earned more than 50 percent of their income from farm-related activities.

8. A core farm household "has more than one male aged over 15 and under 60 who engages in agriculture for more than 150 days a year" (OECD 1983, 209).

9. The *Economist* reports that Japanese consumers in 1981 spent 32 percent of their income on food while U.S. and European consumers (EEC members) in 1983 spent 20 and 19 percent respectively.

REFERENCES

Coyle, E. *Japan's Rice Policy*. Foreign Agricultural Economic Report no. 164. Washington, D.C.: Economics and Statistics Service of U.S. Department of Agriculture, July 1981.

Donnelly, M. "Setting the Price of Rice: A Study in Political Decisionmaking." In T. J. Pempel, ed. *Policymaking in Japan*. Ithaca, N.Y.: Cornell University Press, 1977, pp. 143–200.

Economist. "Repeal the Rice Laws." 4/28-5/4/84.

Fukui, H. "The Japanese Farmer and Politics." In I. Frank, ed. *The Japanese Economy in International Perspective*. Baltimore, Md.: Johns Hopkins University Press, 1975, pp. 134–165.

Gilmore, R. *A Poor Harvest: The Clash of Policies and Interests in the Grain Trade*. New York: Longman, 1982.

"Japan Settles Beef Over Beef." *San Francisco Chronicle*, April 8, 1984.

"Japan's Rice Policy." *JEI Report* no. 2A (January 14, 1983).

Johnston, B., and P. Kilby. *Agriculture and Structural Transformation: Economic Strategies in Late Developing Countries*. New York: Oxford University Press, 1975.

Kihl, Y. "Farm Structure and Rural Policy in Japan." *Food Policy* (1982):332–336.

"LDP Stunned by Election Setback." *Japan Times Weekly* 23 (December 24, 1983).

Moore, B. Jr. *Social Origins of Dictatorships and Democracy: Lord and Peasant in the Making of the Modern World*. Boston: Beacon Press, 1969.

Nakamura, T. *The Postwar Japanese Economy*. Tokyo: University of Tokyo Press, 1981.

Organization for Economic Cooperation and Development. *Review of Agricultural Policies*. Paris: OECD, 1976.

Organization for Economic Cooperation and Development. *Review of Agricultural Policies*. Paris: OECD, 1976.

———. *Review of Agricultural Policies*. Paris: OECD, 1983.

Pyle, P. K. "Changing Conceptions of Japan's International Role." Unpublished paper, 1984.

Ruttan, V., and Y. Hayami. *Agricultural Development*. Revised edition. Baltimore, Md.: Johns Hopkins University Press, 1984.

Sanderson, F. *Japan's Food Prospects and Policies*. Washington, D.C.: The Brookings Institute, 1978.

Schlossstein, S. *Trade War: Greed, Power, and Industrial Policy on Opposite Sides of the Pacific*. New York: Congdon & Weed, 1984.

Vernon, R. *Two Hungry Giants: The United States and Japan in the Quest for Oil and Ores*. Cambridge, Mass.: Harvard University Press, 1983.

Part 3
Public Policies in Developing Agricultural Nations

The chapters in Part 3 address the developmental aspect of the issues raised in preceding chapters. The public policies of several agriculturally developed nations have created incentives for increased food production and, when producers benefit sufficiently, have achieved notable successes. These chapters examine the degree to which developing, import-dependent nations and regions have paralleled these achievements. As noted in the introduction, agricultural growth is occurring in developing countries to the extent that growth in several countries no longer lags behind the developed world partners.

Marvin Weinbaum, in Chapter 8, finds that Middle Eastern agriculture—despite the availability of petrodollars—is held back largely by pricing policies that keep consumer cost low in hope of avoiding political instability. Many other aspects of development, such as private investment, have been checked by political and economic problems that limit investment returns. African development, according to Louis Picard in Chapter 9, has been restricted by domestic political constraints and by inherent weaknesses in the infrastructures and administrative capabilities of most African nations. Governments of these countries accept agricultural dependency in order to secure food in the short run and to foster their own export market for some agricultural commodities.

The lack of good alternatives to dependency helps explain the findings on Latin America of Michael Roberts, C. Micheal Schwartz, Michael Stohl, and Harry Targ (Chapter 10). They find that the self-sufficiency models for development produce only a few of the expected improvements in production and domestic consumption. They also conclude, however, that Green Revolution technology adapted from developed-country agriculture does not necessarily improve production, let alone the nutritional status of Latin American citizens.

The difficulties of dependency for Mexico are apparent in the analysis by Gustavo del Castillo and Rosario Barajas de Vega in Chapter

11. U.S.-Mexican food trade, although advantageous to both countries, has been difficult to sustain for economic reasons. That trade has been carried on at some real food costs to the poorest of Mexico's citizenry. As a result, food—which the United States can produce in abundance— is not being used effectively for basic developmental purposes.

The trade results that these authors describe place them at ideological odds with the authors of earlier papers, at least in terms of market approaches. The negative consequences of these basic differences for Third World countries make it less likely that policymakers in these regions will be as favorable to open market trade as are their developed nation counterparts. Nor will the Third World find its embrace of Green Revolution technology to be the panacea that many hope. Schubert, in particular, provides an excellent example of how internal market forces can result in food being directed from, rather than toward, famine areas. For reasons of this sort, these authors argue more strongly for national self-sufficiency than for interdependent linkages.

8 Food Security and Agricultural Development Policies in the Middle East

Marvin G. Weinbaum

In a region otherwise divided by political ideologies and economic systems, substantial agreement prevails among Middle Eastern governments on the need to improve their nations' agricultural performances and mitigate food import requirements. Policymakers' increasingly convergent views reflect their more realistic assessments of national development options and the pressures of sharply rising consumption. Officials express concern about the absence of reasonable food security and the possible economic and political consequences of an indefinite food dependency. The countries of the Middle East, from Morocco through Pakistan, are not, to be sure, faced in the mid-1980s with a supply crisis of the kind found in sub-Saharan Africa. A number of states have the financial resources to import available food grains and other basic commodities at almost any price. In terms of caloric intake, people in the Middle East are, on an average, among the better fed in the Third World. Per capita protein consumption is low against that of the developed countries but compares favorably with other developing countries. Even so, the Middle East confronts the world's largest food deficit and a mounting food import bill that siphons off much national investment capital and limits the import of critical goods. Trends, moreover, promise spiraling consumption and flagging food production with the possibility that food is destined to become for the Middle East a source of vulnerability not unlike what oil has been for most of the rest of the world. In short, to the Middle East, regional economic security may well be defined by its ability to cope with its problems of food production and consumption.

FOOD DEFICITS AND CONSTRAINTS

The gap between production and consumption of food staples in 1980 stood at more than 16 million tons for countries stretching from Morocco to Iran. It is projected to grow to 22.5 million in 1985 and by the year 2000 may reach 45.5 million (FAO 1982b; World Bank 1982). Moreover, these sobering figures make questionable the assumption that the regionwide food output will more than double during a twenty-year period. In the years between 1970 and 1981, food production had indeed increased in the region by approximately 41 percent. Production growth statistics for the Middle East surpassed those for most other regions and for the developing world as a whole. All but Morocco, Egypt, Jordan, Saudi Arabia, and North Yemen, among sixteen countries, showed at least a 20 percent increase in production during the 1970s.

A different picture emerges, however, from figures on per capita food production through the same period. Overall, regional increases come to barely 4 percent, a smaller increase than was found in all other regions outside of the rest of Africa. In more than half of all Middle Eastern countries, moreover, per capita food production had dropped, in some cases dramatically (FAO 1982a, 75–76, 79–80). States in the region were obliged to import many basic food items for which they had been net exporters only a few years earlier. In the Arab Middle East alone, food imports in 1983 rose to more than $30 billion in value. Even with declining oil export earnings, the value of total imports in the region's Organization of Petroleum Exporting Countries (OPEC) members increased by 8 percent in 1983.

Natural population increases for that region that average more than 3 percent per annum account for much of the demand for food and the outstripping of domestic supplies. Several countries, namely, Syria, Libya, Tunisia, and Israel, have succeeded in boosting food production at rates ahead of population growth during the last decade. However, a larger group of countries—including the populous Egypt, Turkey, Algeria, and Pakistan—just barely managed to keep ahead of domestic population increases. The uphill battle is striking in Egypt where, although the area of arable land has increased by about 17 percent during the past thirty years and yields in some crops have risen by 100 percent or more, the population during this period has more than doubled (*Arab Economist* 1981, 44). The third and largest group of countries—including Iraq, Morocco, Jordan, Sudan, and Iran—register food output gains that badly lag behind an expanding population. In the oil-exporting countries of the Gulf, the massive influx of foreign workers has helped to push up domestic food requirements. Yet the surge in food imports in the Middle East since 1973 is stimulated mainly by changing patterns of food consumption based on rising incomes that favor higher valued and more varied foods. Consumption in Iran rose during the oil-boom years of the 1970s by as much as 12 percent annually.

The ecological constraints on agriculture and food production in the region cannot of course be minimized. Some 83 percent of the land in the Arab Middle East receives, for example, less than 4 inches of rain annually. Among these same countries, all except Syria, Sudan, and Tunisia have in excess of 50 percent of their land area classified as desert, waste, or urban (Kimball 1983, 9–10). Syria, Morocco, Lebanon, Tunisia, and Iraq are alone among Arab countries in having more than one-quarter of their land under cultivation or in pasture. (The 71 percent average of land unsuitable or unavailable for food production compares with just 22 percent in the United States.) Curiously, the most productive agricultural system in the whole region is in Egypt, where a mere 2.8 percent of the land is arable. The 6 million acres in production are of course almost entirely irrigated and multicropped, making Egypt in this respect a unique case. Based on water and soil resources, only Sudan, Syria, Iraq, and Pakistan possess a high potential for further agricultural development. None of these countries ranks particularly high, however, in its effective use to date of means of production, estimated from overall yields, cropping intensities, and labor utilization (Weinbaum 1982, 11).

Government policies bear direct responsibility for the wide gap between demand and domestic supply. Development plans from the 1950s through the early 1970s tended to stress industrial export growth as a major, if not exclusive, means to economic prosperity. Even today, pricing policies and urban food subsidies create unintended production disincentives in the agricultural sector. Official willingness to allow the terms of exchange between domestically grown food and urban goods to run strongly against the rural areas assures a continuing exodus to the cities and weak agricultural investment, public or private. Public funding that still goes disproportionately to industry and city dwellers is predictable in a context where political and economic elites are themselves predominantly urban and count on satisfying urban constituencies to sustain power and influence.

Policymakers also have been overly optimistic about the impact of new technologies and have miscalculated the economic returns from land reclamation. They remain shortsighted in their failure to protect against land lost to urban development and to soil deterioration. Very little has been accomplished in reversing the serious problems of waterlogging and salinity as well as desertification. Many governments have refrained from dealing with injustices in the rules governing access to and the availability of land, water, labor, and capital. Even when these issues are addressed in policy, as in land and tenure reforms, expanded irrigation systems, and public credit for agricultural inputs, the benefits to farmers are usually too narrowly concentrated and the commitment of government funds too limited to effect meaningful and sustained production gains.

Political instability and armed conflict in the region have taken an undeniable toll on agricultural production and development. The most visible tolls are the shortages of labor and transport that prevent or delay the planting and harvesting of crops during civil wars and regional conflicts. To be sure, farmers are normally resilient, prepared to work in their fields in the wake of, or even in the midst of, hostilities when local crops are critical to survival and high prices serve as incentive. But fighting that is prolonged and intense can interfere with the normal distribution of farm inputs, curtail credit, and cut off marketing opportunities. In Lebanon, probably one-half the country's crops were lost in 1983. Farm lands and irrigation systems may be devastated, as in Afghanistan where they have become the direct targets of government and Soviet forces seeking to deny the armed resistance its sources of food in the countryside. More typically, the conditions of regime instability in the Middle East find national leaders preoccupied with the problems of holding or consolidating power and deny the continuity of personnel necessary for long-term economic planning. Governments under pressure prefer policies with short-term payoffs rather than waiting for the slow returns associated with agriculture. The perceived need throughout the region for large standing armies and security forces acts as a drain on national budgets, depriving agriculture along with other non-military sectors of investment of needed funds. At the same time, regimes threatened from within or without may increase food imports in an effort to assure adequate food supplies and ensure regime claim to popular loyalties.

FOOD AND DEVELOPMENT STRATEGIES

National differences in agricultural development potential and financial capacity have resulted in somewhat distinctive approaches in meeting food requirements. A prominent few countries in the region have adopted a strategy that concedes a major food dependency. Saudi Arabia, the Gulf Emirates, and Libya, all with food imports that run more than 60 percent of consumption, have in recent years invested a portion of their lucrative oil revenues in agricultural projects, usually in capital-intensive, technologically advanced schemes and major infrastructural improvements. Programs designed to raise agricultural self-reliance are not, just the same, expected to furnish all national food needs. Although Saudi Arabia has succeeded in increasing production of wheat from 30,000 to 500,000 tons in the early 1980s, the output still accounts for less than one-half of the country's consumption. Food security plans for these countries rest on the assumption that, with oil earnings and foreign investments, these countries will always be in a financial position to compete successfully on international markets for food staples.

A second set of countries that includes Iran, Algeria, Egypt, and Iraq all possess a strong agricultural base and have at one time been largely self-sufficient or run a favorable agricultural trade balance. At least until fairly recently, these countries followed strategies directed at a rapid industrial expansion to be accomplished at least in part by domestic resource transfers at the expense of their agricultural sectors. In all, but only belatedly in Egypt, oil revenues also figured strongly in this push toward an industrial society. As a result, food imports were allowed to rise to 50 percent or more of domestic consumption. By the early 1980s, agriculture had begun to make a larger claim on development budgets, but no country in this group had succeeded, for various reasons, in reducing its foreign food dependence.

States in the region with somewhat lower import requirements but also more limited foreign exchange to spend on food imports make up a third category. Syria, Sudan, Tunisia, and Jordan, all without substantial oil revenues, have refrained from strongly industrial-oriented development strategies. The higher priority given to expanding agricultural production is reflected everywhere but in Jordan in impressive agricultural growth rates since the mid-1970s. With crop yields relatively low in the four countries, there is ample capacity for increased output. Each confronts, however, formidable physical, social, or political obstacles to development, and planning is strongly contingent on generous bilateral and multilateral aid as well as private investment. Sudan has banked most heavily on financial and technical assistance from Western and Arab sources, as is discussed below.

A fourth set of countries already counts on major food exports and nonagricultural commodities to finance development efforts. Turkey, Morocco, Pakistan, Israel, and Lebanon vary in their capacity for future agricultural growth, but each has among the region's highest crop yields. None is, however, free of national food deficits that can be managed only with continued foreign assistance. Most importantly, these nations require for food security wider access to Western markets and higher international prices for their national exports.

Official government rhetoric aside, no country in the region seriously contemplates complete self-sufficiency in all food staples. Whatever the resources and potentials of each country, the economic rationality of pursuing self-sufficiency is weak so long as the principle of comparative advantage has any bearing on cropping choices. Egypt could, for example, produce most of its domestic wheat requirement, but only at the price of relinquishing most of its acreage, which is better suited to growing cotton and other higher value exportable crops. There exists no case in the Middle East of a country prepared to insulate itself from the global market economy, not even those states with close political and economic ties to Eastern Bloc countries. Nor is any country willing to accept the political and social consequences of severely restricted national consumption. Instead, the region's states have settled for a number of agricultural development strategies familiar to the Third World. These approaches are, as elsewhere, interdependent, and no single policy or combination of policies has proven thus far universally applicable or successful.

Investment activities designed to increase food security rest mainly on intensified cropping and the vertical growth of agriculture. Yet, because the region possesses so little arable land, the expansion of areas under cultivation has almost everywhere also been a key component in food planning. Opportunities for land reclamation exist throughout the Middle East; however, the largest, most promising areas are found in Sudan, where only 15 million of a potential 100 million acres are under the plough. Other countries have considerable potential through the extension of water resources to arid or desert land and through careful water management. To date, however, the gains realized have almost everywhere been disappointing. In Egypt, where land reclamation has been going on for at least a century, new land projects have been a government priority since the 1950s and have proven both technologically difficult to open and costly to sustain in production. Less than one-half of the 900,000 acres reclaimed in Egypt since 1952 remain economically viable. Still, Egypt's planners seek to add 150,000 acres of new lands annually, and they cling to the belief that horizontal expansion of agriculture is indispensable if the country is to keep from being overwhelmed by its inevitable population growth and food requirements.

The construction and upgrading of physical infrastructures are the most prominent undertakings designed to increase arable land and raise agricultural production. Activities focus mainly on building dams, irrigation systems, and storage facilities, and improving roads to markets. Egypt's Aswan Dam, completed in the mid-1960s, is of course the most notable achievement. But virtually every country in the region has sought to harness more fully its water resources for urban and industrial as well as agricultural use. Although by the 1980s most of the projects, from Pakistan's Tarbela Dam to Jordon's East Ghor Canal, had been completed, major projects, such as Syria's enormous Tabqa Dam, were still under construction or being planned. Investment in major infrastructural projects captured a large, if now diminishing, slice of development budgets and depended in most cases on international financing and foreign technical assistance.

Development policies throughout the region have been based on the assumption that solutions to food production problems will be found in improved technologies and their related inputs. National plans rely heavily on the introduction of more effective, cost-efficient methods of production. (Israel and most of its occupied territories already have a modern system in place.) Most plans stress greater mechanization of agricultural activities, a direction encouraged by the World Bank and bilateral aid donors. Strategies for raising yields also have predictably focused on the expanded use of improved seed varieties and chemical fertilizers. The region as a whole has not undergone in scope the Green Revolution realized in the Indian subcontinent and elsewhere. Yield averages have in fact trailed those of every region except the less-developed countries of Africa. Agricultural systems in the Middle East have, however, recently set the pace in the Third World in high-cost, esoteric farming methods such as hydroponics and new approaches to dry land farming. Promising results have been obtained in the Gulf Emirates and Jordan. But most gains through the new, usually imported, technologies are thus far limited to export crops and provide a doubtful solution to mass food requirements. Above all, the delivery of advanced research and appropriate methods to most farmers in the region is stymied by the weakness or absence of effective systems of extension. Low social status and poor financial rewards appear to preclude trained and dedicated extension workers.

Reform policies constitute another set of strategies aimed at increasing domestic food production. Beginning with Egypt in 1952, many countries in the Middle East have enacted laws to break up large, ordinarily nonprogressive farm holdings and to distribute land titles to those already tilling the land. Other

reforms have offered tax breaks and given tenant farmers and small owners better economic and legal protections against rural elites. Changes in some countries reflected doctrinal views about foreign and exploitative ownership or, as
in the shah's Iran, were an effort to break the power of a traditional landlord
class. But reforms more often have been pragmatic attempts by governments of
diverse ideological stripe to provide the greater security and incentives to small
farms needed to produce surpluses. In practice, whatever the social benefits,
land reform seldom by itself results in higher production or significant income
redistribution and has often left farmers no less economically vulnerable than
before. In some countries, the reform was, in any case, mostly rhetorical; only
a small portion of the best land was actually resumed by the state. Land reform,
moreover, has failed almost everywhere in the region to address the hardships
of the largest rural class, the agricultural wage laborer.

Recognizing the limits of reform policies, most states in the region have
reorganized the modes of agricultural production. State-managed cooperatives
and collectives and quasi-private agribusinesses have been created from once
large estates or by consolidating already divided land. To overcome inefficiencies and provide support for small units, Egypt eventually reorganized nearly
all its farmers into cooperatives, and Algeria undertook the most extensive approach to large state-operated farms. The shah's regime in Iran attempted a variety of schemes, including the promotion of agribusiness in the early 1970s
that was supposed to attract foreign capital and know-how. In most of the region,
however, reorganization strategies have fallen far short of their production
goals, and initial successes frequently could not be sustained. Nontraditional
modes were undermined in many instances by inadequate public fundings and
unqualified managerial personnel. In some cases, newer structures have been
quietly disbanded and the land redivided. Nowhere in the Middle East has agricultural reorganization given rise to rural institution-building able to provide
for genuine popular participation, local leadership, and decentralization of
authority.

Farm credit and the subsidization of inputs are used as policies in their own
right to spur food production. Nearly all countries in the Middle East have programs to make available fertilizer, seeds, and pesticides at below-market prices;
credit is also frequently available for equipment purchases, including tractors
and tube well pumps. Whether deliberately or not, the underwriting of these
inputs is, as in most of the developed world, usually aimed at the already more
successful farmers rather than at marginal, less creditworthy producers. Although input support policies have helped ease long-standing biases against the
agricultural sectors, these policies have not been extended to provide incentives
to production through higher crop prices paid to farmers. Unfavorable terms of
trade thus continue, as the fixed prices paid to farmers by government agencies
are ordinarily well below the local or international market value. Policies often
proceed on the assumption that agricultural production is not very responsible
to price change and that farmers, therefore, need only be paid enough to keep

them producing. Meanwhile, underpricing enables governments to meet the high costs of urban food subsidies. In effect, the depressed prices farmers receive help to subsidize low fixed-food costs to politically more volatile urban populations. Denial of incentive prices on government-procured crops leads farmers to shift where possible to growing and marketing uncontrolled crops, which, ironically, may defeat national food plans for domestic consumption and exports. Low farm prices also assure that private investment capital will not be attracted to the agricultural sector.

Finally, policies designed to improve education and public health have been undertaken in some countries in an effort to upgrade human resources in rural society. Behind these policies is the belief that a modern agricultural system requires people capable of accepting and using advanced farming methods. Where programs of this kind are a component of a comprehensive rural development approach, they have also included alternative or supplementary employment opportunities for farmers, often in public projects and enterprises. By providing income sources to slow the migration to the cities, governments have also of course sought to keep farm labor costs from rising and to avoid migrants' demands on urban services. A serious commitment to human resource and comprehensive development often fails in countries of the region because it lacks a politically powerful constituency in the capital or continuity in national leadership and policy direction. Conversely, to attack ignorance, poor nutrition, and exploitation may require the kind of social change and income redistribution that only a major political upheaval could effect.

DEVELOPMENT SOLUTIONS AND THEIR COSTS

The slow progress and frequent setbacks experienced by countries in the Middle East in meeting domestic food production goals has certainly dispelled any notions that solutions would be early or easy. After disappointments in trying to industrialize their societies rapidly, many planners expected that agriculture, a traditional economic sphere, would show more responsiveness to increased attention. Large development schemes have in fact usually proven unprofitable in the short term, and nongrowth measures of success are often elusive. Policymakers now better appreciate that agricultural development is bound to be very costly and that even adequate financing may not be enough. Infrastructural improvements can usually be bought, albeit with delays, but large expenditures alone cannot create skilled and dedicated farmers and managers. Nor can money compensate for depleted aquifers or assure markets for exports. Even such apparent success stories as the well-founded Jordan Valley development, with its strong private sector component, has suffered from overproduction and overspecialization as a result of poor marketing and inadequate quality control. National planners are also more apt to recognize food policies as linked with broader social policies, most of all population growth and urbanization. After an infatuation with largely technological solutions to food production, many more concede the indispensibility of an improved administrative capacity and the exercise of political will from the top. Experiences in recent years have also demonstrated that the desired integration of a country's economy into a world trade system and dependence on foreign assistance can carry very real liabilities.

The attraction for many countries of foreign economic assistance in overcoming balance-of-payments problems and severe commodity shortages is diminished by the mounting awareness of the debt burdens being incurred through easily financed food and other imports. Countries strongly dependent on external sources for economic and development aid increasingly find the terms of foreign loans unacceptable and even regional Arab aid sources less than reliable. A slump in oil revenue has cut back sharply Arab donor support for agricultural projects in lower income countries. Support from OPEC and other regional development funds declined steadily from peak levels in 1977. In the case of aid to Egypt, an Arab cutoff of funds after Egypt's rapprochement with Israel demonstrated the political strings attached to Arab aid. The World Bank continues as an important source of assistance, but the specialized international agency set up to assist the Third World's rural poor through agricultural development—the International Fund for Agricultural Development—has faced difficulties replenishing its lending resources from U.S. and OPEC contributions. U.S. food and/or development aid has gone over time to every country in the Middle East, but since the mid-1970s heavy preference for assistance to Egypt and Israel has been openly justified on political-strategic grounds rather than on the basis of economic and humanitarian needs.

No doubt some of the strongest criticisms of food aid are its believed disincentive effect on domestic production. The concessional purchase of wheat and other commodities is frequently blamed for the sluggish growth in output and low levels of public and private investment in the agricultural sector. Commodity aid and development assistance are said to relieve governments of a sense of urgency about their food security and to allow the diversion of domestic resources away from agriculture. Egypt is perhaps the most instructive case. Readily available and affordable U.S. commodity aid lessened pressures for Egypt to increase its own efforts to feed itself. For example, the heavy imports until 1983 of poultry from the United States and its sales at subsidized prices helped bring a steady decline in the domestic production of poultry and eggs. Most serious is the possibility that food aid also facilitates the region's ubiquitous urban food subsidies and low domestic farm prices. Foreign aid has to bear at least indirect responsibility for enabling governments to divert funds to cover subsidies and then to use their budget deficits to justify the depressed crop procurement prices paid to domestic farmers.

Resentment against the United States and other Western donors from government spokesmen in the region is normally focused on the conditions that the donors seek to impose for their aid. Some of the most insistent demands involve budget reforms and, in particular, the reduction of government food subsidies—which the aid givers have indirectly supported. Economists in the recipient countries share the donor's concern that subsidies have the effect of stimulating food consumption. They also appreciate that the subsidies serve as an improper signaling of agricultural and industrial investment choices, thereby introducing distortions into the local economy. The probable incentive effect of raising farm prices is readily acknowledged. Yet, officials in these countries claim that those who give aid are too often insensitive to the domestic political dangers inherent in any policies tampering with food prices or the transfer of resources away from urban centers.

Multilateral aid agencies, and principally the International Monetary Fund (IMF), have demanded the most stringent economic reforms. That countries in the region have been so often willing to submit to IMF's economic preconditions indicates the pressing need for budgetary assistance. Egypt reduced subsidies at IMF insistence in January 1977 on a wide range of food items. Before the higher prices were rolled back, they had provoked widespread urban rioting that nearly toppled the regime of Anwar Sadat. Although the incumbent Hosni Mubarak government has quietly chipped away at subsidies on some luxury goods, Egyptian leaders have tread carefully and, as a result, are repeatedly denied IMF loans. Sudan, pressed by its creditors, managed to survive price increases created by lowered subsidies in spring 1982, but only at the cost of serious civil unrest. In January 1984, Tunisia submitted an austerity program suggested by the IMF and World Bank that carried cutbacks in the estimated $236 million spent yearly on subsidies. A doubling of the price of bread led to disturbances across the country and more than one thousand dead and wounded. As occurred in Egypt, anti-government elements, including Islamic fundamentalists, quickly capitalized on public discontent to mount a challenge to the authorities. Only when president Habib Bourguiba stepped in and announced repeal of the price increases was order restored. To replace higher prices on food staples, the president announced that costs would rise instead on gas, wine, and other alcohols (*New York Times* 1984a).

A few weeks later violence also broke out in Morocco in anticipation of new austerity measures that would push up prices for bread, sugar, and cooking oil. Memories were still fresh of the June 1981 riots when hundreds of people were killed or wounded after the government lowered subsidies and prices rose from 14 to 77 percent on basic commodities (*Washington Post* 1981). King Hassan II assured the public that no new increases were in fact contemplated, but only after as many as 200 people had died in demonstrations the government blamed on communists, Zionists, and followers of Iran's Khomeini (*New York Times* 1984b). The Moroccan government had been negotiating with the IMF for a loan to tide the country over its continuing economic crisis brought on by an extended drought and low prices for phosphate, Morocco's major export. Here, as elsewhere in the Middle East, governments have had to deal with the dilemma of how to meet external demands for economic reforms that they recognize as valid and also keep from violating an implicit social contract to protect the food consumption of the urban poor.

Belief persists that the quest for increased food security by countries of the Middle East must lead ultimately to more regionwide approaches. The Liberal economists insist that trade based on comparative advantage and agricultural development financed by handsome oil revenues gives the Middle East a potential not matched elsewhere in the Third World. Demand for cooking oil, meat, and sugar could, it is argued, be most easily met from regional sources. In the late 1970s, agreements were reached between Iran and Turkey and between Libya and Syria to undertake joint ventures in food production. Egypt and Sudan have a long-standing plan to integrate their economies and expand water resources for agriculture in the Nile Valley. Sudan in the 1970s became a special focus of attention by planners in the Gulf states seeking a reliable local food supplier. Petrodollars were to be combined with Western technology to make the country the Arab world's breadbasket and stockyard. Two states have emerged meanwhile as significant, if not major, sources of food grains. Turkey has run wheat surpluses for several growing seasons, and Pakistan, long an importer, began to export to the region in 1983.

Regional solutions to food security seem, all the same, an elusive goal. Trade patterns remain skewed toward extraregional transactions; less than one-fifth of the Middle East's total exports and imports occur within the region. The food trade flow with the Western industrialized countries, in fact, continues to expand. Sudan is no doubt the deepest disappointment in intraregional trade. It soon became obvious that the country lacked the trained manpower and infrastructure needed to fulfill the prescribed role of producer of food surpluses, much less feed itself. Private Arab investors, on whom development plans had largely rested, lost interest, especially when the Sudanese government was unable to commit the local financing for joint projects. More generally, regional cooperation in agricultural development, whether on a private or public level, seems stymied by competing claims that divert resources and distract the region's policymakers. Disparate ideologies and institutions, uncomplementary agricultural systems, and shifting political alliances across countries also undermine hopes for regional food interdependency.

The United States figures prominently in the Middle East's food security plans. U.S. wheat surpluses are an insurance against poor harvests domestically and low reserve stocks internationally. Programs of concessional food aid remain the best hedge for lower income countries, especially in times of rising world prices. On a regular basis, Egypt takes the bulk of U.S. Public Law 480 food aid, receiving approximately $250 million worth of aid annually. But recipients of substantial concessionally sold agricultural commodities in recent years also included, among others, Pakistan, Morocco, Sudan, and Israel. Roughly 10 percent of the Middle East's food imports are presently from U.S. sources; U.S. exporters have increasingly struggled to remain competitive with Europeans and other sources in sales of grains, poultry, and processed foods. In the 1980s, markets for U.S. agricultural exports on commercial terms have been strongest in Saudi Arabia, Egypt, Pakistan, and Iraq. Iran, once the United States' best cash customer in the region, virtually dropped out of the U.S. market after 1979, but commodity trade is again rising. The Middle East is not, to be sure, a major factor in U.S. agricultural trade worldwide. The region accounted in fiscal year 1982/83 for just 4.5 percent of the value of all U.S. agricultural exports. This compares with 7.3 percent for Africa, 12.7 percent for South and East Asia, and 12.7 percent for Latin America, among the developing regions (World Food Institute 1983, 43).

The stakes for the United States are, in fact, more political than economic. U.S. strategic policy in the region hinges in large part on the survival of moderate regimes in the face of their radical Islamic and Marxist enemies, domestic and foreign. Because few issues in the Middle East have the capacity of food to ignite mass discontent, the United States remains vitally interested in the food deficits and the policies adopted to deal with agricultural growth and access to food by urban consumers. But efforts through the U.S. Agency for International Development and through other means to assure that domestic policies conform to Western concepts of development, sound economics, and a global market system cannot avoid charges that Washington seeks to interfere in others' affairs. Ruling elites throughout the region harbor fears that U.S. food aid and trade may be used to constrain or blackmail them in regard to their foreign policies. It is unlikely for many reasons, however, that food power can ever be wielded with the full potential of oil power, and, indeed, it can be a double-edged sword. Increasingly, U.S. diplomats are concerned that too much overt pressure may act to destabilize cooperative regimes that cannot afford to be seen yielding to outside influences. Farsighted analysts also realize that whatever the possible economic advantages to the United States and its balance of payments of food dependent relationships, greater national and regional self-reliance may be in the longer term in the U.S. political interest if world food demand increases at a more rapid rate.

REFERENCES

Arab Economist 12 (April 1981).
Food and Agricultural Organization. "Supply Utilization Tape, 1982."
International Monetary Fund. *IMF Yearbook 1982*. Washington, D.C.: IMF, 1982.
New York Times, January 7, 1984.
New York Times, January 23, 1984.
Washington Post, August 25, 1981.
Weinbaum, Marvin G. *Food, Development, and Politics in the Middle East.* Boulder, Colo.: Westview Press, 1982.
World Bank. *World Development Report 1980.* New York: Oxford University Press, 1982.
World Food Institute. *World Food Trade and U.S. Agriculture, 1960–82.* Ames: Iowa State University Press, August 1983.

9 Self-Sufficiency, Delinkage, and Food Production: Limits on Agricultural Development in Africa

Louis A. Picard

"Malnutrition," according to Richard Barnet "is the hidden holocaust of our day" (Barnet 1980, 159). During the past fifteen years, staple food production has fallen behind population growth in fifty-three developing countries. By 1979, the less-developed countries (LDCs) had 70 percent of the world population. At the same time, they were producing only 40 percent of the world's food supply (Bryant and White 1982, 277). Further, in a number of LDCs, particularly in Africa, there have been severe absolute declines in food production since the "winds of change" brought independence from Britain, France, and the smaller colonial powers.

Estimates of malnutrition are grim and getting grimmer. Ten years ago there were more than a half billion people in the world who were malnourished. More than one-half of them were children under the age of five. Today, out of a world population of 4.5 billion, as many as 1.3 billion people may be chronically undernourished.

Agricultural and rural development, though plagued with many unanswered technical questions about food production potential, is the single most important item on the agenda of many LDCs for the rest of the century. This chapter's concern is with the domestic capacity of LDCs to grapple with the problems of agricultural self-sufficiency, particularly in the area of food production. Inevitably, throughout the Third World the prospects for rural and agricultural change seem inextricably linked to the expansion of government activities in the rural areas. Rural changes depend on the "strength and integrity of bureaucratic institutions" (Puchala and Hopkins 1979, 10).

Though few question that bureaucratic capacity is a crucial intervening variable in the process of agricultural and rural production, the irony of the last twenty years has been that "in country after country the rural bureaucracy becomes a major constraint upon development itself" (Nicholson 1980, 18). A 1977 United Nations study on the future of the world economy suggested that malnutrition can be eliminated with a 5 percent increase in the production of food worldwide (Leontief 1977). However, "the technological revolution needed to feed the anticipated global population in the year 2000 is within our grasp, but institutional, political and social obstacles stand in the way" (Barnet 1980a, 159–160).

DEPENDENCY REVERSAL

The last two decades have graphically demonstrated the fragility of LDC economies, buffeted as they have been by both natural and manmade catastrophies. Given the impasse between the deepening agricultural crisis in the Third World and the inability of administrative and political institutions to reverse this process, this chapter argues the need to go beyond the usual development administration paradigm and examine the fundamental contradictions between development strategy and the bureaucratic, institutional, and political barriers that hinder development.

There is now a substantial body of literature on the processes, conditions, and effects of dependency on LDCs. Dependency theorists argue that there is a direct relationship between underdevelopment in the LDCs and the high level of economic development in the so-called First World countries. This relationship is historical in origin and related to the built-in structures of poverty that characterize the contemporary international system (Baran 1957; Gunder Frank 1969; Amin 1972b and 1974; Arrighi and Saul 1974; Valenzuela and Valenzuela 1978; and Munoz 1981).

For dependency theorists, terms of trade, choices about what to produce, and patterns of investment are to a large extent not determined by the LDC, and these decisions both strengthen the interests of certain groups within a society (the dependent upper middle classes) and strengthen industrial country dominance over LDCs. Economic and political forces, both internally but most importantly internationally, keep LDCs in poverty but structurally linked to the needs of the industrialized world. LDC middle classes, because of consumption patterns, economic interests, and an imposed value system, look to the industrial world for political and economic direction (Bryant and White 1982, 11–13).

Increasingly, scholars have begun to examine domestic strategies that an LDC can use to reduce or reverse dependency relationships (Munoz 1981). This approach focuses on what the individual LDC can do "taking as given the international rules of the games as they existed circa 1976" (Diaz-Alejandro 1978, 123). This approach moves away from the thrust of many dependency theorists who argue that any attempt to develop a counterdependency strategy "must organize the world into a unified whole without inequality" (Amin 1974, 33).

Four related concepts are involved in the development of a domestic strategy of counterdependency. The first is dependency reversal, which encompasses all of the techniques used to overcome or reverse the dependency relationship between the LDC and the international economic system. The second concept is delinkage. Advocates of delinkage advocate the withdrawal, or at least partial withdrawal, of the state from the international economic system in order to protect fledgling economic activities. The third concept is self-reliance and is of primary concern here. Self-reliance suggests that an LDC should be able to produce its own food as well as other basic needs such as clothing, shelter, educational and medical services, and be able to supply its own nonluxury energy needs.

DEVELOPMENT ADMINISTRATION

The final concept linked to domestic strategies of dependency reversal is the concept of development administration. Sunkel suggests the importance of a development-oriented administrative and political system and "much more administrative and political socialization and local self-reliance and management" (Sunkel 1981, 109).

Development administration grew out of the realization of the 1950s and 1960s that with independence in Africa and Asia, the newly independent state would take a major role in the management and promotion of economic development. Development administration refers both to institutional arrangements—the complex of agencies, management systems, and processes a government establishes to achieve its development goals—and to innovation and movement—"those activities of government that foster economic growth, strengthen human and organizational capabilities, and promote equality in the distribution of opportunities, income, and power" (Esman 1974, 3).

The link between dependency reversal and development administration is not often made. Indeed, there has been "precious little common ground for any meaningful debate between them" (Hirschmann 1981, 473). Much of the criticism of the traditional modernization school of development focuses on the failure of development administration advocates to move beyond the confines of the existing socioeconomic system within the LDC to an understanding of the underlying structural constraints to development (Gould 1977, 349–378). The bulk of this criticism, however, relates to the means/end problem of development administration and failure of many of its advocates to effectively grapple with the political and economic realities of the Third World. According to Hirschmann, development administration should be seen as a more revolutionary strategy than its proponents seem to appreciate. "For instance, in its client-orientation it is administratively conceived, but the consequences, if effective, would be economic as well as political." An ongoing participatory process could lead to a more equitable distribution of benefits (Hirschmann 1981, 473).

Yet, when we examine the recommendations made by dependency theorists to reverse dependency relationships or delink the LDC from the international system, the gap between dependency theory and development administration narrows. Whereas Esman (1972, 1974) defines development administration as activities of government that foster growth and promote equality, Caporaso and Zare emphasize that dependency theory conceives development as including growth and also the qualitative aspect of increasing equality (Caporaso and Zare 1981, 517). For nondependent development to occur, then, there should be decreasing inequality, less marginalization, and more democracy.

It is a major argument of this chapter that dependency theorists, far from dismissing the major tenets of development administration, have developed a series of propositions that buttress the major themes of development administration theorists. An examination of the domestic strategies of dependency theorists will demonstrate the extent to which dependency reversal and delinking strategies bear striking similarity to the approach of development administration proponents.

Dependency theorists offer a variety of suggestions to LDCs that wish to pursue a policy of selective self-sufficiency. The following are the major components of such a policy: (1) The LDC should follow a basic needs strategy of agricultural development—societal needs must come first; (2) focus should be on food and seed production—cash crops should not be allowed to encroach on the production of basic survival agricultural products; and (3) emphasis must be on small-scale irrigation and production. Where rural residents are scattered, however, population relocation should be considered so that services can be more effectively distributed and productivity can be increased by shared use of agricultural implements, extension services, and mechanistic aids; (4) both infrastructure development and production should be based on labor-intensive strategies—meaningful production must be linked to manpower availability and job creation strategies; (5) appropriate technology should be developed within the domestic confines of the LDC and be complementary to cultural, social, and environmental constraints; (6) the management of natural resources should be based on ecologically sound principles; and (7) development activities should be concentrated in the rural areas, if necessary at the expense of the urban areas, so that movement from the rural areas to the urban areas can be severely curbed if not stopped (Green 1976; Munoz 1981; and Diaz-Alejandro 1978).

Agricultural self-sufficiency is directly linked to political and administrative capacities within the LDC. Conditions conducive to agricultural and rural development are "largely a function of government policy and administrative capacity and these in turn result from political considerations that have little to do with agriculture as such" (Puchala and Hopkins 1979, 2). Among the political and administrative strategies suggested for self-sufficiency are the following: (1) Self-sufficiency requires a high degree of political and administrative decentralization to the lowest level of government—mechanisms of participation should be pegged to primary political structures. (2) There should be an increased emphasis on human resource development within the LDC, with a corresponding decrease in dependence on either the overseas expert or the overseas-trained national. (3) Within an overall manpower strategy, LDCs must develop a pool of local development experts "whose loyalty to the national interest of the Southern country is unquestioned and unclouded by links to extranational business centers" (Diaz-Alejandro 1978, 112). (4) At both the national and the local level the LDC must increase its cyclical and emergency economic planning capacity and its capacity to analyze existing economic systems and trends. (5) The leadership in an LDC must go beyond material incentives in its approach to administrative and political elites and cultivate a moral strategy that appeals to elites to curb their inclination toward consumption and economic control. (6) LDCs should promote the development of commercial, financial, and technological links with other LDCs in what Green calls the "regional potential for integrated vectors" (Green 1976, 267). (7) The core aspect of delinkage is a strategy of social mobilization in the rural areas that creates a rural political awareness and stimulates agricultural productivity within the context of that heightened political consciousness. Finally, (8) an overall emphasis should be placed on an equitable distribution of resources within an LDC. Inequity is for dependency theorists the first link in the chain of dependent relationships that link LDC political and administrative elites to policymakers in the industrialized states (Gould 1977, 349–378).

The successful implementation of even a part of the agricultural self-sufficiency strategy advocated by dependency theorists requires both the development structures described by Gant (1979) and the processes of innovation and change proposed by Esman (1974). Green (1970) has argued that internal changes within the LDC must play the dominant role in any strategy of dependency theory. Internal changes alone offer the route to economic independence based on balanced economic development strategies and selective delinking from the world economic system. At issue is whether there are fundamental bureaucratic, institutional, and political barriers to agricultural self-sufficiency in much of Africa and parts of the Third World.

Administrative, institutional, and political constraints are significant barriers to the implementation of a strategy of agricultural development in many LDCs. Although these constraints are crucial in understanding LDCs in Africa, they are of some relevance for LDCs in Asia, Latin America, and the Caribbean as well. To the extent that the constraints discussed in the next few pages have any validity, domestic strategies of agricultural self-sufficiency in much of the Third World are probably doomed to failure.

ADMINISTRATIVE CONSTRAINTS

The legacy of formal colonial rule has precluded the development in newly independent states of administrative systems able to cope with myriad new demands generated by the postcolonial environment. The bureaucratic constraint is largely one of capacity. Third World bureaucracies often lack the capacity to plan, manage, and evaluate agricultural as well as nonagricultural projects that are not of an infrastructural nature. These constraints are manifested first of all at the policy level. Policy is the "commitment of resources in particular patterns; decisionmaking is the act of choice about the use of resources" (Schaffer 1969, 186). Administrators often find it difficult both bureaucratically and politically to determine a policy. Bureaucratic decisionmakers are adaptive rather than innovative, and their "compartmentalization means that it is easier to refer issues elsewhere rather than deal with the complexities of choice" (Schaffer 1969, 194).

At the planning level, there is often a severe inability on the part of a bureaucracy to undertake the physical and project planning necessary to fund or support development projects (Picard 1981, 71–76). This weakness often begins with the inability of the bureaucracy to write the project document itself.

At the field level, implementation often provides the severest test to LDC bureaucracies. Field delivery on a project is often the weakest link in the development process: Rural-based field administrators are usually the least qualified and least able in the civil service.

LDC bureaucracies specifically lack the requisite skills to promote agricultural and rural development. The civil service is by its nature regulative and routine rather than innovative and developmental. Bureaucracies in more developed countries, such as the United States, Britain, France, or Sweden, would be hard-pressed to take on additional activities of a developmental nature (Diamant 1968). Yet, this is exactly what is asked of the administratively "underdeveloped" civil services in the LDCs. Development administration, it has been suggested, is deadlocked because of a low level of administrative development.

Dependency theorists pinpoint another major bureaucratic constraint to the planning and management of agricultural development—the conflict-of-interest problem. By the nature of their role as managers of agricultural or rural development projects, civil servants are meant to be neutral operatives within the wide society. Yet Hirschmann noted the bureaucracy in Africa, as the major component of an emerging local bourgeoisie, has scope for expanding its influence both within that class and on behalf of that class (Hirschmann 1981, 471). In an agricultural society, civil servants are often interested farmers or cattle owners. As a major socioeconomic group in society with major investments in the agricultural sector, the civil service is in a unique position to manipulate public policy on such issues as land use so that as a burgeoning class, civil servants can benefit from such policy (Picard 1980b). As interested parties, civil servants in ministries of agriculture as well as in allied ministries and departments are likely to have a status quo rather than a developmental or change focus.

The weakness of administrative structures in LDCs is often linked to the failure to develop a meaningful system of technical, community development, and administrative training. Policymakers fail to allocate meaningful resources to appropriate training programs and institutions. Promotion within the civil service becomes automatic with the entry point in many African countries at the lower secondary, and in some cases primary, school certificate level. Field staff, particularly those working as agricultural demonstrators and other extension officers, is at the lowest priority in terms of human resource allocation. Lack of qualified staff is part of a circular problem that results in bureaucratic inertia.

International influences often further exacerbate domestic weaknesses. At the operational level, one of the major influences on the domestic administrative process is the presence of significant numbers of foreigners in key positions of influence. Many African countries rely heavily on foreign experts for preparation of their development plans, in part because they lack personnel, in part because countries granting aid may put forward their own experts.

Countries with strong links to the international economy and the industrial powers are not the only ones that have overseas personnel. Tanzania, with a clear policy of self-sufficiency, depended on overseas planners well into the 1970s and as late as 1982 had expatriate planners attached to district headquarters. Even when the foreigners are gone, they may have left a value system among their successors that is detrimental to the development process. Further, external influences and models come from international agencies. In order to implement a project, the donor agency is likely to demand compliance with certain requirements that distort the priorities and procedures of the recipient government.

The international bureaucrat, though often dedicated and hard working, is likely to lack a knowledge of the political, social, and economic environment of the country where he or she works. According to Horesh, "Just as the (expatriate) policy advisor cannot come to grips with the administrative process still less can the professional foreigner understand the most elementary social processes" (Horesh 1981, 612). The lack of host country experience increases the likelihood of the unadapted transfer of agricultural techniques, whether this be the U.S. model of large-scale ranches or the Scandinavian model of agricultural cooperatives.

The role of the international bureaucrat, particularly the technician, is an uncertain one at best in many Third World countries. An unadapted transfer of techniques, to the extent that it increases the risk of failure, is likely to increase the level of suspicion between indigenous policymakers and expatriate advisers. This suspicion is often compounded because of inherent value conflicts about technology transfer (the tractor versus the hoe problem) and cultural resistance to proposed role changes (such as changes in male/female roles in agriculture).

A related administrative constraint on program implementation in an LDC is caused by subbureaucratic competition within the public sector. There are often several nationalities present in an LDC on overseas contracts. Norwegians in a department of animal health may be in competition with Rumanians in an arable agricultural division while U.S. or Canadian advisers kibitz from a rural sociology unit. Obviously, the greater the penetration of overseas personnel into the public service system, the greater the dislocation there will be from subbureaucratic international competition. At a broader level, networks of expatriates tend to operate outside of national communication links. Speaking of this phenomenon, Schaffer notes: "Western academics and experts . . . moved through one sort of network in one sort of way" (Schaffer 1978, 184). Members of the local administration move through in another.

Educational and training institutions are not immune from this kind of competition. Much of the human resource development is delivered through contracts and link arrangements between LDC training institutions and overseas universities and colleges. To cite a current example in a Southern African country, a Cornell University presence in an agricultural ministry was counterbalanced by the University of Wisconsin in a ministry of local government and South Dakota State University in the country's agricultural college. Such competition can also envelop LDC administrators who received all or part of their training overseas. The usual example is the conflict between a Soviet-trained specialist and a U.S.-trained administrator. Less obvious but no less real differences occur between those trained in Britain or France and those trained in North America.

Administrative constraints on LDC capacity exist at a low level of visibility when one examines the implications of dependency theory from the top down. For this reason, administrative constraints are often overlooked when counterdependency strategies are discussed. Equally as important and often equally neglected is the fact that administrative systems operate within an institutional structure. It is to this level of analysis that we now turn.

INSTITUTIONAL CONSTRAINTS

When we examine the capacity of a state to implement a domestic strategy of agricultural self-sufficiency, it is institutional capacity that is ultimately of concern. To what extent are a society's institutional arrangements and structures able to accommodate a self-sufficiency strategy, selective though it may be?

Institutional capacity can be seen in the context of the institutional transfer/institution-building approach to development management. The objective is "to develop an indigenous, long-run, technical . . . facility that can provide, or create, the techniques for solving problems relevant to its environment" (Potter 1972, 1). Without this institutional capacity both in public and the cooperative sectors, there is little possibility of significant agricultural self-sufficiency.

Innovation and implementation are the twin pillars of institutional capacity. For Esman, "the object is to achieve institutionality—meaning that innovative norms and action patterns are valued within the organization and by the larger society and are incorporated into the behavior of linked organizations and groups" (Esman 1972, 67–68). The societal environment becomes supportive of the organizational innovations, and new patterns of action are introduced to support a political commitment to self-sufficiency. When this has been achieved, institutional capacity not only exists but is valued and used by the ministries and departments and accepted by target groups within the LDC.

Institutional capacity is not just the institutional structure, "but a set of continuing patterns of action that encompass both the organization and its transactional relations with its environment" (Siffin 1972, 144). A key factor to be considered in institutional development is time. A major argument of the institution-building school is that the institutionalization process takes a long time no matter how modest the project or task. An institution-building process should be approached in terms of decades rather than years, and a minimum of ten years will have to be invested to even begin to turn institutional patterns in a different direction.

The time factor is a crucial one and one that will have to be dealt with as LDCs map out a strategy of agricultural self-sufficiency. A Food and Agriculture Organization (FAO) paper on institutionalization of in-service training makes this clear and argues that "rapid institutionalization is undesirable as it may lead to the concomitant undesirable institutionalization of trainers" (FAO 1980, 6). This suggests that the strategy of agricultural self-sufficiency, if it is to be successful, must be seen in the long term, and any "quick fix" operation is probably doomed to failure.

For the institution builders, the issue of implementation is a crucial factor as LDCs seek to modify patterns of action inherited from the colonial period. If strategies of agricultural self-sufficiency are to be successfully established by an LDC, a great deal of attention will have to be paid to an implementation strategy. It is critically important "to make the difficulties of implementation a part of the initial formulation of policy" (Pressman and Wildavsky 1979, 143).

The key to a government strategy in rural and agricultural development is the promotion or transformation of rural institutions such as production and training units, financial and credit facilities (i.e., banks and cooperatives), research and extension services, and farmers' organizations (Puchala and Hopkins 1979, 11). The past two decades of LDC postcolonial experience suggest that institutional incapacity is the weak link in any strategy of rural development. Much of the ensuing problems can be linked to international influences on the LDC. Nicholson has pointed to the negative influence of institutional transfer in the area of agricultural research. The U.S.-style research system, for example, has been exported without adaptation to a great many LDCs (Nicholson 1980, 9). Much of the pattern of both bilateral and multilateral technical assistance is based on unadapted institutional transfer.

Institutional failure is considered a major source of a loss of confidence in the rural area. Government projects that may fail because of an inadequate attention to institutional capacity quickly cause the rural farmer to lose confidence in governmental agriculture strategies. LDC farmers operate on a very low level of marginality. The marginal subsistence farmer simply cannot afford to gamble. Nicholson has found a flaw in recent assumptions that small farmers will be "rational" in adopting new technology that increases per acre yields; he notes that much of this technology is unsuited to the small farmer's resource factor endowments and must therefore be rejected by him on "rational" grounds (Nicholson 1980, 6).

A strategy of agricultural self-sufficiency requires a capacity for organization and management based on correct assumptions about conditions in the rural area. Increased productivity requires "both considerable decentralization but also a highly participatory structure in which farmers play a key role in defining problems and setting priorities" (Nicholson 1980, 13). Yet it is at the level of rural extension and service delivery that LDCs are particularly vulnerable. The farther away from the capital city a public institution operates, the more likely the probability of an institutional failure. Bryant and White note, for example, that agricultural extension agents "are few and far between, ill paid, ill trained, ill equipped with a technical package, and consequently very poor in quality" (Bryant and White 1982, 291).

Agricultural and rural development must be based on a level of administrative and institutional development beyond the capacity of many LDCs. Both administrative and institutional capacities are necessary but not sufficient conditions for a dependency reversal strategy that depends on agricultural self-sufficiency. Neither should be seen as separate from the domestic and international political environment of which administrative and institutional constraints are a part. These political constraints ultimately make a domestic strategy of agricultural self-sufficiency and rural development difficult.

POLITICAL CONSTRAINTS

It is at the level of political constraints that the dependency literature is most useful. The development administration school assumed that the thrust of state policy in LDCs was a positive one and that the political and administrative leadership played at least a "neutral" if not a prodevelopment role in the evolving LDC. Dependency theorists, by pointing to the evolving socioeconomic class system and its relationship to policymaking, have restored political analysis to its proper role in the discussion of development and underdevelopment. Politicians, like bureaucrats, represent an evolving socioeconomic class and are generally conservative about change. Like other members of the socioeconomic elite, politicians have a vested interest in the economic system (Arrighi and Saul 1974).

One of the most disturbing aspects of development strategy in many development countries has been the general lack of priority for agricultural development. Policymakers generally emphasize urban priorities at the expense of rural needs. Where priority is given to agricultural projects, the focus of agricultural priorities has been to provide support for "master farmers" (large commercial farmers) rather than smaller commercial or subsistence farmers. Arguments of economies of scale and the need for foreign exchange mask a clear and widespread bias against rural development as opposed to agricultural growth. As Puchala and Hopkins point out (1979, 16), "When higher earning export crops or cheaper food imports (e.g., food aid) create incentives to move away from food production, this shift will also affect the urban-rural terms of trade because cheaper food prices generally favor the urban population." There is a line of argument that many Third World politicians would feel very comfortable with that "the rich (i.e., successful) farmer should not be discriminated against" (oral interview with local politician in Botswana, June 1982). In the postcolonial period, the state, in the guise of serving the general welfare, is "used to manipulate and deflect the consciousness of the subordinate classes, so serving the interests of the politically and economically dominant classes" (Hirschmann 1981, 470). Programs that discriminate in favor of the poor/subsistence producer receive scant support from most LDC politicians.

If one steps back from dependency theory to look at individual level political behavior, the situation becomes hardly less bleak. At the behavioral level there may be a conflict between elite political requirements and the agricultural and rural development needs of an LDC. Politicians even in a one-party or dominant-party state perceive the need for mass support (Picard 1979; 1980a; and 1980c). Gaining mass support most likely means an emphasis on physical or infrastructure change rather than attempts at social transformation. Buildings (schools, health posts) and roads have an immediate impact of a kind that a long-term arable agriculture program or a training or a human resources development program lacks (Picard 1979, 294).

For some political leaders political control may be a concern. Developmental programs in the rural areas are dangerous in that they may stimulate rising expectations that government may not be able to meet in the future. For many LDC leaders, there has been a temptation to give priority to industrialization and/or mineral exploitation at the expense of agricultural production in the hope, particularly in the mining sector, there may be a quick payoff. Thus, there is a net decline in agricultural production, the LDC shifts from a net exporter to a net importer of foodstuffs, and as visible urban development takes place, migration from rural areas generates the urban slums characteristic of LDC cities.

The central dilemma of agricultural development is that politicians often perceive the peasant as "conservative" and unwilling to change or adapt to the current needs of government policy. For the subsistence farmer the adaptation to the vicissitudes of government requires a trade-off of what the farmer knows in terms of agricultural production for an uncertain future with a new policy whose benefits are far from assured. For the farmer this may be a rational calculation. Development in a very real sense means austerity for someone—capital accumulation means the lack of basic goods as saving occurs. In all likelihood, it will be the rural dweller at the subsistence level, not the urban politician and bureaucrat, who sacrifices.

Part of the gap between the "conservative" peasant and the policymaker is a function of a critical communication problem common to many LDCs. The distance is great, both physically and psychologically, between the subsistence level rural dweller and the administrator in a ministry of agriculture. This distance has been exacerbated in many countries by the failure of local level political institutions such as local councils and district and village development committees. At the same time, there is a mistrust on the part of central government officials in many countries of local traditional leaders (ethnic, feudal, or religious) who are likely to maintain communication links with rural farmers.

Domestic political constraints on agricultural development are reinforced by political constraints that are international in origin and are a part of the nature of bilateral and multilateral technical assistance. The IMF/World Bank austerity program to manage and eventually ensure LDC debt repayments is well known. At the broadly political level the donor agencies (whether bilateral or multilateral) do have a major influence and do place political constraints on the developmental process. Donor requirements have set priorities for Third World countries. The dynamic of the donor project is money—often big money for a project that may or may not relate to country needs. LDCs find it very difficult to turn down major donor projects, but as a result the type of agricultural emphasis is often then taken out of local policymakers' hands.

Selective diluting of donor funds can limit the excessive influence of technical assistance but cannot eliminate the problem altogether. Through the 1970s, for example, when Tanzania experimented with a self-sufficiency strategy, technical assistance continued to contribute significantly to its development budget and its development strategies.

Projects, even those involving large sums of money and several years duration, tend to be written very quickly. A consultant on a project team is sent in for three or four weeks to write a project paper. That brief visit then becomes the basis of massive donor and LDC expenditure. The result is often a project emphasizing activity rather than impact, with a visual effect (the gift of a new machine or an officer going overseas on a study tour) at the apex. Project priorities are more likely to reflect bureaucratic and political needs in the donor capital rather than LDC needs.

Donor projects from various countries often do not sync with one another or with domestically funded projects within the LDC. That the various parts do not make up the whole is a problem of interdonor communication. The various donors, even in relatively small countries, tend not to talk to each other about what they are doing, and the LDC government or supervising ministry often does not have the leverage to bring the donors together.

The technical assistance process is, of course, influenced by the international political competition of which donor programs are a part. This competition occurs at a number of levels. Fundamental to international rivalries is competition about values and patterns of economic control and influence. At the broadest level, superpower politics and competition determine foreign aid. The economic strategies of Third World countries are often captives of both national and international political alliances, financial arrangements, and foreign policy considerations. The strings attached to foreign aid are just as real whether they link collectivization with the Soviet Union's assistance or individual land tenure with Western aid. At the value level, fundamental assumptions are made by technical advisers about such crucial questions as the ownership and control of land and individual or collective land tenure, assumptions that are divorced from a historical or a cultural context.

CONCLUSION

At the international level agricultural development strategies remain to a large extent in conflict with international market constraints. Part of what has been seen as a decline in Third World agriculture is a perceived decline in the agricultural market for Third World commodities. Given that food markets are hard to find, it is easy to understand Nigeria's higher priority for oil than for ground nuts. Dependency theorists have thoroughly documented the fundamental limitations that LDCs face in terms of marketing, trade, and resource allocation. There are simply no good solutions for Third World countries given the nature of the current international economic system.

There is a fundamental dilemma for LDC policymakers as they try to set priorities in their relationship with the world, particularly the industrialized north. Proponents of a growth-oriented strategy of development argue the need for integration with outside economic systems. Focus under these circumstances is usually on large-scale agricultural production of export commodities (plantation-scale agricultural business). The weakness of this strategy is made clear by dependency theorists. Not only does this leave the LDC dependent on external investment and influence, but it also requires the LDC to compete against the industrial north in an area where the LDC is often weakest—commercial agricultural production. The historical evolution of the world economic system precludes a fundamental shift of advantage to the majority of LDCs. LDCs are thus faced with no satisfactory alternatives.

The alternative strategy is increased autonomy and selective agricultural self-reliance. This has been tried by a number of LDCs, the most prominent of which is Tanzania. Such efforts have usually had their limitations as well. This chapter suggests that there are fundamental administrative, institutional, and political barriers to the effective use of a domestic strategy of dependency reversal based on agricultural self-sufficiency and rural development. Often in the shift to self-sufficiency, basic commodities seem to disappear from grocery shelves just about the time that foreign exchange reserves disappear. The shift toward self-sufficiency, particularly in concert with a new agricultural strategy, is often combined with an increased use of coercion. Coercion is then followed by an increased resistance to the new policy. At the same time, the most productive and competitive sectors of society are discouraged.

The dilemma of satisfactory alternatives points to the problem of incentives as they relate to the alternative value systems of the planned versus the market economy. Although the market economy may provide material incentives for the few, neither strategy provides much economic incentive for the majority of rural subsistence agriculturalists. The planned economy on the other hand has failed to demonstrate that ideology or "rhetorical incentives" are successful alternatives.

REFERENCES

Amin, S. "Underdevelopment and Dependence in Black Africa: Origins and Contemporary Forms." *The Journal of Modern African Studies* (1972a): 503–524.

Amin, S. *Neo-Colonialism in West Africa*. New York: Monthly Review Press, 1972b.

Amin, S. *Accumulation on a World Scale: A Critique of the Theory of Underdevelopment*. New York: Monthly Review Press, 1974.

Arrighi, G., and J. S. Saul. *Essays on the Political Economy of Africa*. Nairobi: East African Publishing House, 1974.

Baran, Paul. *The Political Economy of Growth*. New York: Monthly Review Press, 1957.

Barnet, R. J. *The Lean Years: Politics in the Age of Scarcity*. New York: Simon and Schuster, 1980a.

Barnet, R. J. "The World's Resources: Part I, The Lean Years." *New Yorker* (March 18, 1980b): 45–81.

Bryant, C., and L. G. White. *Managing Development in the Third World*. Boulder, Colo.: Westview Press, 1982.

Caporaso, J. A., and B. Zare. "An Interpretation and Evaluation of Dependency Theory." In H. Munoz, ed. *From Dependency to Development: Strategies to Overcome Underdevelopment and Inequality*. Boulder, Colo.: Westview Press 1981, pp. 43–56.

Diamant, A. "Tradition and Innovation in French Administration." *Comparative Political Studies* (July 1968): 251–274.

Diaz-Alejandro, C. F. "Delinking North and South: Unshackled or Unhinged." In A. Fishlow et al., eds. *Rich and Poor Nations in the World Economy*. New York: McGraw-Hill, 1978, pp. 87–123.

Esman, M. J. "Some Issues in Institution Building Theory." In D. W. Thomas, H. R. Potter, W. L. Miller, and A. F. Aven, eds., *Institution Building: A Model for Applied Social Change*. Cambridge, Mass.: Schenkman Publishing Co., 1972, pp. 65–90.

Esman, M. J. "Administrative Doctrine and Developmental Needs." In E. P. Morgan, ed. *The Administration of Change in Africa: Essays in the Theory and Practice of Development Administration in Africa*. New York: Dunellen Publishing Company, 1974, pp. 3–26.

Food and Agriculture Organization. "Institutionalization of In-Service Training." Prepared by the Policy Analysis Division, Food and Agriculture Organization, and presented at the Expert Meeting in In-Service Training Approaches for Agricultural Project Analysis in Small Developing Countries. Katmandu, Nepal, February 18–20, 1980.

Gant, G. F. *Development Administration: Concepts, Goals, Methods*. Madison: University of Wisconsin Press, 1979.

Gould, D. J. "Local Administration in Zaire and Underdevelopment." *Journal of Modern African Studies* (1977): 349–378.

Green, R. H. "Aspects of the World Monetary and Resource Transfer System in 1974: A View from the Extreme Periphery." In G. K. Helleiner, ed. *A World Divided: The Less Developed Countries in the International Economy*. Cambridge: Cambridge University Press, 1976: pp. 251–283.

Gunder Frank, A. *Latin America: Underdevelopment or Revolution*. New York: Monthly Review Press, 1969.

Hirschmann, D. "Development or Underdevelopment Administration? A Further Deadlock." *Development and Change* (July 1981): 459–479.

Horesh, E. "Academics and Experts or the Death of the High Level Technical Assistant." *Development and Change* (October 1981): 611–618.

Leontief, W. W. *The Future of the World Economy*. New York: Oxford University Press, 1977.

Munoz, H., ed. *From Dependency to Development: Strategies to Overcome Underdevelopment and Inequality*. Boulder, Colo.: Westview Press, 1981.

Nicholson, N. L. "The Political Economy of Agricultural Research in Developing Countries: The Case for Farming Systems Approaches." Paper presented to Farm Structure and Rural Policy Symposium, Ames, Iowa, October 20–22, 1980.

Picard, L. A. "Rural Development in Botswana: Administrative Structures and Public Policy." *Journal of Developing Areas* (April 1979):238–300.

Picard, L. A. "Socialism and the Field Administrator: Decentralization in Tanzania." *Comparative Politics* (July 1980a):439–457.

Picard, L. A. "Bureaucrats, Cattle, and Public Policy: Land Tenure Changes in Botswana." *Comparative Political Studies* (October 1980b):313–356.

Picard, L. A. "Attitudes and Development: The District Administration in Tanzania." *African Studies Review* (December 1980c):49–67.

Picard, L. A., with Klaus Endresen. *A Study of the Manpower and Training Needs of the Unified Local Government Service, 1982–1992*. Gaborone, Botswana: Government Printer, 1981.

Potter, H. R. "Introduction." In D. W. Thomas, H. R. Potter, W. L. Miller, and A. F. Aven, eds. *Institution Building: A Model for Applied Social Change*. Cambridge, Mass.: Schenkman Publishing Co., 1972, pp. 1–5.

Pressman, J. L., and A. Wildavsky. *Implementation*. Berkeley: University of California Press, 1979.

Puchala, D. J., and R. F. Hopkins. "The Politics of Agricultural Modernization." In D. J. Puchala and R. F. Hopkins, eds. *Food, Politics, and Agricultural Development: Case Studies in the Public Policy of Rural Modernization*. Boulder, Colo.: Westview Press, 1979, pp. 1–20.

Schaffer, B. B. "The Deadlock in Development Administration." In C. Leys, ed. *Politics and Change in Developing Countries*. London: Cambridge University Press, 1969, pp. 177–212.

Siffin, W. J. "The Institution Building Perspective." In D. W. Thomas, H. R. Potter,

W. L. Miller, and A. F. Aven, eds. *Institution Building: A Model for Social Change*. Cambridge, Mass.: Schenkman Publishing Co., 1972.

Sunkel, O. "Development Styles and the Environment: An Interpretation of the Latin American Case." In H. Munoz, ed. *From Dependency to Development: Strategies to Overcome Underdevelopment and Inequality*. Boulder, Colo.: Westview Press, 1981, pp. 93–114.

Valenzuela, J. S., and A. Valenzuela. "Modernization and Dependency: Alternative Perspectives in the Study of Latin American Underdevelopment." *Comparative Politics* (July 1978):535–557.

10 The Policy Consequences of the Green Revolution: The Latin American Case

Michael K. Roberts, C. Micheal Schwartz,
Michael S. Stohl, and Harry R. Targ

The hopes and success of the Green Revolution have found a sympathetic audience in a United States imbued with the ideology of the technological fix. A recent article by Stevens is an informative exemplar: "High-yield grains, tractors, irrigation, chemical fertilizers, pesticides and advanced farming techniques have made the Punjab into by far the most prosperous state in India" (Stevens 1982, 4). Stevens continues, reporting that in one village ninety people farm a total of 200 acres. Each family owns a tractor, and the village is served by electrically operated tube wells providing underground water to the acreage. The families grow wheat and rice, reaping a profit of $10,000 a year. About $3,500 is reinvested for new land and buildings. In the state as a whole, Punjabis consume 3,000 calories per day compared with 2,000 throughout India.

The example speaks well of the Green Revolution. The Green Revolution is a shorthand term for a set of agricultural development policies that encourage the utilization of high-yield grains, fertilizers, pesticides, and advanced agricultural machinery to increase agricultural productivity. It is an approach to agriculture that is encouraged by the industrial capitalist states and their allies among Third World leaders to build a more productive agricultural base than that provided by traditional agriculture.

The Green Revolution is designed to facilitate the production of food exports as well as food for domestic consumption. In fact, the agricultural policies of Third World countries attracted to the Green Revolution have emphasized food exports as a centerpiece of economic growth. Fertile land in the countrysides of many Third World nations has been transformed from hundreds of small farms to small numbers of native- or foreign-owned large "factories in the fields," producing strawberries, citrus fruits, bananas, carnations, and other ex-

---

This research is part of a larger project on the world food system that was supported by a U.S. Agency for International Development Title 12 Strengthening Grant to Purdue University.

port crops for markets in the United States and other developed nations. The assumption of the Green Revolution is that the earnings from these export platforms will trickle down to the populace of the exporting country and will facilitate capital accumulation for broadbased economic growth. It is further assumed that these increased earnings and food production will raise the caloric intake of the local population.

Cheryl Payer cites a World Bank paper on rural development that states that bank policy (and indeed the policy of aid-giving industrial capitalist states, agribusiness multinational corporations, and Third World elites) is concerned with "the modernization of rural society" and with the "transition from traditional isolation to integration with the national economy" and the international economy. Core capitalist states and institutions seek "greater interaction between the modern and traditional sectors, especially in the form of increased trade in farm produce and in technical inputs and services" (Payer 1982, 221).

Multinational agribusinesses sell the machinery, fertilizers, seeds, and other inputs for the Green Revolution to Third World "farmers" who can afford to purchase them or who are perceived as good risks for World Bank loans. It is hoped that the recipients of these Green Revolution inputs will produce crops with increased yields that will be available for export, and hence, will generate foreign exchange earnings for the country. It is also believed that the processes of production and exchange catalyzed by the Green Revolution will increase the capacity of Third World nations to more equitably distribute food and ultimately provide more adequately for the food needs of the people.

By using certain types of indicators of agricultural productivity or by selecting examples of economic growth in a sea of stagnation, the high-technology agriculture associated with the Green Revolution is often portrayed in a positive light by its defenders. Some agricultural researchers, however, have begun to identify settings in which Green Revolution agriculture has been less than successful in fulfilling the food needs of a given population (Burbach and Flynn 1980; Caldwell 1977; Christensen 1978; George 1977; de Janvry 1981; Lappé and Collins 1978; Payer 1974).

Frances Lappé and Joseph Collins (1978) write about the experiences of Mexico and the Central American nations during the 1960s and the 1970s. Northern Mexico has been transformed into a vast area for the production of asparagus, cucumbers, tomatoes, and other crops for the U.S. market. Large agribusinesses such as Del Monte, General Foods, or Campbell's contract with Mexicans to produce crops once produced more cheaply in the United States. In 1973, U.S. asparagus farmers received 23 cents a pound for their produce from Del Monte. Mexican contractors received 10 cents a pound. Mexican seasonal agricultural workers were earning 23 cents an hour.

Lappé and Collins report that Mexico is supplying more than one-half of many of the winter and spring vegetables sold on the U.S. market. They say that from 1960 to 1974 U.S. imports of onions from Mexico increased fivefold. From 1960 to 1976, cucumber imports increased from 9 to 196 million pounds.

Eggplant imports increased ten times and squash 43 times in just twelve years. Strawberries and cantaloupes from Mexico now make up 33 percent of U.S. consumption of those fruits (Lappé and Collins 1978, 281–282).

The dollar value of Mexican imports of agricultural machinery more than doubled between 1965 and 1975 ($42.6 million to $103 million). Imports of fertilizer increased 60 percent, and imports of pesticides rose by about 15 percent. U.S. direct foreign investment in Mexican food production more than tripled between the late 1960s and the first half of the 1970s. The dollar value of agricultural imports increased by 800 percent, and the value of agricultural exports rose by 60 percent between 1965 and 1975. Meanwhile, the consumption of calories and proteins on a per capita basis did not change between the middle 1960s and the 1970s.[1]

In discussing the impacts of Mexican agricultural developments on food consumption, Lappé and Collins suggest that it was not long ago that Mexican national fruit and vegetable production was sufficient to provide some quantities of these commodities at prices that poor families could occasionally purchase. Now, they say, such crops are crowded out to grow luxury crops grown for the "global supermarket." They claim that "land growing crops for the Global Supermarket is land the local people cannot use to grow food crops for themselves." Even beans have become a luxury for the poor people of Mexico (Lappé and Collins 1978, 281–282).

If we focus on the five Central American nations, we find that by 1969 more than 19 percent of their total acreage was planted with fruits and vegetables for export. Another 29 percent of the cropland was used for growing coffee, sugar, cotton, and bananas and for cattle raising (Lappé and Collins 1978, 283). Table 10.1 illustrates the pattern of machine imports, agricultural exports, and food consumption per capita of the five Central American countries in 1965 and in 1975. Although the dependent variable percentage of daily caloric requirements on a per capita basis is an inadequate measure of the gross inequalities of food distribution, the table does suggest the limited impacts of the importation of sophisticated machinery and the exports of agricultural commodities on caloric intake or food consumption.

For example, Costa Rica, El Salvador, and Honduras dramatically increased their importation of agricultural machinery, yet El Salvador and Honduras still did not provide an adequate daily requirement of calories for its peoples. All five Central American countries dramatically increased their agricultural exports; however, only Costa Rica improved the caloric intake of its citizens above the daily requirement. Although the data reported in Table 10.1 are not conclusive as to the impacts of the Green Revolution and of export-oriented agriculture, such data and the anecdotal evidence of writers like Lappé and Collins raise questions about the efficacy of the high-technology Green Revolution and export agricultural policies of Third World states in providing food for their people.

Therefore, the mixed findings concerning the Punjab and Central America stimulate a series of questions about the relative merits of a high-technology agriculture, an export-oriented agriculture, a Third World agriculture that is inextricably bound to the needs of the core capitalist states, and a core capitalist state policy that encourages this high-technology, export-oriented agriculture in the Third World. This chapter examines the merits of the case for and against the Green Revolution by examining data on Latin America in the 1960s and 1970s. To structure the investigation, two competing explanations for agricultural development are presented: the Green Revolution Agricultural Model and the Radical Model of the World System. The chapter concludes with a discussion of the agricultural policy implications of the findings for both core capitalist and Third World states.

THE AGRICULTURAL DEVELOPMENT MODEL: THE GREEN REVOLUTION

The central premise of the Green Revolution is that utilization of advanced agricultural technology will result in significant increases in agricultural and food production. This increase in agricultural production is expected to lead to a direct increase in domestic food consumption because of increases in the supply of food. Export earnings are projected to generate valuable foreign exchange, some of which can be used for overseas food purchases. Further, by enhancing the financial resources of a nation, it is hoped that foreign exchange will stimu-

Table 10.1

Machine Inputs, Agricultural Exports, and Caloric Intake in Central America[1]

COUNTRY		IMPORTS OF AGRICULTURAL MACHINES (1000 DOLLARS)	EXPORTS OF AGRICULTURAL PRODUCTS (1000 DOLLARS)	PERCENTAGE OF DAILY CALORIC REQUIREMENTS (PER CAPITA) (%)
Costa Rica	1965	$ 3,100	$ 92,600	104
	1975	16,843	340,372	111
El Salvador	1965	4,200	147,400	80
	1975	15,850	348,551	91
Guatemala	1965	7,700	157,350	98
	1975	9,000	434,187	98
Honduras	1965	2,400	90,900	98
	1975	12,736	166,459	92
Nicaragua	1965	8,600	124,800	112
	1975	9,814	227,177	109

[1] Data derived from various editions of the FAO Production Yearbook.

late domestic food consumption through increased income available to purchase domestic food commodities.

When the Green Revolution was first posited by agricultural researchers in the 1940s, it was correctly assumed that major agricultural technologies would soon be available for food production around the world. The succeeding decades saw the utilization of high-yield seeds, chemical fertilizers, modern pesticides, and advances in agricultural machinery. The application of seeds, chemicals, and machinery in Third World countries has been encouraged by agriculturally rich countries, by international agencies such as the World Bank, and by the huge agribusiness multinational corporations who produce the Green Revolution inputs and who process food grown in the Third World for sale in rich industrial capitalist markets.

To explore the impact of the Green Revolution, four hypotheses derived from the Agricultural Development Model based on the Green Revolution are subjected in this chapter to empirical investigation. They are:

1. Utilization of Green Revolution inputs leads to an increase in domestic food production.

2. Increases in domestic agricultural production leads to increases in domestic food consumption *and* increases in agricultural exports.

3. Increases in agricultural exports lead to increases in domestic food consumption *and* increases in food imports.

4. Increases in agricultural imports leads to increases in domestic food consumption.

THE RADICAL MODEL: THE WORLD FOOD SYSTEM AND HUNGER IN THE THIRD WORLD

Those who challenge the efficacy of the Green Revolution from the standpoint of food distribution and consumption underscore the transforming character of high-technology agriculture on power, social classes, and occupational structures in Third World countries. The Green Revolution, it is argued, stimulates and indeed requires technological dependence, large landholdings, small numbers of crops, and long-term indebtedness due to the start-up costs of the new machinery. Consequently, limited local markets lead to the need for overseas customers: Large quantities of sugar, coffee, bananas, and winter vegetables must be sold to wealthy customers in core capitalist countries.

The goal of Third World policy planners therefore becomes one of selling foodstuffs overseas. The initial concern for increasing food consumption becomes reconceptualized to that of creating a viable export-oriented agriculture. Whether the crop is wheat, soybeans, or pineapples, agricultural policy is transformed into a concern with increasing export sales and moves away from its original purpose of feeding hungry people. With a Green Revolution-oriented agriculture, food for the Third World's hungry will have to come from the profit gained from export sales. The land in Third World nations is removed from subsistence agriculture and turned over to export agriculture.

In addition to the transformation of Third World countries to a high-technology, export-oriented agriculture encouraged by the core states, multinational agribusinesses, and international institutions, a transformation occurs in Third World class formations and hence in the distribution of wealth and power. Most peasants are not able to purchase the Green Revolution inputs, nor do they own sufficient land for profitable cultivation. Wealthy peasants and large landholders are the only actors in the Third World able to purchase high-technology inputs to produce quantities sufficient to make profit. The wealthy in the countrysides then purchase or expropriate land held by poor peasants. These peasants become farm laborers in the money economy or an unemployed labor-seeking reserve army displaced by capital-intensive agricultural machinery. The last three decades have seen a radical transformation in landholding patterns in the Third World nations that have attempted the Green Revolution.

In sum, the Radical Model argues that despite increases in agricultural production due to the Green Revolution and increases in food export earnings coupled with increases in food imports, masses of Third World peoples receive less food because of social structural transformation in the countryside that exacerbates gaps between rich and poor. Poor peasants, once subsistence farmers, are thrust into the money economy but do not have the income to purchase needed food. The Radical Model, on the basis of the causal chain leading from the global economy to the poor peasant in the countryside, predicts an exacerbation of hunger needs as industrial capitalist and Third World states opt for policies supporting the Green Revolution and an export-oriented agriculture. The five hypotheses below are derived from the Radical Model and are subjected to empirical examination in this chapter:

1. Utilization of Green Revolution inputs will lead to an increase in agricultural exports, a decline in the percentage of labor employed in agriculture, and an increase in equality.

2. Increases in agricultural exports will lead to increases in agricultural imports and reductions in the level of domestic food consumption.

3. Increases in agricultural imports will not lead to increases in domestic food consumption.

4. Declines in the percentage of the labor force employed in agriculture will lead to an increase in inequality.

5. Increases in inequality will lead to decreases in domestic food consumption.

METHODOLOGY

The empirical investigation of the hypotheses derived from proponents and critics of the Green Revolution policy consists of a cross-sectional analysis of fifteen Latin American nations from 1965 to 1977.[2] During this period, most of the nations were the recipients of large dollar amounts of Green Revolution inputs (seeds, fertilizers, pesticides, machinery).

Data was gathered for seven variables. *Domestic food consumption* is measured by per capita caloric intake.[3] The Food and Agriculture Organization (FAO) obtained this figure by dividing available food supplies by population. Of course, this measure, although the best available, is insensitive to the actual distribution of food for consumption purposes. As a measure of Green Revolution inputs, imports of *agricultural machinery* were selected, as analysis demonstrated that these imports were highly correlated with imports of fertilizer, pesticides, and seeds. Measures of *agricultural imports* and *exports,* including all crops and livestock products, were also gathered. *Agricultural and food production* is measured as the value added to the Gross Domestic Product by agriculture (GDP Agriculture) and includes agriculture, forestry, hunting, and fishing. The *percentage of labor employed in agriculture* measures the number of laborers in agricultural activities, including farming, forestry, fishing, and hunting, as a percentage of the total labor force. Finally, the measure of income inequality is measured by the *income received by the lowest 20 percent* of the population.

All monetary figures provided by the *World Tables* and the *FAO Production Yearbook* have been converted into U.S. dollars when domestic currency had originally been reported. Controlling for inflation, all U.S. dollar figures have been converted into constant (1969) U.S. dollars. These figures were then divided by the corresponding country and year population estimates. This provides a standardized metric that facilitates the pooling of data for the time period under consideration in this study. The unit of analysis is the country. Bivariate correlational analyses were performed on the data to test the hypotheses posited.

LATIN AMERICA EXPERIENCES THE GREEN REVOLUTION:
1965–1977

Table 10.2 indicates the relationships found among seven variables for fifteen nations from 1965 to 1977. Generally, the predictions derived from the Agricultural Development Model, which gave support to the Green Revolution, were not confirmed. There was no significant relationships between the Green Revolution indicator, agricultural machinery, and food production. However, there was a significant correlation between agricultural and food production and

Table 10.2
Pearson Correlation Coefficients
Among All Variables

VARIABLES	1	2	3	4	5	6[1]	7[1]
1) Domestic Food Consumption (Caloric Intake)	---	r=-.01 N=(60) P=.459	r= .04 N=(60) P=.389	r= .06 N=(60) P=.335	r= .30 N=(58) P=.011	r=-.71 N=(30) P=.001	r=-.13 N=(17) P=.306
2) Green Revolution Inputs (Agricultural Machinery)		---	r= .73 N=(120) P=.001	r= .27 N=(120) P=.001	r= .03 N=(118) P=.271	r=-.14 N=(30) P=.234	r=-.12 N=(17) P=.323
3) Agricultural and Food Production Imports			---	r=-.05 N=(120) P=.300	r= .32 N=(118) P=.001	r=-.29 N=(30) P=.059	r=-.22 N=(17) P=.193
4) Agricultural and Food Production Exports				---	r=-.18 N=(118) P=.025	r= .06 N=(30) P=.385	r= .60 N=(17) P=.005
5) Agricultural and Food Production (GDP in Agriculture)					---	r=-.40 N=(43) P=.004	r=-.20 N=(24) P=.171
6) Percent of Labor in Agriculture						---	r=-.31 N=(24) P=.067
7) Percent of Income of Low 20%							---

[1](Because of the low number of cases, caution needs to be used when interpreting this column. See comments in the text.)

r = the Pearson correlation coefficient
N = the number of cases. (The number of cases will vary because the socio-demographic variables were not available for each year under study.)
P = the level of significance

domestic food consumption. This suggests that as food production increased so did food consumption. This finding did not conflict with the Radical Model. The Radical Model suggested that there was no relationship between an export-oriented agriculture fueled by the Green Revolution and food consumption; as the model was postulated here it did not address the question of food production and consumption *in isolation from the Green Revolution.*

Further, contrary to the predictions of the Agricultural Development Model, increased food production did not lead to a direct increase in agricultural and food exports. In fact the data suggest that as food production increased during the years studied, food exports decreased. Table 10.2 also indicates that the export of agricultural commodities did not stimulate either domestic food consumption or the importation of foreign food commodities. No significant associations between these variables were noted.

Finally, it was predicted that an increase in agricultural and food imports would lead to an increase in domestic food consumption. No significant relationship was noted between imports and consumption. The data suggest that the world food system of trade did nothing to enhance the domestic food consumption of Latin American peoples. Domestic food consumption increased only when domestic food production increased.

The data tend to give greater support to predictions based on the Radical Model. For example, one of the strongest correlation coefficients is the relationship between the Green Revolution inputs and agricultural exports. The more a country imports Green Revolution inputs, the more agricultural and food commodities it exports. As the model suggests, landowners purchase inputs and then must place their commodities on the world market in order to make a profit to recoup the large capital expenses. Further, as suggested above, although the dollar value of Green Revolution inputs soared in the period under examination, the data indicated that Green Revolution inputs did not correlate with increases in overall food production in the fifteen Latin American countries studied.

Because the newer high-technology agriculture forces the concentration of lands in large holdings and is capital-intensive, it was predicted that as inputs rose, the percentage of the work force in agriculture would decline. This relationship was modestly confirmed. Another major premise is also modestly supported by the data. As Green Revolution inputs increase, a wider gap between the rich and poor in Latin America becomes noticeable. The lower 20 percent of the population receives a smaller amount of the total income of the population.[4]

The data do not conform to the Radical Model predictions concerning agricultural exports, imports, and food consumption, but at the same time the data did not give support to the Agricultural Development Model. The data indicated that there was not a significant relationship between exports and imports as the Radical Model assumed. However, there was no relationship at all between agricultural exports or imports and food consumption. Consequently, the international agricultural market bore *no* constructive relationship to the food needs of Latin Americans.

The last two hypotheses derived from the Radical Model were not supported by the data at all. Contrary to expectation, as the percentage of the agricultural labor force declined, the percentage of income of the lower 20 percent of the population increased. However as noted earlier, findings related to these two variables may be artifacts of the measures themselves. One likely explanation of an outcome opposite to the prediction of the model is that although peasants, forced off their lands as farms became factories, are forced into the money economy as marginalized workers, they increase their reported income and hence appear from the statistics to have increased their real income. Consequently, their money income increases the amount acquired by the bottom 20 percent of the population.

Finally, it was predicted that an increase in inequality would lead to a decrease in domestic food consumption. The data indicated that as inequality became greater, food consumption increased. A possible explanation for this finding contrary to expectation is that as one class gains wealth, incomes of other classes rise also, but modestly. Another explanation is posited by George (1977), who claims that although per capita figures of caloric intake may show an increase, larger percentages of the population of a nation may be increasingly malnourished. This is so because the dependent variable, caloric consumption per capita, cannot be sensitive to actual food distribution in towns, cities, and rural areas.

The aggregate data analysis so far rejects the relationship between the Green Revolution, an export-oriented agriculture, and the diminution of world hunger, while giving modest support to some predictions derived from the Radical Model. To further examine the two models and to provide increased specificity to the analysis, the fifteen countries examined were divided into those that fell above the fifteen-country mean in caloric intake during the time frame studied and those that fell below this mean. Those that were above the mean in caloric intake per capita were Argentina, Brazil, Chile, Costa Rica, Mexico, Nicaragua, Panama, and Venezuela. Those with a per capita caloric intake below the mean were Colombia, the Dominican Republic, Ecuador, El Salvador, Guatemala, Honduras, and Peru.

Disaggregating the countries indicates whether Green Revolution agricultural policies were more applicable in settings of high or low caloric intake. It was conceivable that the Green Revolution policies had a constructive role to play in food production and consumption in more agriculturally developed countries and an equally negative role to play in the most agriculturally underdeveloped countries. In this prediction, capital-intensive agriculture would more negatively impact on class inequality in poorer countries where gaps between rich and poor are more extreme and only would be made worse by the new modes of production. Or on the other hand, it may be that greater positive Green Revolution impacts on food production and consumption occurred in the poorest countries in terms of production and consumption.

Tables 10.3 and 10.4 report the findings for the two groups of countries. Table 10.3 indicates that among the above-caloric-mean countries, caloric intake is negatively correlated with Green Revolution inputs and agricultural imports. Among the below-caloric-mean countries, the Green Revolution inputs have no effect on caloric intake. Both country group findings reinforce the rejection of the Agricultural Development Model. Agricultural imports also are not related to calories in either group of countries.[5]

In reference to interrelationships between Green Revolution inputs and elements of the Agricultural Development Model, there were relationships found between agricultural machinery imports and agricultural imports in general and increases in agricultural machinery and exports in below-caloric-mean countries. Similarly, a relationship was found between agricultural exports and agricultural imports in below-caloric-mean countries.

In the seven countries that had a caloric intake below the mean, increases in agricultural exports and increases in agricultural productivity correlated strongly with increases in the share of income of the bottom 20 percent of the population. However, there was a strong negative correlation between the narrowing of the income gap and caloric intake. Therefore, even in the case of very poor countries, increases in agricultural productivity and exports and decreases in income inequality (usually no more than 1 percent) were not reflected in greater food consumption. This suggests that some peasants and farmers improved their income through the newer agriculture, but the results did not positively impact on the vast majority of the nation's citizens.

Table 10.3
Above Caloric Mean Countries, Pearson Correlation Coefficients
Among All Variables

VARIABLES	1	2	3	4	5	6[1]	7[1]
1) Domestic Food Consumption (Caloric Intake)	---	r=-.41 N=(32) P=.010	r=-.39 N=(32) P=.012	r=-.09 N=(32) P=.296	r= .14 N=(32) P=.215	r=-.62 N=(16) P=.005	r= .28 N=(10) P=.209
2) Green Revolution Inputs (Agricultural Machinery)		---	r= .77 N=(64) P=.001	r= .24 N=(64) P=.026	r=-.07 N=(63) P=.303	r=-.08 N=(16) P=.386	r=-.22 N=(10) P=.269
3) Agricultural and Food Production Imports			---	r=-.03 N=(64) P=.396	r= .26 N=(63) P=.022	r=-.28 N=(16) P=.144	r= .18 N=(10) P=.305
4) Agricultural and Food Production Exports				---	r=-.23 N=(63) P=.032	r= .10 N=(16) P=.353	r= .44 N=(10) P=.104
5) Agricultural and Food Production					---	r=-.38 N=(23) P=.037	r= .17 N=(15) P=.270
6) Percent of Labor in Agriculture						---	r=-.33 N=(15) P=.113
7) Percent of Income of Low 20%							---

[1](Because of the low number of cases, caution needs to be used when interpreting this column. See comments in the text.)

r = the Pearson correlation coefficient
N = the number of cases
P = the level of significance

Table 10.4
Below Caloric Mean Countries, Pearson Correlation Coefficients
Among All Variables

VARIABLES	1	2	3	4	5	6[1]	7[1]
1) Domestic Food Consumption --- (Caloric Intake)	r= .01 N=(28) P=.477	r=-.12 N=(28) P=.264	r=-.34 N=(28) P=.038	r= .09 N=(27) P=.312	r=-.48 N=(14) P=.041	r=-.67 N= (7) P=.050
2) Green Revolution Inputs --- (Agricultural Machinery)		r= .16 N=(56) P=.107	r= .42 N=(56) P=.001	r= .04 N=(55) P=.381	r= .24 N=(14) P=.205	r= .11 N= (7) P=.409
3) Agricultural and Food Production Imports ---			r= .44 N=(56) P=.001	r= .12 N=(55) P=.188	r= .43 N=(14) P=.065	r= .41 N= (7) P=.182
4) Agricultural and Food Production Exports ---				r= .41 N=(55) P=.001	r= .08 N=(14) P=.391	r= .75 N= (7) P=.025
5) Agricultural and Food Production (GDP in Agriculture) ---					r=-.31 N=(20) P=.091	r= .63 N= (9) P=.033
6) Percent of Labor in Agriculture ---						r=-.21 N= (9) P=.294
7) Percent of Income of Low 20% ---						

[1](Because of the low number of cases, caution needs to be used when interpreting this column. See comments in the text.)

r = the Pearson correlation coefficient
N = the number of cases
P = the level of significance

POLICY IMPLICATIONS FOR DEVELOPED AND DEVELOPING NATIONS

The competing claims concerning the impacts of the Green Revolution on economic growth and food consumption in the Third World were the stimuli for the empirical analysis described above. Fifteen Latin American nations were analyzed from 1965 to 1977 in the light of seven variables related to the Green Revolution, an export-oriented agriculture, and food production and consumption. The data indicated that

1. There was no relationship between the Green Revolution and food production.

2. Food production increases did not lead to increases in food exports.

3. There was no relationship between food exports and imports and domestic food consumption.

4. There was a relationship between the Green Revolution inputs and agricultural exports.

5. There was a (slight) relationship between Green Revolution inputs and the decline of workers in agriculture.

6. There was a (slight) relationship between Green Revolution inputs and income gaps between rich and poor people.

The analyzed data did not give strong statistical confirmation to all of the hypotheses derived from the Radical Model. This might be an artifact of the data gathered, sample size, or statistical technique. Of course, refinements in the theory and hypotheses may be in order as well. What does seem clear, however, is that there is no empirical confirmation for elements of the Agricultural Development Model. There is no evidence to suppose that, in the Latin American case, a high-technology, export-oriented agriculture has in any way alleviated the food deficiencies of the peoples of Latin America. It is this finding that raises questions about public policy in the food area for both the nations and peoples victimized by hunger and the industrial capitalist states (particularly the United States) and international institutions that give support to high-technology, export-oriented agricultural policies in the Third World.

For the typical Third World nation, all government encouragement should be given to the creation of an agriculture base that accepts as its first priority the production of food for domestic consumption. Although the evidence here does not fully confirm the Radical Model, some of the data and other literature suggest the need to provide land for marginalized agricultural workers for the purpose of replacing low wages with the basic tools for producing food for direct consumption. Surplus food production could then be sold on international markets, preferably with the receipts made available to direct producers or to the society at large. It is likely that a policy of food self-sufficiency for Third World nations requires a radical transformation of the class structures throughout their societies such that glaring gaps in wealth and power are removed. Food self-sufficiency is impossible in a country such as El Salvador, for example, where 2 percent of the country's 5 million people receive 50 percent of the nation's income and own 60 percent of the cultivated land (Barry, Wood, and Preusch 1983, 188–190). Further, as Burbach and Flynn (1980) indicate, in Guatemala, 87 percent of all government credit between 1964 and 1973 went for export production while basic staples such as rice, beans, and corn received only 3 percent. The Brazilian case is also typical as small farmers who produce 75 percent of the staples of the country receive only 5 percent of all agricultural loans. "Three of Brazil's major staple crops (black beans, manioc, and maize) received only 13 percent of government-subsidized credit from 1970 to 1977, while huge amounts of credit were channeled to export production" (Burbach and Flynn 1980, 104).

Susan George offers a prescription for social change that stands in stark contrast to these cases when she argues that underdeveloped countries should reduce the amount of land devoted to cash crops, stop incurring external debts by importing expensive agricultural equipment, end the practice of educating Third World young people in agricultural programs in U.S. universities, end borrowing from foreign banks, and stop encouraging multinational corporations to come to their countries—"in a word, put an end to dependency" (George 1977, 247). This means an end to foreign dependency and dependency on indigenous economic oligarchies that benefit from the policies supporting high-technology, export-oriented agriculture.

For Lappé and Collins, this approach constitutes a policy of "food self-reliance." Food self-reliance involves the democratic control of agricultural resources so that agricultural production serves the local population. They believe that control of productive assets by local majorities will increase the prospects of production for local consumption (Lappé and Collins 1978, 458).

Third World food self-reliance can be given encouragement by U.S. and other industrial capitalist states in two ways. The United States could adopt a minimalist policy that would dramatically reduce the penetration of the U.S. economy into Third World nations. This would mean reducing aid projects that stimulate big capital projects in support of export agriculture at the expense of self-sufficiency. Further, U.S. policies could reduce the incentive for foreign investment in Third World agriculture and/or require that a certain percentage of profits earned by multinational corporations from the sale of Green Revolution inputs, from crops grown on foreign-owned lands in Third World countries, or from food processed out of Third World raw materials, be returned to the Third World nation where the profits were made to be employed in domestic food production for direct consumption.

A maximalist approach to world hunger would require technical and financial aid to nations that have adopted a food self-reliance model and have moved to increase the control of productive assets among the rural population at large. Although policies supporting food self-reliance are unlikely to be adopted or even sought as long as the Agricultural Development Model and the Green Revolution are accepted (and will be opposed by huge agribusiness and food processing multinationals), the data suggest that traditional agricultural policies may not be adequately fulfilling the food needs of Third World peoples. Given the stakes for human survival, more research is needed to investigate the efficacy of food self-reliance as a policy to reduce hunger in the Third World.

NOTES

1. The data reported here as well as the aggregate data analyses that follow are

derived from the *FAO Production Yearbook* for various years and *World Tables*. Although the accuracy of Third World development data should always be considered with caution, these sources provide the most comprehensive examination of the agricultural developments under consideration. The most intellectually precise impressions of the impact of the Green Revolution can best be achieved by on-the-spot experiences in diverse locations. For most researchers concerned with public policy at the global level such experiences are difficult to achieve.

2. The countries are Argentina, Brazil, Chile, Colombia, Costa Rica, the Dominican Republic, Ecuador, El Salvador, Guatemala, Honduras, Mexico, Nicaragua, Panama, Peru, and Venezuela. These are the nations in Latin America and the Caribbean for which relatively complete data were available.

The actual dates for which data have been collected and analyzed are: 1960, 1965, 1967, 1970, 1971, 1973, 1975, and 1977. It was necessary to include 1960 for variables that are only reported by the recording source at five-year intervals (percentage of labor force in agriculture and percentage of income received by the lowest 20 percent).

3. The caloric estimate is highly correlated with other possible nutritional variables such as protein consumption.

4. The magnitudes of the coefficients in the last two relationships were quite low, and serious anomalies may exist (i.e., relationship between "percent of labor in agriculture" and "percent income of lower 20 percent"). However, this problem may not be as much a problem in theory as it is a problem in methodology. The social and demographic indicators in the data set contain much missing data. These indicators have not been obtained for every year in every country. If the data were complete, the problem might be eliminated. The variable "percent of labor in agriculture" and "percent of income of low 20 percent" especially have a very low number of cases. In many instances only one year was available in the period under study. Therefore, the reader should be cautioned as to the interpretation of the data. The decision to have these variables in the model was made for theoretical reasons. It is the hope of the authors that as the data become available, the models can be tested without large numbers of missing data.

5. Although not central to the hypotheses tested here, it was noted that in both above- and below-mean-caloric nations, there was an inverse relationship between agricultural development assumptions about agricultural modernization, changing occupational structures, and increased access to food that have some basis in historical fact. However, the data may be showing that the poorest countries, from a caloric standpoint, are those that have witnessed the least opportunities for higher paying jobs in urban centers while their peasantry is progressively being deprived of land to grow adequate supplies of food for consumption.

REFERENCES

Barry, Tom, Beth Wood, and Deb Preusch. *Dollars and Dictators*. New York: Grove Press, 1983.

Burbach, Roger, and Patricia Flynn. *Agribusiness in the Americas*. New York: Monthly Review Press, 1980.

Caldwell, Malcolm. *The Wealth of Some Nations*. London: Zed Press, 1977.

Christensen, Cheryl. "World Hunger: A Structural Approach." In Raymond F. Hopkins and Donald J. Puchala, eds. *The Global Political Economy of Food*. Madison: University of Wisconsin, 1978, pp. 171–201.

Food and Agriculture Organization. *FAO Production Yearbook*. Rome: FAO, various years.

George, Susan. *How the Other Half Dies*. Montclair, N.J.: Allanheld, Osmun and Co., 1977.

Jain, Shail. *Size Distribution of Income*. Washington, D.C.: World Bank, 1975.

de Janvry, Alain. *The Agrarian Question*. Baltimore, Md.: Johns Hopkins University Press, 1981.

Lappé, Frances Moore, and Joseph Collins. *Food First*. New York: Ballantine Books, 1978.

Payer, Cheryl. *The Debt Trap*. New York: Monthly Review Press, 1974.

Payer, Cheryl. *The World Bank: A Critical Analysis*. New York: Monthly Review Press, 1982.

Stevens, William K. "Punjab Farmers: A Shining Example." *New York Times*, October 7, 1982, p. 4.

World Bank. *World Tables*. Washington, D.C.: World Bank, 1980.

11 U.S.-Mexican Agricultural Relations: The Upper Limits of Linkage Formation

Gustavo del Castillo and Rosario Barajas de Vega

This chapter deals with four aspects of Mexican agriculture. First, it explains the current trends in peasant agriculture, including the relationship of peasant to commercial agriculture. Second, it explores how these trends have developed given the articulation between the agricultural producer and the Mexican state. Third, it addresses the most immediate question of public policy—that is, what are the short-run problems that Mexican policymakers must address in relation to Mexico's agricultural sector? Finally, it outlines the interrelationships between Mexican and U.S. agriculture that have important policy implications.

AGRICULTURE AND SOCIETY

The debate about Mexican agriculture has been an ongoing concern since the decade following colonization in 1515. The debate then as now has been about decreasing production surpluses. Part of the past problem was the decimation of the producing population due to European-generated epidemics. (Obviously, today's problems are not due to epidemics, but have to do with a reduction of production surpluses.) Colonial Mexico regenerated its population with the introduction of slavery and by relying, in ever increasing ways, on wage labor—i.e., by freeing community-based peasants to encourage their entrance into the emerging labor force of the time.

The central concern of eighteenth century decisionmakers was the issue of political stability. During the nineteenth century, Mexican liberal thinkers foresaw the achievement of justice in the rural sector as crucial in guaranteeing political stability. Some years before Marx's *Communist Manifesto* was published, Mariano Otero in Mexico published a classic piece on Mexico's class structure that dealt with the unequal distribution of societal benefits and the threat this posed to internal stability. In effect, Otero was analyzing a readily observable phenomenon—Miguel Hidalgo's independence movement of 1810, which was born out of frustration by the peasant sector in some of the most productive agricultural areas of the country, the *bajoi*. The recognition of the peasant as an agent of change has been a Mexican concern from the start. The history of Mexico's independence movement can be read as a debate between liberals and conservatives about which role the peasant would play in modernizing Mexico.

Mexico's contemporary history also indicates the role that an unsatisfied rural sector can play as an agent of change. In Morelos, the peasantry who had been driven from the land saw the armed uprising of 1910 as a solution to the question of ownership (Womack 1969). The 1910 revolution was in its initial stages a rural movement to redress the process of unequal exchange. The social and economic importance of the peasantry took on a strategic importance during the revolution; yet discussions at that time concerning the peasantry never isolated the "peasant" issue from what public policy ought to have been in order to control armed uprisings or to increase peasant production.

These public policy issues became of central importance after the revolution. The new state's functions became those of a guiding agent of development and those of an arbiter between conflicting visions of the direction that Mexican society ought to take after the conflict. Laissez-faire economics was to be tolerated within the new parameters imposed by the state, which became the agent for a developing nation.

This reinforced role of the character of the state in the development process found its maximum expression after the revolution with the Reforma Agraria, which began in 1936 with the expropiation of lands in the Comarca Laqunera, Yucatan, and Michoacan. In these areas, and under the administration of President Lazaro Cardenas, the state took an enormous step to guide agricultural production and at the same time gain a political clientele that answered to this administration. Martinez (1980) characterizes the process that developed in the Laquna as "the social costs of a political victory." This step in public policy was necessary because differences still existed among the revolutionary family as to the exact role that the state would play in the agricultural sector (Brandenburg 1964). A very important figure of this family, ex-president Plutarco Calles, favored the privatization of land leading to the development of a farmer culture instead of the collectives that were being developed under Cardenas (Table 11.1).

Regardless of the direction agricultural development would take in Mexico before World War II, the most immediate questions in the short run had to do with issues of public investment in agriculture. Investments had to be made within the context of the limits faced by Mexican agriculturalists in a post-reform stage. To overcome these limits, investments helped develop irrigation systems on a large regional scale to obviate the uncertainties of the Mexican weather. A second line of investment made credit available to agricultural producers who were constantly faced with a shortage of the capital necessary to

Table 11.1
Land Tenancy in Mexico, 1930-1970

	EJIDOS (%)	COMMUNITIES (%)	PRIVATE FARMS (%)
1930	6.3	4.6	89.1
1940	22.5	4.7	72.8
1950	26.7	5.2	68.1
1960	26.3	5.2	68.5
1970	43.3	6.6	50.1

Source: Compiled from data appearing in Yates 1981, 154.

turn the land into a productive enterprise. Cardenas' efforts, shown in Table 11.2, resulted in an actual transformation of the role played by collectivized agriculture in Mexico.

The *ejidos,* or collectives, became by 1940 the major producers in Mexican agriculture in terms of the actual value of production. There is little doubt that these changes in agriculture resulted from direct and massive state intervention. These same factors that led to the rapid development of the collectives in the decade 1930–1940 also were responsible for their decreased importance after 1940 in the face of state actions and the public policies of President Alvaro Camacho, Cardenas' successor. The actual development plans from this date on read like a carbon copy of each other. An evaluation of the agricultural situation by the Office of the Counselor for Agricultural Affairs of the U.S. Embassy (1980, p. 14) in Mexico City found that most Mexican officials felt rural

Table 11.2
Value of Production by Type of Tenancy

	PRODUCTION		PERCENT
1930	Total		100
		Private	89
		Ejido	11
1940	Total		100
		Private	49
		Ejido	51
1950	Total		100
		Private	63
		Ejido	37
1960	Total		100
		Private	59
		Ejido	41

Source: From data appearing in Hewitt de Alcantara 1976, 7.

Table 11.3
Public Investment in the Agricultural Sector
as a Percentage of Total Public Investment

1965	9.2%	1969	9.7%	1973	15.4%
1966	9.8%	1970	10.3%	1974	16.7%
1967	10.4%	1971	12.8%	1975	18.2%
1968	10.0%	1972	13.0%	1976	17.6%

Source: Based on data provided by the Dirección General de
Inversión Públicas. Secretaria de Programación y Presupuesto,
Departamento de Información y Registro.

residents to be "both the cause and solution" for most major social and economic problems within the country. But if this has been the perspective of the
role of Mexican agriculture in Mexican society, public policy toward this sector
apparently contradicts official pronouncements. A good indicator of agriculture's actual importance is reflected in the levels of public expenditures in that
sector. Table 11.3 shows expenditure levels since 1965.

An important aspect of the relationship between the agricultural sector and
Mexican society that ought to be pointed out is that, in formal terms, the participation of agriculture as part of the Gross National Product (GNP) has been declining during the years, as shown in Table 11.4. One could probably justify
the overall low levels of investments in this sector given its decreasing importance to the national economy. But if this represents the logic that is followed,
the implications for peasants and other small agriculturalists seem rather
clear—they will be displaced to an increasingly peripheral position within Mexican society. It should also be clear that the seeming decrease in the relative
importance of agriculture within the economy, as measured by the GNP, gives
but a false sense of security because the multiplier effects of agriculture are
wide-ranging. These effects will be reflected in the employment levels, on the
demand side for agricultural implements, and in commerce. In this sense, the
agricultural sector in Mexico, if not a majority sector, is still an immensely
large sector influencing the course of national society. This does not change the
peripheral or marginal position of individual peasants or of farming communities. This has been the lot of the peasantry worldwide, at least since the
Industrial Revolution. The real issue that must be addressed is whether a marginal peasantry can continue to produce agricultural surpluses for the urban sector
and whether in the process of unequal exchange political stability can be maintained.

RECENT TRENDS IN MEXICAN AGRICULTURE

The fact that since the early 1970s Mexico has been a net importer of food
staples is usually seen as the best indicator of a failed agricultural policy, a

failed *ejido* system, and the failure of the agricultural reform that began in 1936. Asking why agriculture has failed, however, is the wrong question. The point to be made is that agricultural trends do not develop independently of state intervention, but as the result of state policy and of whatever adaptive strategies peasants, *campesinos,* or farmers use to counteract state actions. It must be kept in mind that since colonial times the peasantry has had a close relationship with the economy so that at the present time the articulation of the peasantry to the state is not the only meaningful relationship; the relationship of *campesinos* with other productive sectors of the economy is also of critical importance. These relationships, although operating in a more or less free economy, are very frequently the subject of state intervention. Since colonial times the state has played an important regulatory function for the peasantry.

THE PROBLEM OF THE PEASANTRY

The particular concern here is with the productive role of the peasantry during the last quarter century, and specifically from 1980 through 1984. Later in this discussion the issue of the survival of the peasant as a social entity is addressed.

In a very general way, peasants have been the main agricultural producers for most societies, and the exchange process between peasant society and urban-industrial society has been regarded by most analysts as being inherently unequal. A fundamental concern for policymakers in Mexico and around the world has been to elaborate the terms of exchange between the larger society and the peasantry. That is, the exchange process itself will be unequal, and the question to be resolved is whether the peasantry will be deserving of a larger or lessened proportion of the surplus produced (speaking of resources in general and not of agricultural products). The question for the peasantry is whether to

Table 11.4
Participation of Agriculture as Part of GNP[1]

1940	10.0%	1971	7.0%
1950	11.6%	1972	6.4%
1960	9.8%	1973	6.0%
1965	9.4%	1974	5.9%
1966	8.9%	1975	5.6%
1967	8.4%	1976	5.5%
1968	7.9%	1977	5.7%
1969	7.3%	1978	5.6%
1970	7.1%	1979	5.0%

[1] These figures do not include the cattle and fishing industries.

Source: Banco de Mexico, S.A. Producto Interno Bruto y Gasto. Cuadernos 1960-1979 and 1970-1979. Serie Información Economica. Mexico 1978 and 1980. Also, Banco de Mexico, S.A. Informe Anual, 1978. Mexico, 1979. Nacional Financiera, S.A. La Economia Mexicana en Cifras. Mexico, 1978.

continue producing surpluses that subsidize the urban world. Also, at the present time, a critical question is whether the capitalist mode of production presents any alternatives for peasant society: Can peasants continue, in any terms, to be integrated under any conditions with the larger society?

Both of these questions relate to the issue of how a society obtains its surpluses, from what sectors, and under what conditions. For the Mexican peasant, surplus production has diminished significantly, and the policy problem is whether, given existing conditions, peasants are in any position to produce surpluses. One last issue must be made clear—especially when dealing with the question of peasant production. As far as Mexico is concerned, there are regional peasantries with distinctly different problems. Specifically, different regional settings force the peasants to develop strategies that differ in nature because peasant articulation with the state and regional economies as well as peasants' relations with local or regional elites differ from case to case. Bee farmers in Chan Dom, Yucatan (Merrill 1983) have little in common with corn farmers in the Cienega de Chapala in Michoacan (Duran 1982).

In order to highlight the problem of peasant production, it is necessary to look at the issue of the "marginalization" of the peasantry, its implications in terms of what is actually being produced and by whom, official state actions in driving the peasantry to abandon production of crops for human usage, and the emergence with state aid of large transnational corporations in association with Mexican agrocapitalists dedicated to the production of grains for animal feed and consumption by the urban well-to-do (Barkin and Suarez 1982). In a sense, state behavior toward peasants and other small agricultural producers not only has determined the role of these sectors in the productive process, but it also has determined which sectors will continue living with a precolumbian high carbohydrate diet and which will be able to afford high protein diets. Early income shifts in the 1960s were responsible for changing demand as per capita beef and beer consumption increased while corn and bean demand decreased (York 1981, 30).

A major transformation has taken place with respect to which crops are being planted, as can be seen in Table 11.5. But it is important to specify what is being substituted, especially because different crop substitutions affect Mex-

Table 11.5
Cultivated Surface Dedicated to Animal and Human Consumption

	TOTAL HECTARES CULTIVATED (% CHANGES)	FOR HUMAN USE (% CHANGES)	FOR ANIMAL USE (% CHANGES)
1940–50	3.8	2.1	–
1950–60	3.5	2.0	–
1960–70	2.1	0.3	23.1
1970–80	1.2	-0.3	7.0
1940–80	2.6	0.9	13.1

Source: Barkin and Suarez 1982, 58.

Table 11.6
Maize: Land Cultivated (Hectares), and Total Production

YEAR	IRRIGATED	PERCENT	RAINFED	PERCENT	TOTAL	PERCENT	TOTAL PRODUCTION (tns)
1970	396,883	5.3	7,044,66	94.7	7,440,949	49.7	8,912,538
1975	1,133,530	16.4	5,786,455	83.6	6,919,985	44.2	8,842,822
1976	1,291,443	18.3	5,772,520	81.7	7,063,963	46.0	8,716,123
1977	979,251	13.1	6,490,398	86.9	7,469,649	45.3	10,173,737
1978	946,867	13.2	6,244,212	86.8	7,191,079	43.5	10,909,000*
1979	853,492	15.3	4,715,339	84.7	5,568831	37.1	8,752,000*

*Ministry of Agriculture and Water Resources, as shown in Banco Nacional de Mexico Statistical Data, 1970-1980.

Table 11.7
Beans: Land Cultivated (Hectares), and Total Production

YEAR	IRRIGATED	PERCENT	RAINFED	PERCENT	TOTAL	PERCENT	TOTAL PRODUCTION (tns)
1970	71,634	4.1	1,676,677	95.9	1,748,311	11.7	925,902
1975	390,256	21.6	1,411,550	78.4	1,801,806	11.6	1,085,972
1976	316,789	22.8	1,069,378	77.2	1,386,167	8.9	823,711
1977	166,120	10.2	1,462,889	89.8	1,629,009	9.9	762,191
1978	206,214	13.0	1,374,013	87.0	1,580,227	9.5	948,713
1979	203,946	19.4	836,964	80.6	1,040,910	6.2	

Sources for Tables 11.6 and 11.7: From 1970-1976, MEB Sector Agropecuario y Forestal, various tables. From 1977-1979, SARH Direccion General de Economía Agrícola. Información Agropecuario.

ican agriculturalists in differential manners and because the substitutions tend to link Mexican and U.S. agriculture together. An important issue is whether the links that are being established tend to increase the articulation in policymaking, whether it be in the area of agriculture or in other economic or political activities between the two countries.

One of the most important trends in contemporary Mexican agriculture has been the overall decline in the cultivation of what had been historically Mexico's principal crops. An important question that has to be answered, and its implications questioned, is what these processes mean to the peasantry. The data in Tables 11.6 and 11.7 are indicative of this process.

There are two points to emphasize with respect to the data presented above. The first is that corn and beans planted in irrigated land have increased during the 1970s, while both of these crops grown in rainfed land have decreased. Yet bean production on irrigated land is not constant; increases and downturns have occurred, with a high point in 1976 and an intermediate point during 1979. One could look at the data and argue that the losses and gains tend to average out and that, most probably, the gains outrank losses due to higher productivity of irrigated land. However, peasants are not the producers in irrigated land. The Mexican Revolution has not yet benefited them to this extent. One must ask what is happening within peasant society that corn production is decreasing? Is it a question of lagging productivity? Of abandoned land? Of their inability to produce because of lack of credit? An observer of Mexico's peasantry could probably name several factors to explain the overall decrease in corn and bean production. One of the most notable concerns the overall land under cultivation.

An analysis of the 1970–1980 decade indicates that land under irrigation increased 266 percent from 1970 to 1976, the year of maximum utilization of irrigated land. This growth reflects an attempt by the state to bring marginal land under cultivation, especially in the Sexenio of Luis Echeverria (Barkin and Suarez 1982). Yet an analysis of yearly trends indicates a 24 percent decrease in the utilization of irrigated land from the maximum in 1976; 2,337,522 rainfed hectares previously planted with corn, beans, wheat, and sorghum have been taken out of cultivation.

This decrease of 24 percent offsets the increase in hectares planted with these same four crops on irrigated land: 982,695 more hectares of irrigated land as opposed to 2,337,522 fewer hectares of rainfed land during this same period of time. This change may indicate that the previous production of more than 2 million rainfed hectares could, in 1976, be produced on 980,000 hectares of irrigated land.

Decreases in the total area of cultivated rainfed hectares from 1976 to 1979 amount to 17 percent (approximately 1,285,666), substantially less than the 31 percent decrease during the same period for irrigated land utilization. However, although 1976 is the peak year for utilization of irrigated land, the peak for rainfed land (after the original decrease from 1970 to 1975) is 1977. From this year of maximum utilization to the low year of 1979, the decrease in rainfed hectares planted in these four crops was 2,794,754 hectares, or 31 percent—the same decrease as for irrigated land for the period 1976 to 1979.

When one addresses the question of whether the declines in cultivated area of both of these major crops are outweighed by gains in productivity, the answer is unfortunately a negative one. Data during a thirty-year period, from 1940 to 1970, indicate decreased yields for both of these staple crops (Table 11.8). Unfortunately, these decreasing yields also occurred during the periods when there were the greatest increases in resources invested in irrigation. Thus, out of the federal resources invested in the agricultural sector in these thirty years, the great bulk went into irrigation districts (Table 11.9).

What is not surprising is that yields obtained in wheat production increased significantly during this thirty-year period, most likely due to wheat plantings in irrigated land. The data presented so far leads to one conclusion: In the case of corn and beans, there has been both a reduction in acreage planted as well as insignificant yield gains. These failures led to a massive program of grain imports from the United States that began during 1980. Does responsibility lie with public policy or faults in peasant society?

Part of the explanation for the general decreases affecting the production of these two staple crops is the shift toward opportunity cost crops. Some producers have found it more profitable not to produce these staple crops, but rather to go into an area of activity that yields higher utility. In part, the shift toward opportunity cost crops derives directly from decisions in public policy. How do agricultural producers derive higher utility as a result of public decisions? One clear factor has been Mexico's use of subsidies to maintain low prices of certain critical commodities. Agricultural subsidies also have redi-

Table 11.8
Average Annual Rates of Growth in Cultivated Area
and Yields for Two Selected Crops

CROPS	1940–60	1940–50	1950–60	1960–70
Corn Cultivated area	1.5	2.1	0.3	2.9
Yield	2.6	2.8	2.5	2.0
Beans Cultivated area	2.7	3.9	1.4	2.7
Yield	3.5	2.0	5.1	2.8
Wheat Cultivated area	2.1	0.6	3.5	0.5
Yield	3.4	1.8	4.9	7.2

Source: From data appearing in Hewitt de Alcantara 1976, 105.

Table 11.9
Sectoral Public Investment and Irrigation

YEARS	AGRICULTURAL SECTOR (%)	INDUSTRIAL SECTOR (%)	IRRIGATION (%)
1940–44	16.4	9.7	80.0
1945–49	20.7	18.2	95.8
1950–54	17.8	27.6	72.1
1955–59	13.0	36.0	99.2
1960–64	10.1	37.5	85.5
1965–69	10.6	41.0	98.4

Source: From data appearing in Barkin and Suarez 1982, 64–65.

rected private efforts in directions that the government chooses so that new and varied crops are planted that fit into foreign exchange.

An analysis of the government's pricing strategy through subsidies for corn and beans yields ambigious results. All guarantee prices appear to have been increasing annually from 1970 through 1975. Yet, in 1976, there was a decrease for standard quality beans as well as for sorghum, supposedly a highly commercial crop and one that falls in the category of an opportunity cost crop. These two crops show negative changes or only slight increases for the years through 1979. Thus, in contrast to a 243 percent increase in the guarantee price for beans for the period 1970–1975, the price for this same product rose only 25 percent from 1975 to 1976. In marked contrast with these decelerating price changes, corn continues to be highly subsidized through the government guarantee price program. Although prior to 1975 corn showed the slowest rate of price increase, after 1975 corn far and away led in price subsidies, enjoying a 1979 guarantee price 83 percent higher than its price in 1975 (Table 11.10).

With the advent of the 1982 crisis in Mexico and the imposition of an International Monetary Fund (IMF) austerity program, there have been significant free-market price increases for these two staples indicating sharp decreases in the subsidy program. Still, during the decade 1970–1980, the commodities that averaged the greatest increases in guarantee prices were those used in industry (Table 11.11).

The least that can be said of the guarantee price policy is that it has not been consistent; this inconsistency does not give agriculturalists any clear direction as to which crops might be desirable to plant. In the worst case, guarantees deter others from actually planting crops that could be profitable. Undoubtedly, agricultural policy has additional components other than crop subsidies. An important aspect of Mexico's agriculture is farm credit provided by the federal government. In this respect, Lamartine Yates (1981), an expert on Mexican agriculture, comments that the National Rural Credit Bank directs the major part of its lending toward commercial farming.

One must conclude that Mexican agriculture reflects the duality that appears characteristic of Mexican society—that is, Mexican agriculture is an integral part of Mexico's socioeconomic phenomena and reflects those phenomena. Just as there are those in the urban-industrial sector with very high or very low incomes and substantially different life possibilities, such is also the case for Mexican agriculturalists. There are the modern agricultural sector (commercial), which is receiving government support, and the sector composed of marginal and forgotten peasants.

An important problem for Mexico that deserves careful attention is whether this duality has made Mexico a dependent country in terms of its import necessities. For the purposes of this chapter, this question could be phrased in these terms: What are the linkages between Mexico and the United States that result from this agricultural asymmetry and interdependency?

PUBLIC POLICY AND U.S.-MEXICAN LINKAGES

The trends cited above are brought about by policy decisions originating in Mexico, but have implications in the United States where decisions must be made in response to Mexican events. The cycle of substitution determines the lives of peasants and small farmers, depending on the different combinations of surpluses or shortages in and outside Mexico. Political factors that the Mexican state takes into account in order to mollify its different clienteles are also important.

When dealing with Mexican exports (primarily to the United States), an immediate policy link is established between the public sectors of the two countries. For instance, short- and long-term policy decisions are made in Mexico

Table 11.10
Guarantee Prices

PRODUCT	(Mexican Dollars per Ton)		
	1970	1975	1980
Corn	940	1,900	5,000
Wheat	800	1,750	4,600
Beans (standard quality)	n.a.	6,000	12,000
Beans (extra quality)	n.a.	5,000	12,000
Rice	1,100	3,000	4,500
Sorghum	625	1,600	2,900
Safflower	1,500	3,500	7,600
Soybeans	1,300	3,500	8,000
Sesame	2,500	6,000	11,500

Source: Ministry of Agriculture and Water Resources data

Table 11.11
Decade-Long Selected Guarantee Prices Increases

	(Mexican Dollars per Ton)
Corn	406
Beans	1025
Rice	340
Sorghum	227
Soybeans	670
Sesame	900

Source: Ministry of Agriculture and Water Resources data

City with respect to the types and quantities of subsidies or export incentives given to Mexican vegetable exports to the United States. At the same time, the United States must formulate policies regarding countervailing duties on Mexican agricultural products. Long-term discussions take place within the bureaucracy. Interagency competition arises out of such discussions where competing interpretations are made of U.S. trade law and where the pressure of conflicting interest groups is readily felt (Mares).

In the process of exporting Mexican agricultural products, new policy needs are created, and additional linkages arise between the United States and Mexico. New policies must be constantly adopted in the United States as a result of continuous changes in export-directed crop plantings in Mexico. New and related industrial requirements for agricultural products then create new import needs from the United States. As a result, Mexico's agricultural policies affect both the U.S. public sector, which must respond to satisfy U.S. foreign policy requisites toward Mexico, and its own internal clientele with interests as diverse as Iowa farmers and Cargill grain transnationals.

In the intervening process, linkages are also established, and old linkages are reinforced between new sets of actors. Massive grain imports by Mexico during 1981–1985 have linked in very formal ways the public and private sectors of both nations. The linkages being established are indicative of the degree of integration of the agricultural sector within both countries. In other words, what Mexico decides will be quickly felt in Washington and vice versa; and what either of them decides will impact on agricultural production in both countries. For Mexico this specifically affects the livelihood of small farmers and peasants.

Recent research indicates that decisionmaking between Mexico and the United States obeys junctural conditions, while at the same time there is a tendency toward increasing linkages. These linkages result in two areas of activity, that of agriculture and, to some extent, that of trade.

Because of its agricultural processes, Mexico has become a net importer of different grains from the United States. This large importation process began in 1980 when Mexico bought approximately 10 million tons of grains from the

United States. The primary actions began within the White House where President Carter took a leading role along with the Office of the Special Ambassador. Top officials in the White House contacted the Mexican ambassador in Washington to gauge Mexico's interest in buying U.S. grains, and he in turn contacted the head of the National Company for Popular Subsistence Goods to obtain the reaction in Mexico City. On this occasion, Mexico insisted that representatives of the U.S. Department of Agriculture (USDA) not only contact the selling companies, but that these same representatives sit with Mexican officials, take the bids for the grain sales, and announce the Mexican decisions to the grain companies. Mexico's representatives wanted Washington officials to act as brokers between the Mexican government and the grain companies, a role that, according to informants, Washington had never played and felt very uncomfortable playing. In previous grain sales to Mexico, the Mexican government had gone directly to the companies without Washington's intervention. One possible reason for Washington's acceptance of Mexican conditions has to do with the importance of the grain sale to President Carter and to the special ambassador. Also, because the Mexican government was conscious of this fact, it set this condition knowing that Washington would probably go along because of the political necessities involved. In other words, the Mexicans were negotiating out of a strong position combined with the fact that the Carter administration saw Mexico and the bilateral relations between the two countries positively.

The most recent grain sales to Mexico demonstrate changed conditions with staggeringly different results. After the initial sales of 1980, Mexico and the United States entered into agreements committing the former to purchase predetermined amounts of grain during a period of years. Part of the agreements covered purchases in 1984. However, these agreements were undermined by the 1982 Mexican fiscal crisis brought on by Mexico's inability to pay part of its foreign debt and the subsequent entrance of the International Monetary Fund, the U.S. Treasury Department, and the U.S. Federal Reserve Bank. The negotiated package involved the sale of grains to Mexico through the Commodity Credit Corporation (CCC). Department of Agriculture officials, who had felt so uncomfortable in their role as brokers between Mexico and the supply companies in the 1980 sale, saw the contemporary situation as one that made it possible for them to withdraw from active participation. Mexican officials then had to deal with the grain companies under the watchful eye of the CCC. The crisis atmosphere since 1982 saw the added involvement of government agencies besides the USDA. Because of the financial crisis, the Federal Reserve Bank played a major role in securing new credit for Mexico, contingent on the sale of Mexican oil to the U.S. Strategic Reserve. This was, in effect, a barter agreement in which Mexico traded oil for vital subsistence commodities.

The linkages that result from this last operation are hard to explain and more difficult to interpret. It should be obvious that one linkage that came into existence in 1983 that had not been present in 1980 is the presence of oil in the agreement. In the present situation there are two linkages that must be un-raveled. The first is the quasi-barter procedures involving grains and oil. The second and probably more important linkage is between one productive sector in one country (Mexican oil) and the agricultural sector of the United States (grains).

What are the elements of public policy in this last case? For Mexico, it involved deciding whether to sell oil to a Strategic Reserve system that, in many public pronouncements, it had declared it would not do. More importantly, de-cisions were made whether to exchange a nonrenewable resource for a renewa-ble resource. In macroeconomic terms, this involved the acceptance of the theory of comparative advantage, which in this case means the acceptance of food dependency. In other words, Mexico has the capacity to produce oil, while at the same time it is dependent on the purchase of strategic commodities from the United States. U.S. policy choices center around how the United States will use or exploit Mexico's food dependency. It is certainly not a question of the United States deciding to withhold much needed food to Mexico. Given the present Mexican situation, public policy with respect to food utilization in the United States and Mexico's own agricultural policy are being made at increas-ingly higher levels in Washington. The decision to stock the Strategic Oil Re-serve with Mexican oil in exchange for U.S. grains was certainly not made in the Department of Agriculture. Within the bilateral relationship between Mexico and the United States, actors are being incorporated whose world of expertise is not Mexican agriculture, its peasant base, and the peasants' histori-cal role. Nor are the concerns of these actors necessarily agricultural. The focus for current U.S. policymakers is on questions and issues of appropriate U.S. and Mexican public policy linkages that may incidentally relate to agriculture and food production.

What are the upper limits of the linkages that can arise between Mexico and the United States? It should be clear that the upper limits are reached when the participating actors are those concerned with questions of national security. In these cases, there is little or no opportunity to achieve any agricultural inte-gration because the questions before these actors involve national sovereignty and are not alienable. Other upper limits are reached when issues such as the sale of grains to Mexico are linked to larger issues of foreign policy so that con-flict about "peripheral" issues intervenes to block possible agreements, or where actors from nonspecialized jurisdictions intervene with new procedures and institutional settings utilized in discussions foreign to the issues under con-sideration.

REFERENCES

Barkin, David, and Blanca Suarez. *El fin de la autosuficiencia alimentaria.* Mexico, D.F.: Editorial Nueva Imagen, 1982.

Barkin, David, and Blanca Suarez. *El fin del principio: Las semillas y la seguridad alimentaria*. Mexico, D.F.: Ediciones Oceano, S.A., 1983.

Brandenburg, Frank. *The Making of Modern Mexico*. Englewood Cliffs, N.J.: Prentice Hall, 1964.

Duran, Juan Manuel. "Transformación agricola y migración en La Ciénega de Chapala." Presented in the IV Coloquio de Antropoligia e Historia Regionales, Colegio de Michoacan, Zamora, 1982.

Hewitt de Alcantara, Cynthia. *Modernizing Mexican Agriculture: Socioeconomic Implications of Technological Change, 1940–1970*. Geneva: United Nations Research Institute for Social Development, 1976.

Mares, David. "The Evolution of U.S.-Mexican Agricultural Relations: The Changing Roles of the Mexican State and Mexican Agricultural Producers." Research Report, # 16. La Jolla, Calif.: Center for U.S.-Mexican Studies, University of California, San Diego, undated.

Martinez S., Tomas. *El costo social de un exito político*. Chapingo, Mexico: Colegio de Postgraduados, 1980.

Merrill, Deborah. "Commercial Beekeeping or Migrant Wage Labor: Alternative Cash Strategies in the Peasant Economy of Chan Kom, Yucatan, Mexico." Presented at the 1983 Society for Applied Anthropology, San Diego, California, April 1983.

Otero, Mariano. *Ensayo sobre el verdadero estado de la cuestión social y política que se agita en la República Mexicana*. Mexico, D. F.: Ediciónes del Instituto Nacional de la Juventud Mexicana, 1964.

U.S. Department of Agriculture. "Mexico and its Agriculture: A Developing Market." Mexico, D.F.: Office of the Counselor for Agricultural Affairs, U.S. Embassy, July 1980.

Womack, John Jr. *Zapata and the Mexican Revolution*. New York: Alfred A. Knopf, 1969.

Yates, P. Lamartine. *Mexico's Agricultural Dilemma*. Tucson: University of Arizona Press, 1981.

Part 4
Dependence, Development, and Interdependence

The difficulties of escaping dependence are the concerns addressed in Part 4. The experiences of developing nations have not been successful, by and large. Under economic pressures the governments of these nations have been more inclined to exploit rather than develop their agriculture; no established agricultural interests exist within these countries to force related food issues to the forefront of national agendas. Under these conditions, as Ross Talbot points out, the world must recognize the necessity for international food assistance. Those who cannot afford to purchase in the world market in order to satisfy basic needs must otherwise have these needs translated into food demand. Talbot finds this the appropriate role of world food organizations.

James Schubert examines the efficacy of food aid, with a somber assessment of the political consequences of mass hunger or famine. Earlier chapters have documented the fear within governments of being blamed for food shortages. He concludes that food shortages do generate political aggression, and once strength is restored following famine, it is accompanied by a will to punish the government. Hunger is, in the last analysis, extremely destabilizing, so food aid may serve the interest of peace. Schubert believes the political effects of food aid are so mixed that aid should be justified for humanitarian rather than political reasons. However, Schubert finds that the "creedal passion" described by Talbot has been a nominal motive in U.S. food aid for many years.

Don Hadwiger notes that even opposing systems have forged desirable relationships. In the great power interactions between the United States and the Soviet Union, goals are narrowly economic, and linkages are with agricultural sectors only. Efforts by the United States to embrace wider issues and linkages have been disastrous. For developing countries, by contrast, food dependency is likely to involve many sectors such as banking, the military, and industry. Even so, there is reason to hope that food dependence, as a short range "necessity" for some developing nations, will contribute to the evolution of a more balanced interdependence. Hadwiger discusses some findings relevant for future U.S. food policy.

12 The Role of World Food Organizations

Ross B. Talbot

The headquarters of four world food organizations are in Rome—the Food and Agriculture Organization (FAO), World Food Council (WFC), World Food Program (WFP), and the International Fund for Agricultural Development (IFAD). Several other international agencies, notably in Geneva, Vienna, Washington, D.C., and New York, have functions and responsibilities that complement, supplement, and sometimes conflict with those in Rome, but these functions are not the concern of this chapter.

The role of these agencies is examined in this chapter with particular reference to U.S. relations with the Rome agencies. A major premise is that in this world of multiple interdependencies and dependencies, U.S. agriculture is becoming increasingly dependent on rich, middle-income, and even low-income nations. Said another way, the U.S. farm economy has become at least moderately dependent on the growth of the economies in Third World nations, in Eastern and Western Europe, and in Japan. Given this premise, world food organizations might be viewed as useful agencies in the pursuit of a positive-sum strategy for food distribution in which all the major participants would be winners, although some more so than others.

THE U.S. CREED AND THE ESTABLISHMENT OF THE WORLD FOOD ORGANIZATIONS

The thesis propounded here is a modification of Samuel Huntington's (1981) concept of the U.S. Creed.[1] The modification is really an addition to, not a revision of, Huntington's proposition. That is, an important element in U.S. "moralism" is a powerful belief in food humanitarianism—namely, that those who are hungry, really hungry, must be fed. Just why this belief is always true, although much more intensely during times of "creedal passion," cannot be examined here in any detail. Nevertheless, the creed probably has its roots in natural law and natural rights theory, the beliefs of the English Puritans, and in some political ideas forthcoming from the period of the Enlightenment, among other historical sources. The essence of the problem this belief poses is, however, that the ideal of freedom from hunger, food for peace, food for freedom, succoring the poorest of the poor exceeds the grasp of U.S. political institutions. That is, those in the world who encounter economic and social conditions that result in severe malnutrition, and perhaps starvation under certain extreme circumstances, seem to number some 500 million human beings. Overwhelmingly, they live in Third World countries, in nation-states that are independent, sovereign, distrustful, and proud. There is a broadly based consensus that therein lies a world food problem of some considerable, if not gigantic, proportions. The world food institutions in Rome are functioning in a minimal to moderate manner to alleviate that terrible condition, and, as will be argued later, they could do even better work if U.S. policymakers would reassert the former U.S. role of positive leadership toward the policies and programs of these agencies. Huntington has devised a simple quadrant to explain U.S. responses to this gap between U.S. ideas and institutions. His terms have been modified here, perhaps more than slightly, by substituting the category of "realism" for "cynicism" (Table 12.1).

The second proposition of this chapter is that the period of the World Food Conference, which was held in Rome in November 1974, constituted a kind of conclusion to Huntington's fourth period of creedal passion, i.e., the 1960s to 1975. For whatever reasons, and they continue to be debated, that period was haunted by the specter of potentially mass starvation in the Third World. Fortunately, relatively good cereal harvests in 1975 and 1976 caused the specter to diminish, but draw up a more dismal scenario, and the results would be terribly frightening. The ideal that grew from the conference was the "Universal Declaration on the Eradication of Hunger and Malnutrition," and probably the most moving and influential speech leading up to that declaration was delivered by that modern Metternich, Henry Kissinger, who was then U.S. secretary of state. In his words:

The profound premise of our era is that for the first time we may have the

Table 12.1
U.S. Responses to the IvI Gap

INTENSITY OF BELIEF IN IDEALS	PERCEPTION OF GAP	
	CLEAR	UNCLEAR
High	Moralism	Hypocrisy
	(eliminate gap)	(deny gap)
Low	Realism	Complacency
	(tolerate gap)	(ignore gap)

Source: Huntington 1981, 64.

technical capacity to free mankind from the scourge of hunger. Therefore, today we must proclaim a bold objective—that within a decade no child will go to bed hungry, that no family will fear for its next day's bread, and that no human being's future and capacities will be stunted by malnutrition.

Our responsibility is clear. Let the nations gathered here resolve to confront the challenge, not each other. Let us agree that the scale and severity of the task require a collaborative effort unprecedented in history (Kissinger 1974, 2–3).

One could argue, to be sure, that this is just one more splendid example of Machiavellian realism. But leaving aside any judgment concerning motives, the end result was that the United States had asserted itself once again as the world leader in the "war on hunger."

WHY THE DECLINE IN U.S. SUPPORT?

What must now be examined is this question: Why has the United States chosen not to pursue this self-chosen responsibility through, at least in part, a more aggressive and constructive utilization of the services of these four Rome-based organizations?

Before trying to answer that question two background comments need to be made. First, the FAO and the WFP are really the godchildren of the United States. Certainly the FAO was a U.S. progeny. The Hot Springs Conference in 1943, at which the FAO Charter was drafted, was called at the initiative of President Franklin Roosevelt. In the case of the World Food Program, U.S. leadership is somewhat less overwhelmingly evident. The U.N. General Assembly had assumed some initiative in this matter in 1960, calling on the FAO to study the feasibility of an international organization that might mobilize and distribute surplus food to developing countries. But it was primarily because of George McGovern's involvement, as director of President Kennedy's Food for Peace office, that an experimental three-year program was begun, largely using U.S.-contributed food, on January 1, 1963 (Wallerstein 1980).

The World Food Council and the International Fund for Agricultural Development were products of the 1974 World Food Conference. The U.S. delegation had gone to Rome with an unofficial instruction of "no new world food organizations." Ambassador Edwin Martin's case study (he was Kissinger's principal lieutenant at the conference) shows how the World Food Council came into being (Martin 1979). The Official Report of the U.S. Delegation to the WFC makes clear that, in the U.S. view, the WFC would have only a coordinating role: "It would have no authority beyond moral suasion to force action on the part of governments or U.N. bodies" (U.S. Department of State 1974, 29).

Likewise, IFAD was not a U.S. creation. Apparently the prime movers were the Arab Organization of Petroleum Exporting Countries (OPEC) member states. According to the Official Report of the U.S. Delegation:

> The U.S. supported the proposal [to establish IFAD] in hopes that it will be used as a vehicle for promoting development by the countries with surplus oil revenues, but the U.S. has no present intention of contributing to the Fund, and will continue directing its substantial multilateral contributions through existing institutions (U.S. Department of State 1974, 30).

Moreover, since 1974 the U.S. government has been an avowed supporter of FAO, WFP, WFC, and IFAD, but U.S. support has been a kind of begrudging, unenthusiastic acceptance. At best one might characterize the U.S. strategy as a form of reluctant standpatism—i.e., a "you should do better with what you already have" attitude. Some of the U.S. officials who have been directly involved in U.S. relations with the Rome agencies will likely see this characterization as unfairly pessimistic. But it appears that U.S. strategy has primarily been one of "defend the status quo."

In a nutshell, the United States was initially the predominant actor in both FAO and WFP, but during the last decade this role has changed to that of only a major actor. Concerning IFAD, the United States was first pushed into a major role, and now seems to be insisting on a lesser position. Regarding the World Food Council, U.S. support has been unenthusiastic and reluctant, although avowedly positive. Thus, a major question arises: Why has the support of the United States toward the activities of these world food organizations been on the decline or, at best, only lukewarm?

The first reason for the decline in, or at least the tepid nature of, U.S. support is the lessening of U.S. influence therein. Membership in FAO has gone from 39 in 1945 to 156 in 1983. As is true throughout the United Nations and the specialized agencies, the new (developing) nations have the votes, and they have institutionalized that strength in the form of the Group of 77. One should be cautious here: The Group of 77 has the votes, but the Organization for Economic Cooperation and Development (OECD) nations have the financial resources. An international conference is a meeting of negotiators, a kind of push-hold political environment in which the Group of 77 does the pushing (but not too much), while the OECD nations use holding tactics (with only modest success). Within this unique process of negotiation, the United States is usually the principal member-state engaged in the tactic of restraint, or hold the line.

The second reason proceeds logically from the first: Policy innovations from WFC, FAO, WFP, and IFAD will quite likely cost money. Who will pay the new bills? Primarily the OECD nations, with some assistance from the Arab OPEC members, particularly in the case of IFAD. Overall, the United States has encountered a gradual weakening of its budgetary control over the finances of the Rome agencies. Again these generalizations are open to amendment, but the budgetary process, which is somewhat different for each Rome agency, has a common characteristic. The director-general of FAO, the executive director of WFP, the executive director of WFC, and the president of IFAD will predictably be attempting to increase the size of their budgets, or proposing programs that, if adopted, would require modest to substantial amounts of new funds. Keep in mind that these organization heads are negotiators, not dictators. They are practitioners of the art of the possible, plus a bit more.

Table 12.2 is a quick review of FAO's biennial budgets for a selected number of biennia. For the Regular Budget, the U.S. share (25 percent, by Congressional mandate in 1961) can be calculated with a fair amount of accuracy. For example, the Regular Program will cost the U.S. government approximately $113 million for 1984–85. Extrabudgetary sources, primarily from the World Bank, UNDP, and trust funds mostly from Western European nations, are difficult to calculate in terms of the U.S. contribution. But, using an arbitrary 15 percent estimate, the cost to the United States would be almost $98 million making a total of almost $211 million for the 1984–85 biennium. Relative to the Regular Budget, FAO's director-general obviously has engaged in a substantial amount of incrementalism, although when those budget increases are adjusted for inflation, the increases become much more modest.

In turn, Table 12.3 surveys the volume of food aid of cereal grains during much of the last decade, predominantly supplied by OECD nations and the United States in particular. About 20 percent of this food aid is handled by the World Food Program. Some one hundred nations make voluntary contributions to WFP at a pledging conference held in New York each biennium. For every biennium since 1969–1970, the pledging targets have increased ($1 billion for 1981–1982, $1.2 billion for 1983–1984). Originally the U.S. share was set at

Table 12.2
Resources Available to FAO for Selected Biennia

BIENNIUM	REGULAR BUDGET (U.S. DOLLARS)	EXTRA-BUDGETARY RESOURCES (U.S. DOLLARS)	TOTAL (U.S. DOLLARS)
1946–47	8,361,000		8,361,000
1956–57	13,400,000	17,589,000	30,989,000
1966–67	49,974,000	112,039,000	162,013,000
1976–77	167,000,000	389,783,000	556,783,000
1978–79	210,150,000	437,168,000	647,318,000
1980–81	278,740,000	581,120,000	859,860,000
1982–83	368,016,000	683,047,000	1,051,063,000
1984–85	451,627,000	653,502,000[*]	1,105,129,000

*Estimated

Sources: 1. Ralph W. Phillips. FAO: Its Origins, Formation and Evaluation, 1945-1981. Rome: FAO, 1981, 78.

2. Food and Agriculture Organization, The Director-General's Programme of Work and Budget for 1982-1983 (and for 1984-85). Rome: FAO, 1981 and 1983, 56 and 211.

Table 12.3
Volume of Food Aid Contributions (Grains)

COMMODITY/COUNTRY	1975/76	1976/77	1977/78	1978/79	1979/80	1980/81	1981/82	ESTIMATED ALLOCATIONS 1982/83	1983/84
				1,000 metric tons					
Grains	7,121	10,893	10,887	10,817	9,197	9,338	8,780	8,847	8,915
Argentina	0	15	32	30	38	67	20	47	45
Australia	261	230	252	329	315	370	485	450	450
Canada	1,034	1,176	884	735	730	600	600	764	675
European Economic Community*	928	1,131	1,394	1,159	1,205	1,263	1,449	1,650	1,650
Finland	25	33	47	9	19	29	20	20	20
Japan	33	46	135	352	688	893	494	400	450
Norway	10	10	10	10	11	40	39	40	40
Sweden	47	122	104	104	98	94	119	80	100
Switzerland	36	33	32	32	32	16	22	43	35
United States	4,637	7,940	7,663	7,552	5,649	5,631	5,087	5,000	5,050
Other	199	157	354	505	412	324	445	353	400

*Aid from individual EEC countries as well as from the entire commission of European Community.

Source: U.S. Department of Agriculture, Economic Research Service, World Food Aid Needs and Availabilities, 1983. Washington, D.C.: Government Printing Office, July 1983, 15 (modified).

not more than 50 percent of the total pledged, then that was reduced to 40 percent, and by 1977–1978 the U.S. pledge came to about 25 percent of the $750 million target. In sum, the United States is still, by far, the major contributor to WFP. However, "in volume terms, U.S. food aid has declined for six years. In absolute amounts, however, U.S. food aid still represents more than half of the world total of food aid" (U.S. House of Representatives 1983). Since 1974, the U.S. strategy regarding the World Food Program has been cautiously positive in support thereof, but negative in its constant complaints that the pledging target is set unrealistically high and that more nations, and OPEC nations in particular, should be major contributors.

The budget of the World Food Council has consistently received the quiet support of the United States. But WFC is primarily a think-tank and coordinating operation, with a small professional staff of some thirty persons—and thus far its executive director has always been from the United States. In brief, the United States supports the WFC as an institution, but seldom does the United States move out in a leadership role to transform the WFC's policy recommendations into realities.

The political responses of the United States to requests for IFAD's funding have taken on a strange complexion. As stated earlier, the initial reactions of the United States to the establishment of IFAD were, at best, tepid, but of the initial three-year fund of a little more than $1 billion, the U.S. Congress contributed $200 million, about one-fifth the total. This was for the years 1978 through 1980. Then IFAD's Governing Council set a figure of $1.1 billion for the first replenishment, of which the United States agreed, in principle, to contribute $245 million. The Reagan administration reduced this figure to a commitment of $180 million.

Negotiations for the second IFAD replenishment, which was originally to have covered the 1984–1986 period, had yet to be completed as of the end of 1985. Eight "consultations" have been conducted by IFAD's president, with no conclusive result. This is a complicated controversy but it would appear likely (*Christian Science Monitor* 1985) that the total amount of this replenishment will be $530 million, with the Reagan administration stubbornly insisting that the U.S. contribution will not exceed 17 percent of that total—i.e, $90 million. On July 31, 1985, Congress passed a foreign aid authorization bill for fiscal 1986 and 1987 in which $50 million was specified as a first-stage allocation to IFAD. However, late in 1985, Congress appropriated only $30 million for fiscal 1986 (the administration had requested no funds), and it should be noted that "when the full effects of the Gramm-Rudman-Hollings Balanced Budget Act are felt, foreign aid programs will likely be cut still further" (Interfaith Action for Economic Justice 1986, 1).

This leads to other reasons for the indifference strategy of the United States: inflation and very high budget deficits at home. The first condition appears now to be under control; the second seems not to dissuade the Reagan administration from requesting a substantial greater amount for the defense establishment, while Congress continues in its refusal to believe that the moral commitment by the United States to replenish IFAD's funds, for example, is a matter of any particular concern. These conditions imply one more reason for the declining support of the world food organizations: weak interest group/constituency support. The Rome agencies are not complete political orphans in the Congressional view, but they approach that condition. The Interfaith Action for Economic Justice is certainly active on the Hill and often effective at the margins; the same can be said about Bread for the World. There are numerous U.S.-based international relief agencies engaged in lobbying activities, discreetly or openly—e.g., Church World Service, CARE, Lutheran Relief Service—but their political clout in Congress and with the executive is distinctly limited even when the African food situation was of crisis proportions.

Then there is what might be termed "the weariness syndrome." No one seems to understand the how and the why of this kind of political pathology, but the disease is prevalent and serious. Reverting to Huntington's terminology, realism has hardened into cynicism, complacency is the tranquilizer of the day, and the U.S. population is plagued by an overdose of hypocrisy. This condition is not only, or even primarily, directed at the world food agencies, one should quickly note; all international organizations (perhaps the World Bank and the International Monetary Fund are marginal exceptions) are the victims of this national malaise. But whatever the causes, the effects are of substantial consequence when measured in terms of the short-, medium-, and long-range needs of the low-income developing nations.

Finally, it seems that U.S. policymakers believe that "food policy begins at home." As Destler argues (1980), four "conflicting but legitimate policy concerns" are exhibited in U.S. food policy, but the "global welfare and development policy" concern is surely, and consistently, accorded the lowest order of priority.[2] Although this is playing with the numbers somewhat, the U.S. commitment to the World Food Program would be roughly equal in 1983 to 1 percent of the cost of the domestic PIK (Payment in Kind) program. Even then, the U.S. allocation to the World Food Program is really a suballocation of funds from Title II of P.L. 480. There is a certain amount of uncalculated magnanimity in these food aid shipments, at least on the part of the untutored U.S. public. But the sharp realities come to the fore when farmers are distressed because, among other reasons, agricultural exports have declined by some $10 billion during 1982–1984. Under this kind of economic stress, it could be expected that a prominent staff member of a major U.S. farm organization would testify before a Senate Agricultural Subcommittee as follows: "We are going to press harder for the administration to use all authorities and means at its disposal to stimulate farm exports, which are vital to both farm income and our national economy" (American Farm Bureau Federation 1984, 1). Among these stimuli will be an increase in P.L. 480 funding for fiscal 1985 and 1986.

But this argument must be kept in some balance and in a clear perspective. A central thesis of this chapter is that conditions of starvation and gross malnutrition have always, at least in this century, aroused the creedal passions of the U.S. people. There seems to be a present consensus that "famine stalks Africa," to use the headline of a recent publication of a Washington-based religious interest group (Interfaith Action for Economic Justice 1984, 1). Significantly, this African food crisis (which has been monitored and predicted by the FAO since 1981) took a great deal of time to become a true media event in the United States, and it moved rather lethargically toward that status. The weariness syndrome, the creedal passion of "feeding the hungry," and low U.S. farm prices are interlocked in a kind of unfathomable political struggle.

The frustrations and concerns of the world food organizations are neatly characterized in a recent statement of U.S. Senator John C. Danforth (Rep., Missouri), who had just returned from a tour of some of the drought and hunger areas in Africa: "America . . . represents a value system most of us believe in very strongly. That value system has to do with the worth of human beings, whoever they are, wherever they are. We believe that lives are worth saving, and our fellow humans must be fed" (*World Development Forum* 1984, 1–2). There would certainly be little dissent from the world food agencies to that humanitarian proposition. But the business of the Rome agencies is development, not only or primarily the alleviation of conditions of starvation. Stated simply, their mission is to assist the poverty nations to move toward economies that are rationally self-sufficient—i.e., economies in which food can be grown and processed domestically or purchased in the world market with hard currencies that have been earned through the sale of exports. This kind of a positive-sum strategy is extremely difficult, some would say impossible, to bring into effective operation. It depends, to grossly oversimplify, on whether the nation under discussion is an NIC (a newly industrialized country), an MIC (a middle-income country in the process of developing), or an LIC (a low-income country, with a per capita income of some $400 a year, which may or may not be in the socioeconomic process of developing).

Understandably, given present economic conditions, U.S. policymakers respond enthusiastically to the often stated belief that U.S. food assistance builds cash markets for recipient countries. It is an attractive, sometimes accurate, perhaps seductive claim, which could more realistically be subdivided as follows: NICs, yes; MICs, possibly; LICs probably not, at least in the short run. But in terms of U.S. policy toward the world food agencies one must ask: What should be done now? The alternatives are fairly obvious: Do more, about the same, or less. During the last decade the policy response has been: about the same, hold the line. But this kind of political leadership is unbecoming in a great nation. The United States is badly shirking its international responsibilities; and one can be properly critical, even stern, in demanding a change in attitude and considerable improvement in our posture of standpatism.

WHAT MIGHT PUBLIC POLICYMAKERS DO?

One would like to come forward with some stimulating and forward-looking proposals and predictions at this point regarding the topic at hand. The Food Security Act of 1985 contained few provisions relating to the four world food organizations, and that is just as well. These periodic efforts to rewrite a national farm and food policy take place, by and large, in the House and Senate Committees on Agriculture (plus Forestry and Nutrition in the Senate's title). The act, almost surely, was not a truly national food policy legislation, but rather a replay of Lowi's characterization of U.S. farm legislation—ten titles wrapped into one bill, with each title less than satisfying to a major farm commodity group (Lowi 1979, Chapter 5).

But if we forswear realism and assume that a national food policy bill could be written, even then we would have to argue that these standing committees have so neglected their monitoring and oversight functions regarding the strong interdependencies and dependencies that surround the world food system, that they or the committee staffs—or even in the short run, the USDA's Economic Research Service—are unable to draft a title (section) concerning the role of the world food organizations in the international food system. There are advantages and there are disadvantages in using a multilateral organization as an instrument of U.S. domestic and international policy, but these pros and cons have not been explored in any systematic, hardly even episodic, manner.[3]

Both the House Committee on Agriculture and the Committee on Foreign Affairs did hold hearings in 1983 relative to the world food situation. These efforts, among others during the years, should not be discounted, but again one must return to the starvation-development debate. The immediate problem is starvation, to which the U.S. creedal passion will respond, but the medium- and long-run concern is development assistance, and here the United States seems to permit complacency, if not hypocrisy, to take command and lull most people into a state of moderate indifference and unconcern.

Another problem, hardly unique to farm and food legislation, is the matter of committee jurisdiction. That is, if the House Committee on Agriculture attempted to write a title within any future farm bill that concerned provisions for a program of planned incrementalism toward the world food organizations, numerous and serious turf and boundary controversies would quickly arise. Probably bureaucratic machinery could be designed to overcome, or at least placate, this matter of jurisdictional disputes; but it seems doubtful that the effort would result in any kind of a favorable cost-benefit ratio that was based on the concept of a national food policy.

An alternative, and one that has been discussed within the food and agriculture network, is the establishment of a House, Senate, or joint Select Committee on Hunger. On February 22, 1984, the House did pass a resolution that authorized the establishment of a Select Committee on Hunger. A seventeen-person committee has now been set up and charged with the responsibility to "conduct a continuing and comprehensive study of the problems of domestic and international hunger" and "provide a channel for direct and uninterrupted focus on this critical problem." The United States shall have to wait a few years in order to judge the committee's value. However, this select committee is directed to focus "on the diverse and complex issues associated with domestic and international hunger" (Hall 1984, 758–759).[4] A single-purpose committee, with a specialized staff, will likely concentrate on policies and programs directed more toward food quality, environmental concerns, and nutritional needs, and less on production, exports, and surpluses. The positive contributions of the Senate Select Committee on Nutrition and Human Needs, which did its work from the mid-1960s through the first half of the 1970s, come to mind. Nevertheless, one must recollect that this Senate committee functioned in a quite different political environment than the one that prevails in 1984. To reiterate, the central problem is poverty in the LICs; and the specific problems, accordingly, center around the role that the world food organizations, among several others, perform in that regard and how their activities correlate with the national interests of the United States.

A third consideration—although, again, not one to write into this legislation—is the role of the executive bureaucracies. More specifically, the activities of the world food agencies are principally the concern of the USDA, the State Department, and the U.S. Agency for International Development (AID), with the Office of Management and Budget and the Treasury in the role of more than interested observers. But policymaking by intragovernmental bureaucracies has its own set of problems. There does seem to be some considerable merit in the 1983 proposal by the Commission on Security and Economic Assistance (the Carlucci Commission) to set up a single organization—the commission would name it the Mutual Development and Security Administration (MDSA)—to integrate and coordinate all of our international programs with those particular concerns. Others will see this as too much overkill, and particularly dangerous because of the tying together of bilateral and multilateral programs and the connecting of economic with military assistance. These concerns are matters worthy of considerable debate, and such debate might be of value in pushing the whole issue to a higher position on the political agenda.

In 1980, the Presidential Commission on World Hunger proposed that the International Development Cooperation Agency (IDCA) should be "significantly strengthened," but it is difficult to believe that the Reagan administration will ever give much credence to this recommendation. The point is, however, that there needs to be a revitalization of legislative and bureaucratic leadership in these important matters of producing, distributing, and consuming food by, for, and to those in a condition of poverty and hunger.

There are three other quasi-legislative considerations. One concerns farmer interest groups, general and commodity. The House and Senate agriculture committees could not, of course, dictate the content of farm group testimony, but they could request farm interests to include within that testimony some reference to the "proper" role of world food organizations. U.S. farm organizations have been remarkably neglectful of what goes on in Rome—an attitude of uncalculated indifference, one might rightly term it. A close look would probably provide farm groups with convincing evidence that the world food organizations do, for the most part, function in ways that enhance the economic interests of U.S. farmers and are therefore, if for no other than humanitarian reasons, worthy of concerted U.S. support.

A second consideration is related to the nongovernmental organizations (NGOs) that are involved in world food matters, notably in the Third World. There are many praiseworthy observations that could be made about the dedication, skill, and effectiveness of those who administer these NGOs but, in this instance, one should point to a handicap. A major portion of NGO resources, at least in the NGOs' roles as distributors of food to the hungry nations, comes from Title II shipments under P.L. 480—as does U.S. food committed to the World Food Program. There is a conflict of interests here between NGO and U.S. policies that at least needs to be carefully examined—or, perhaps P.L. 480 needs a Title IV, a specific and carefully considered allocation of food and transportation funds to WFP. Finally, the world hunger network seems to revolve around a Washington, D.C.–New York axis. There is really meager grass-roots involvement "out in the provinces." Bread for the World has been struggling to set up local chapters. Paradoxically there is a considerable amount of elitism in this NGO world food network. Whether there is any practical (i.e., economically and organizationally feasible) way to overcome this undesired elitism is, admittedly, open to much discussion.

To summarize and conclude, the major argument herein has been that the United States played a central role in the establishment of two of the world food organizations (FAO and WFP) and an important, albeit somewhat reluctant, role in the founding of the World Food Council and IFAD. But in recent years (since the mid-1970s) U.S. policy toward these international organizations has been less than negative, but also less than forward looking. It has been characterized herein as a status quo, conservative, hold-the-line strategy. Some of these policy attributes of modest neglect and circumspect indifference can be accounted for by the condition of the U.S. economy—food policy, among other things, begins at home. But the further argument herein has been that hunger, malnutrition, and especially starvation are human conditions that, in terms of demands for their relief, have constantly been an incipient concern within the terms of the U.S. Creed. Furthermore, this creed, even at its weakest stages, has always been like fire in the ashes, and under certain conditions it can, and has been, stoked into a true passion. Whether the current food crisis in Africa will bestir U.S. policymakers into a revitalization of U.S. leadership in setting world food policy seems doubtful at the moment. In any respect, the utility of these four world food organizations, even if measured only in terms of a U.S. positive-sum strategy, needs to be more thoroughly evaluated by Congress.

NOTES

1. Huntington's thesis, very succinctly, is that there is a U.S. Creed (beliefs in democracy, freedom, individualism, distrust of power, etc.) that has pervaded the U.S. political culture throughout our history. But only in four historical instances (1760–1770, 1820–1830, the 1890s, and 1960–1975) has the gap between these ideals and the performance of U.S. political institutions been so in conflict that we have encountered a period of "creedal passion"—the ideals versus institutions (I v. I) gap. Moreover, this U.S. Creed moves in cycles—creedal passion to realism (cynicism is his preference), to complacency, to hypocrisy.

2. The other three concerns are farm policy, domestic economic policy, and general foreign policy.

3. It should be noted that several of the congressional staff agencies—and, in particular, the General Accounting Office—have reviewed and criticized the activities of the Rome agencies in recent years, and especially U.S. involvements therein.

4. The debate was far more concerned with "domestic" rather than "world" hunger.

REFERENCES

American Farm Bureau Federation. *Farm Bureau News,* February 27, 1984.

Christian Science Monitor, November 5, 1985, pp. 9–10.

Commission on Security and Economic Assistance. *A Report to the Secretary of State.* Washington, D.C.: Department of State, November 1983.

Destler, I. M. *Making Foreign Economic Policy.* Washington, D.C.: Brookings Institute, 1980.

Food and Agriculture Organization. *The Director-General's Programme of Work and Budget for 1982–1983 (and for 1984–85).* Rome: FAO, 1981, p. 56; and 1983, p. 211.

Hall, Tony. *Congressional Record,* 98th Cong., 2nd sess., no. 17, February 22, 1984, pp. 758–759.

Huntington, Samuel. *American Politics: The Promise of Disharmony.* Cambridge, Mass.: Harvard University Press, 1981.

Interfaith Action for Economic Justice. *Policy Notes,* Note 84–10. Washington, D.C.: IAEJ, March 16, 1984.

———. *Congress Cuts Foreign Aid Funding,* Note 86–1. Washington, D.C.: January 10, 1986, p. 1.

International Fund for Agricultural Development. *Press Release* (FIA/83/47). Rome: IFAD, December 8, 1983.

Kissinger, Henry. *Official Report of the United States Delegation to the World Food Conference.* Washington, D.C.: U.S. Department of State, 1974.

Lowi, Theodore, J. *The End of Liberalism: The Second Republic of the United States.* New York: W. W. Norton, 2nd edition, 1979.

Martin, Edwin McC. *Conference Diplomacy, a Case Study: The World Food Conference, Rome, 1974.* Washington, D.C.: Institute for the Study of Diplomacy,

Georgetown University, 1979.

Phillips, Ralph. *FAO: Its Origins, Formation and Evaluation, 1945–1981.* Rome: FAO, 1981, p. 78.

Presidential Commission on World Hunger. *Overcoming World Hunger: The Challenge Ahead.* Washington, D.C.: U.S. Government Printing Office, 1980.

U.S. Department of State. *Official Report of the United States Delegation to the World Food Conference.* Washington, D.C.: U.S. Department of State, 1974.

U.S. House of Representatives, Committee on Agriculture. *Hearing: Review of the World Food Problem.* 98th Cong., 1st sess., October 25, 1983. Washington, D.C.: U.S. Government Printing Office, 1983.

Wallerstein, Mitchell B. *Food for War—Food for Peace.* Cambridge, Mass.: MIT Press, 1980.

World Development Forum, March 15, 1984.

U.S. Department of Agriculture, Economic Research Service. *World Food Aid Needs and Availabilities, 1983.* Washington, D.C.: Government Printing Office, July 1983, p. 15.

13 The Social, Developmental, and Political Impacts of Food Aid

James N. Schubert

This chapter addresses the social, economic, and political impacts of food aid. Logically, such an assessment could address impacts with respect to both donor and recipient countries. This discussion focuses on impacts in recipient countries. The task of assessing impacts in recipient countries may be distinguished as follows: Do the conditions addressed through aid involve continuing problems of food insecurity/insufficiency, chronic problems of the same nature, or acute emergency problems of food crisis and famine? The chronic problems are revealed in Food and Agriculture Organization estimates on percent of population below basic metabolism requirements in calorie consumption that have a mean and median of 25 percent with a standard deviation of 12 for fifty-six less-developed countries (LDCs) in 1969–1970 (FAO 1977). The acute problems that threaten or involve mass starvation are highlighted by press reports that people were reduced to eating tree bark in Mozambique in early 1984—a classic indicator of a population under critical nutritional stress in the context of severe famine (Walford 1970; Aykroyd 1974). Indeed, a significant portion of the African continent is presently affected by severe drought and impending or current famine. Although chronic and acute problems are very much interrelated, they constitute separate dimensions of food aid impacts. Both problems are addressed here.

Ideally, the methodology for assessing the impacts of food aid would proceed from theoretical modeling of probable or posited effects to empirical studies employing rigorous designs to yield replicable findings describing the effects of aid. However, what little systematic cross-recipient evidence marshaled to date on the impacts of food aid must be regarded as tentative, and other data are primarily drawn from case study literature. The discussion that follows draws on relevant bodies of theory to model probable effects and utilizes the diverse sources of available data to evaluate hypotheses.

SOCIAL IMPACTS: FOOD AID AND HUMAN WELFARE

International food aid is a broad concept that encompasses both bilateral and multilateral aid transfers, through both private and official channels. Historically, the United States has accounted for a major portion of international food aid, nearly 90 percent during the period of greatest aid flows in the 1960s. To some extent, assessment of impacts must account for program goals, and these goals have certainly been many and diverse in U.S. food aid policy (Toma 1967; Stanely 1972; Wallerstein 1980), including promotion of economic development, improving nutritional conditions, and securing political objectives. One has only to briefly peruse the U.S. Agency for International Development's (AID) periodic reports in *Overseas Grants and Loans* on PL 480 allocations to appreciate the political nature of aid giving. Nevertheless, a humanitarian component has been among the nominal objectives of the program, at least since the early 1960s, and legislative revisions have reinforced this component over time. It is, therefore, reasonable to ask whether or not food aid does enhance the well-being of hungry and malnourished peoples. This is certainly a controversial question and one that is a prerequisite to assessing other impacts of food aid. Although the distinction between aid addressed to chronic problems and aid designed to relieve outright crises tends to get lost in many discussions of food aid, the effects of food aid on human well-being are most evident in the context of food crises and famine.

Food Aid in Famine Relief

Famines in the modern world are more political than natural disasters (Schubert 1983a; Dando 1980). A survey of case studies of famine, ranging from the Ethiopian famines of the early 1970s to famines in sixteenth and seventeenth century England and also including cases in Russia, Ireland, India, and China, suggests certain general patterns in both the incidence and relief of food crises.[1] These cases fall in a category of accidental rural famines—accidental in the sense that they were not deliberately induced through public policy, nor directly related to international war, as in Russia in the 1930s, the Netherlands in 1944, Kampuchea in the 1970s, or possibly East Timor in the 1970s. It is necessary to briefly examine the causal framework underlying famine to assess the impact of food aid in famine relief.

The explanation of the onset of rural accidental famines requires a two-stage model: one predicting the vulnerability of populations to famine and a second describing precipitating causes. In case after case, vulnerability or "risk" in populations is produced by the interaction of several background conditions (Schubert 1983b). These conditions include a high rate of population growth, a semi-feudal peasant economy, pressures for commercialization in agricultural production, and a marginalized or already impoverished and chronically or cyclically undernourished population. Pressure on food supplies comes from both the increased demand brought on by population growth and from commercialization that orients production away from consumption and toward exports. Agricultural productivity is undercut and crop vulnerability enhanced by cultivation of marginal land, monocropping, and poor land management and conservation strategies. Populations in such settings are vulnerable or at risk. It is in this context of vulnerability that drought, flood, frost, blight, or other natural causes of crop failures or harvest shortfalls may precipitate famine (Schubert 1983b).

People, however, do not begin to starve because harvest shortfalls occur. In times of impending shortage, speculators begin to hoard supplies and prices rise. People do begin to starve only when they can no longer pay the price for food. By this time, they have sold their livestock and possessions of marketable value and are largely bereft of resources (Currey 1981). Although destitution may occur quickly in populations at risk, governments typically have several weeks or even months to act to prevent the full-scale onset of famine. Typically, in what Green (1975, 1977) refers to as the "acknowledgment" problem, they do not act until mass starvation is well under way. Thus, lacking standard operating procedures, as in India's Famine Code, efforts to devise early warning systems without appropriate bureaucratic reaction systems are likely to prove ineffective. It is in this sense that accidental rural famines are political disasters. Famines have an underlying etiology rooted in the political-economic conditions of vulnerable populations (who are by no means independent of international market structures).[2]

With regard to food aid and famine relief in such settings, it should be clear that normal market forces are unlikely to be effective in relieving conditions. Objective demand for food is high, but effective demand is practically nil: Starving people do not have the means to purchase food, regardless of price. Food supplies that often provide minimal nutrition quite adequately, even in periods of food crisis and given optimal distribution, do not naturally flow into, but out of, famine areas. Thus, Ethiopian granaries were tapped during the heights of the 1973 famine, not to feed the starving, but to exploit the higher prices available in neighboring countries (Shepard 1975). Given the inefficacy of normal market forces, the potential role of food aid to relieve famine conditions is quite strong.

The potential to learn from past experience in international food aid for famine relief is also strong. A survey of historical cases of famine (Schubert 1983b) indicates that one overarching lesson of history is that food aid to starving peoples is quite effective in limiting population mortality and an array of significant and destructive social, economic, and political impacts that are caused by high mortality. Abuses, misuses, corruption, mismanagement, and poor coordination of relief agencies and activities are certainly not exceptional in famine relief and to some extent may constitute a norm (Sheets and Morris 1974). With the exception of the Indians, who have apparently learned to cope with food crises, there is enormous room for improvement in famine relief to maximize the positive effects of food aid. However, where serious efforts have been made to relieve crises through direct food aid, both in modern and historical cases, mortality has been significantly lower than it would otherwise have been. International food aid has played a significant role in most successful efforts to relieve famines, at least during the last one hundred and fifty years.

Four general types of policy approaches to famine relief are observed in the case study literature. These types are identified on the basis of patterns of policy choices made by governments of affected countries. Choices are first distinguished along administrative dimensions of relief policy: (1) financial responsibility for relief (national/local); (2) administrative responsibility (national/local); (3) terms of aid (loans/grants); and (4) primary relief channels (official/private). Choices are also elaborated according to programmatic dimensions: (1) provision of food or money; (2) transfer of assistance directly or indirectly (e.g., via wages for public employment); and (3) the domain of distribution (at-risk population or targeted subgroups, such as children or elderly). Finally, policy choices are made on the basis of regional and international food trade: to restrict or allow free trade with respect to food exports and to stimulate or allow free trade with respect to food imports.

At different periods within famine cycles, in different famines, and in different countries, alternative patterns of policy choices along these dimensions may be observed. The four types of policies representing different patterns of choices vary along a continuum based on the degree of state intervention to relieve conditions. In a direct intervention policy, financial and administrative responsibility is borne by the national government; relief is provided through official channels and emphasizes direct transfer of food to the population at risk, while food exports are banned and imports stimulated (including international aid). Many governments appear loath to adopt this total relief approach, apparently because of cost and the possible creation of long-term public welfare responsibilities.

Historically, a laissez-faire approach has been more popular. It maximizes local financial and local administrative responsibility, loans to relief institutions, use of private channels, provision of money in preference to food, provision through wages for public works employment, and selective targeting of any more direct relief (e.g., communal feeding or soup kitchens, etc.) to the disadvantaged. Without addressing the normative foundations of such policies, they have commonly been premised on the assumption that gratuitous relief is degrading to recipients (and/or too costly). Under a laissez-faire approach, free trade is maintained in food trade policy—exports are not restricted, and imports are not stimulated.

Combining elements of both the direct intervention and laissez-faire approaches is a third, partial intervention, approach. Here, a concern for minimizing governmental interference in the market is modified by the need for direct intervention to prevent death from starvation. Typical of this approach was the action of the British government in 1845 to import maize from North America to help relieve the food crisis in Ireland. The intent of the program was not to feed the population, but to hold down the general rise in food prices by introducing a food foreign to the Irish market at concessional prices. Patterns of policy choices are mixed in this approach; thus, burdens of relief may be borne nationally, but administration is decentralized, and both public and private channels are employed. Exports tend to be restricted, imports stimulated, and aid welcomed.

The fourth type of policy may be labeled as inaction. Here, no attempt is made to relieve famine conditions—sometimes on the nominal premise that reliance on normal market forces would be more effective (e.g., British policy late in the Irish famine and again in India in 1865–1866) (O'Neill 1957). Other factors that appear to be involved include official embarrassment and concern for regime instability that might follow upon official recognition of famine conditions. A related factor involves concern about the potentially destabilizing mass political effects of exposing isolated peasant populations to foreign relief workers (Robbins 1975).

The choice of famine policy apparently has had a great effect upon mortality rates. Data on mortality in populations under famine conditions are imprecise, and estimates of mortality can vary substantially. However, ranges of mortality estimates do vary systematically with policy types along the continuum involving degree of policy intervention. Estimates of population mortality in famines relieved through direct intervention are below 1 percent. They range from 1 to 2 percent with partial intervention policies and from 3 to 10 percent under laissez-faire policies. Estimates of mortality for affected populations in famines characterized by policies of inaction range from 15 to 33 percent of total population. Of course, death rates are a good deal higher for selected groups, especially young children, infants, and the elderly. Actual policies may also vary along the continuum through different periods or cycles in prolonged famines, producing changes in mortality rates.

It is impossible in this brief review to do more than sketch the dimensions of the role of food aid in famine relief. There has been very little systematic study of famine and the role of food aid. Case study materials have largely become available only within the past few years, and the first comprehensive bibliography of food crisis literature did not become available until 1981 (Currey et al. 1981). However, available data do reveal that international food aid has traditionally played an import role in famine relief. The activities of OXFAM, the American Friends Service Committee, and the International Red Cross, among other private transnational efforts, have been crucial in famine relief for the past one hundred years. Private relief committees were formed in the United States during the Irish famine of 1845–1852, and United States private and official efforts played a role in relieving the Russian famines of 1891–1892 and 1921–1922 (Weissman 1974) as well as more recent famines. In general, historical data on famines indicate that a fundamental impact of food aid for famine relief is to significantly reduce mortality.

Food Aid and Chronic Malnutrition

There is no standard as clearcut as population mortality against which to assess the impact of food aid on chronic hunger and malnutrition. Such aid is provided through different channels for different purposes, in quite different recipients, and serves diverse policy goals, some of which may be contradictory. High mortality and morbidity related to malnutrition result from a complex set of causal factors where malnutrition serves as an antecedent and contributing source of effects, but its role cannot easily be singled out for aid impact assessment. It is nevertheless plausible to advance the proposition that where food aid is given in significant amounts, it has positive effects on nutritional status in recipient populations. Aid may enhance individual consumption by helping to keep prices down for food commodities generally and/or by directly reaching the needy—via direct feeding and nutritional intervention programs.

There are several arguments current in relevant literature that contradict this general proposition. First, it is argued that by depressing food prices, food aid undermines the incentives for farmers to produce. Because of this so-called "price disincentive effect," farmers will produce less food for human consumption, leading to a net decline in domestic food production (Shuman 1977) and, presumably, an increase in international food import dependence. Some case study evidence suggests that price disincentive effects may cause farmers to switch to crops not in competition with aid commodities, but no systematic net decline is observed (Goering and Witt 1963; Aktan 1964; Srivastava 1975). India used "fair price" shops to sell concessionally priced foods that were avoided for social reasons by those with sufficient purchasing power, creating a differentiated market that minimized price disincentive effects.

A second argument is that much of the food aid targeted for undernourished segments of LDC populations never reaches its intended recipients. Thus, it is proposed that diversion of aid from intended recipients through waste, corruption, and mismanagement is so great that the impact of aid on nutrition is trivial. Certainly, anecdotal evidence abounds of food aid supplies rotting in warehouses, provided in forms people would not or could not consume, and of aid supplies sold on the black market by corrupt recipient country officials. However, even aid supplies diverted by local elites and sold in the open market should help depress or limit prices for food and, thereby, promote consumption. There is also some case study evidence to indicate that high proportions of food aid commodities have gone into consumption by target groups in such countries as India, Colombia, and Egypt (Goering and Witt 1963). Although there is little doubt that significant amounts of aid are misused, with respect to the ultimate impact of food aid on human well-being the question is whether enough aid gets to intended recipients to improve their nutritional status at all.

A third, and perhaps more critical, argument assumes that food aid does in fact reach targeted recipients. On this basis, it is proposed that the net impact of food aid may be to increase the gross number of people living on the margin of starvation, rather than to increase the nutritional status of individuals. Thus, malnutrition is a major contributing cause of infant and child mortality in under-nourished populations. If improved nutrition functions to reduce mortality and morbidity in LDCs—to reduce death rates in relation to birth rates—such improvement would provide a contributing cause of high population growth rates. However, it is also commonly observed that high rates of infant and child mortality are causally related with high rates of fertility. In terms of demographic transition theory (Marden et al. 1982), improvements in human well-being are prerequisite to reduction in fertility and the development of equilibrium in birth and death rates. Certainly, since the mid-1970s, food aid programs have been complemented by at least nominal family and population planning policies in a large and growing number of aid recipient countries. If malnutrition is a cause of high fertility and if food aid is accompanied by population policy implementation, then this general criticism loses much of its strength.

Ideally, the impact of food aid on chronic conditions of hunger and malnutrition would be assessed through the type of multi-indicator nutritional surveys employed in the United States, utilizing anthropometric, biochemical, and diet recall measurement (Schmandt et al. 1980). Lacking such data for most recipient countries, an alternative approach to measurement involves inferring nutritional conditions in a population from food supply balance sheets. Such aggregate data permit estimates of per capita, per day consumption in relation to estimated daily requirements of protein, calories, and dietary fat content (indicating intakes for energy and fat-soluble vitamins). Of course, such aggregate data can yield only crude estimates of nutritional conditions, and they do not account for maldistribution within populations. One approach to the distributional problem has been to average aggregate data by index scores for income inequality (FAO 1977; Reutlinger and Selowsky 1976); however, such data have not been available for a time period permitting analysis of change in conditions. An alternative approach is to break data down by animal and vegetable sources. Although meat products are highly subject to distributional inequalities, vegetable products are far less so, and cereal foods provide the staple in the diet of most of the world's hungry and malnourished peoples.

One pilot study (Schubert 1981) utilizes such aggregate data to yield a set of preliminary findings on the impact of U.S. P.L. 480 food aid on nutritional status in LDCs. In this study, data on total P.L. 480 aid receipts from 1962 to 1975 for eighty-nine LDCs were normed by population size and divided by the number of years in which LDCs were independent and eligible for P.L. 480 aid. On the basis of these per capita, per year food aid data, the LDCs were divided into high- and low-aid groups. The resulting sixteen high-aid LDCs and seventy-three low-aid LDCs were compared on aggregate indicators of nutritional status for 1960–1965 and for change in nutritional conditions during the period of measured food aid flows: Nutritional data measured change from 1960–1965 through 1972–1974. Changes in per capita, per day scores for animal and vegetable protein, calories, dietary fat content, and calories and protein as a percent of estimated individual requirements were computed on both net difference and percentage change indices between the base years 1963 and 1975.

The two groups did not differ significantly in nutritional status in statistical pretests for between group differences in 1963. At the end of the 1963–1975 period of measurement, the group receiving higher aid did show significantly greater improvement in nutrition than the lower aid group. Thus, the higher aid group had a significantly greater drop in the estimated protein deficiency than the lower aid group and significantly greater improvement in total calories. Change over time in animal and vegetable protein was also tested for significant differences within each group. Findings indicate a significant improvement in both animal and vegetable source protein in the food supply, of 2–3 grams per capita, per day on each variable, for the higher aid group, but no significant change for the lower aid group.

The groups were also compared for various other possible intervening conditions—including growth in food production, growth in Gross Domestic Product (GDP), nonfood economic aid, Gross National Product (GNP) per capita, exports per capita, and rate of population growth—and no statistically significant differences were observed. Using partial correlation to control for GNP/per capita, population growth rates, growth in domestic food production, other economic aid, and nutritional status in 1963, statistically significant fifth order partial correlations of .32 were observed for the relationship between average annual per capita food aid and change in total protein and percent protein deficiency in the sample of eighty-nine LDCs. When countries receiving no P.L. 480 aid were removed from the sample, the partial correlations rose to the .39 level (p<.01). In short, a modest, positive, significant association is observed in aggregate data for the impact of food aid on nutritional status in LDCs.

Two conclusions may be drawn from these data. First, in the long term, food aid does appear to improve nutritional conditions somewhat. Second, relatively few of the more needy LDCs are receiving significant amounts of aid. Food aid may work to improve nutritional conditions in poor societies, but poor societies as a group are not receiving aid in proportion to their needs. Estimates of nutritional deprivation from food supply balance sheets remain appalling, and these data underestimate the incidence of hunger and malnutrition within populations.

In summary, food aid does appear to have a positive social impact with respect to both chronic and acute nutritional problems. In times of current and impending famine, food aid has long played a vital role in limiting population mortality and establishing the socioeconomic conditions for recovery. In addition to its crisis role, food aid may also affect population nutritional status more generally and help address problems of chronic hunger and malnutrition. These findings do not imply that problems of hunger and malnutrition are being effectively addressed through current patterns of food aid. They do suggest that food aid is an instrument that could be used effectively to help solve these problems.

POLITICAL IMPACTS: FOOD FOR PEACE?

One of the nominal suppositions underlying much international food aid is that it retards collective violence and promotes political stability in recipient countries. This assumption is based on a model that proposes a causal relationship between hunger and malnutrition and mass political aggression—including riots, demonstrations, strikes, assassinations, and support for organized subversive movements. Thus, food aid would promote peace by alleviating hunger and, thereby, reduce one cause of political instability in LDCs. However, just as there are contrasting models of the effects of food aid on human well-being, there are also contrasting models of the effects of hunger on political violence and, by inference, the effects of food aid on political stability (Schubert 1982a).

One model proposes a positive relationship between hunger and violence. This model draws upon the frustration-aggression hypothesis in social psychology (Dollard et al. 1939) as it has been employed in the literature of comparative politics (Gurr 1970). The fundamental argument supporting this model is that hunger is a frustrating experience for affected individuals and produces a behavioral predisposition toward angry aggression (Davies 1962, 1963). More recent formulations of frustration-aggression by Berkowitz (1978) emphasizes noxious physical sensations as the basis of aggression-related frustration. Hunger appears to qualify quite well as both a psychologically and biologically frustrating experience and, in terms of this literature, should be quite clearly correlated with political aggression (Dougherty and Pfaltzgraff 1971, 245). Case study evidence lends support to this frustration-aggression model in periods of food crisis.

The onset of famine is often accompanied by mass political aggression—i.e., spontaneous demonstrations, riots, strikes, and assassinations of elites—rather than organized subversion. In several historical cases of famine, the initial onset of scarcity was associated, even in the nineteenth century, with expectations by the poor that government would intervene actively to prevent widespread suffering and starvation. The absence of effective official relief was often met with aggressive mass behavior at public buildings, granaries, public work sites, village centers, and at borders, railroad stations, and other points where the actual export of food supplies from affected areas took place.[3] There is a clear functional quality to such behavior in that it centers on food and food policy–related themes. However, as conditions worsen and population mortality rates climb as a function of nutritional deprivation, mass aggression rates may decline and, at least in the Irish famine, be replaced by a wave of terrorist assassinations of landlords, agents, and public officials. Mass-based revolutions rarely, if ever, occur in the midst of severe food crises, although they frequently follow them.

A second model of the relationship between hunger and violence emphasizes the biological effects of malnutrition and progressive starvation. Although there is inadequate space in this chapter to systematically discuss the impacts of malnutrition on human development and behavior, a few key effects require mention. In sheer quantitative terms, protein-calorie malnutrition involves deprivation of energy. Thus, in addition to a host of deleterious consequences for growth and development (Mitchel 1976), quantitative malnutrition predicts to behavioral passivity. Qualitatively, malnutrition also involves vitamin and mineral deficiencies that are pervasive in poorer societies. A principal consequence of Vitamin B and iron deficiencies, for instance, is anemia. Qualitative deficiencies frequently co-occur with protein-calorie malnutrition, thereby reinforcing the disposition toward behavioral passivity. Attitudinal correlates of malnutrition include apathy, anomie, irritability, hostility, and paranoia (Keys et al. 1950). Thus, the main biological consequence of malnutrition relevant to this discussion is a physical and political lethargy. It is on the basis of this biological model that regimes are accused, on occasion, of attempting to starve unruly populations into passivity (George 1977). Certainly, as hunger and malnutrition grow increasingly severe in a population, mass political aggression appears less likely.

In sum, relevant and substantial bodies of literature support two apparently contradictory models of the relationship between hunger and violence. A frustration-aggression hypothesis supports a positive effects model, while an anemia-passivity hypothesis supports a negative effects model. To deal with the impact of food aid on political instability and political violence requires resolution of the apparent contradiction of these competing models.

First, it may be observed that humans can experience up to a 10 percent loss in body weight before personal energy levels begin to fall and negative effects are experienced. The attitudinal and behavioral correlates of malnutrition are observed under moderate to severe conditions of deprivation. On this basis, it is reasonable to propose an integrated model of effects that accounts for both a psychological predisposition to aggression and a biological disposition to passivity. Under conditions of mild to moderate deprivation, as associated with cyclical chronic malnutrition and the early stages of food crisis, the biological disposition toward passivity is not likely to be strong. At the same time, the psychological frustration and physical discomfort associated with nutritional deprivation should be enhanced under these milder conditions—hunger sensations, for instance, actually decline in more advanced stages of starvation, although appetite remains. As conditions of deprivation become more extreme, biological factors predisposing passivity are likely to overwhelm any psychological predisposition toward aggression. Moreover, under severe deprivation, almost all activity must be oriented toward very short-term consumption goals; behavior with longer term payoffs, whether demonstrating for increased relief or promoting revolution, have little survival value for the individual. Considering the relative influence of both psychological and biological factors under conditions with varying degrees of deprivation, an integrated psychobiological model predicts a curvilinear relationship between hunger and violence, describing political aggression as a second order polynomial function of malnutrition (Schubert 1982b). Aggression increases with greater malnutrition up to the point where the biological disposition toward passivity surpasses the psychological disposition toward aggression in the strength of their effects on behavior.

Assuming that food is effective in improving nutrition in affected populations under chronic and acute conditions, food aid introduces a dynamic dimension into the model of malnutrition and political violence outlined above. Thus, in any relevant context, nutritional conditions are improving, static, or deteriorating. The result of effectively delivered aid will be improved mass nutritional conditions or minimized decline. Where the magnitude or level of nutritional deprivation is mild to moderate—where psychological effects on behavior outweigh biological ones—improvement in conditions, from aid or other causes, should reduce the disposition toward aggressive political behavior, while deterioration in nutritional conditions should increase it. However, where the magnitude or level of nutritional deprivation is moderate to severe, improvement in conditions is likely to minimize the biological disposition toward passivity and, thereby, permit an angry population to express frustration in aggressive political behavior. Dirks (1979, 1980) discusses "relief-induced agonism" in people recovering from acute conditions that involves greater aggressiveness or irritability and may be physiologically associated with hypoglycemia. Such physiological effects in groups recovering from famine or cyclic periods of malnutrition might well interact with psychological dispositions toward aggressiveness. In this context, it is no wonder that although revolution seldom accompanies famine, it frequently follows it (Sorokin 1976; Schubert 1983a).

Historical as well as modern accounts indicate that hungry people do blame governments for their plight. The material situation of food deprivation provides what Muller (1979) calls "normative justification" for political aggression. Psychological frustration and physical discomfort may interact to provide the behavioral disposition toward aggression. Improvement in physical capacity to act permits the hungry to express their disposition in actual behavior. Food aid impacts on the normative, psychological, and biological factors in the relationship between hunger and violence to promote political stability when it is used to avert crises or to prevent mild conditions from worsening. However, when governments allow food crises to develop unfettered and already bad conditions to grow worse, then the introduction of food aid may increase the capacity of the affected population to express its disaffection with government through political aggression. Thus, food aid that improves mass nutrition, but inadequately to remove significant chronic or acute widespread deprivation, may enable deprived populations to act on their grievances. Thus, where deprivation is more substantial and need is great, food aid may not promote stability, but rather may promote politically aggressive and destabilizing mass behavior.

Tentative findings from a pilot study designed to assess the broad relationship between food aid and political instability through cross-national aggregate data analyses do not contradict the predictions derived from the model described above (Schubert 1982b). Data on U.S. P.L. 480 food aid flows—total receipts, Title I and II receipts, and total per capita receipts—were related to aggregate events data on political instability (Banks 1979), including riots, strikes, demonstrations, assassinations, and guerrilla attacks, for the period 1965–1975. Statistical controls were introduced for levels of instability and malnutrition at the beginning of the observed period. Preliminary findings did not indicate any significant positive impact of aid on political stability. To the contrary, stronger and significant correlations suggest an inverse relationship between aid and peace—the greater the aid, the greater the riots and demonstrations—even with baseline levels of hunger and instability controlled. The model presented above is quite capable of explaining such findings, if they are supported in subsequent research. In many recipient countries, if effective but inadequate aid receipts go hand in hand with the normative justification provided by official corruption, mismanagement, or the otherwise apparent insensitivity by government to the plight of the hungry, it is quite plausible that aid and violence are statistically related.

To explore shorter term effects of aid (Schubert 1982b), data were developed on food aid flows and political instability during the 1969–1972 period that brackets the world food crisis period of the early 1970s. Net change in aid flows from 1969–1970 to 1971–1972 were related to net change on indicators of instability for a sample of sixty-five LDCs broken down by FAO (nutritional) classifications into most seriously affected (MSA) and non-MSA groups. Findings indicated that an increase in aid flows was associated with a decrease in levels of mass political aggression for the non-MSA group of LDCs. No significant correlations were observed among the MSA LDCs. Thus, preliminary findings suggest that short-term aid in a period of crisis to populations in which hunger and malnutrition are not normally severe problems was effective in promoting political stability—and this does appear to have been a context of "food for peace." These findings are also quite consistent with the model of hunger and violence discussed above.

An obvious lesson to be drawn from this discussion of the mass political effects of food aid is that the relationship is complex. The bivariate, unicausal models often used to predict the political effects of food aid are simplistic and inadequate. Under specified conditions, aid is likely to enhance political stability in recipient countries. Under other conditions, it is likely to help undermine stability. Given the nature of the policy process, it is of course unlikely that international food aid allocations would be based upon theoretical modeling and prediction of probable impacts on mass political behavior. However, it is also inappropriate and unwise to premise or evaluate food aid on the basis of expectations that it will somehow work to promote political stability or peace. Quite often, food aid may not promote peace, and unfulfilled expectations may contribute to reaction formation among relevant elites in donor countries. Perhaps the overriding lesson to be drawn from the admittedly limited available theory and research on the political impacts of international food aid is that such impacts are sufficiently problematic that allocations might be better based on nonpolitical criteria altogether.

DEVELOPMENTAL IMPACTS OF FOOD AID

The preceding discussion has focused on the biosocial effects of food aid on human well-being and on political impacts that derive from those biosocial effects. It may be apparent that there is a measure of absurdity in policy discussions about the promotion of democratic political development in societies where large proportions of the population experience cyclic or continuing nutritional deprivation. Psychobiological correlates of hunger and malnutrition describe anemic, lethargic, apathetic, and sometimes aggressive or antagonistic populations under moderate to severe nutritional stress. Populations in such straits on a cyclic or continuing basis lack the prerequisites for democratic political development and provide fertile ground for the organization of revolutionary opposition movements. In populations under periodic acute nutritional stress, memories and resentments of governments that fail to prevent food crises linger long in the mass political culture, providing a direct disposition toward revolutionary change (Sorokin 1975; Robbins 1975; Woodham-Smith 1962). In China, Russia, Ireland, India, and even Ethiopia, organized political aggression and revolutionary movements have followed periods of mass hunger. Food aid in relief of crises is not likely to minimize this effect, although such aid may incidentally function to enhance it. Rather, food for peace is food aid that serves to prevent crises. It is aid that addresses the background conditions that place populations at risk or in vulnerability to crises and mass starvation. Famine is a class phenomenon, and it is only people who live with chronic and continuing problems of hunger and malnutrition that starve in times of famine. Thus, food for peace is ultimately food for socioeconomic development.

An important criticism of international food aid is that it promotes political-economic dependence in recipient countries. Commercialization in agriculture in societies with pervasive hunger and malnutrition, coupled with urbanization, undermines food self-sufficiency and contributes to conditions of vulnerability to food crisis among the poor. This is not just a modern phenomenon but a model that appears to hold throughout centuries and across continents (Dando 1980). Given high rates of population growth and urbanization in the hungriest populations, growing dependence on production on marginal lands, and in-

creasing food import dependence, the future of those who are chronically malnourished in poor societies appears in ever greater jeopardy. In the foreseeable
future, there are three possible outcomes. LDCs might make dramatic progress
toward food self-sufficiency, minimize food import dependence by major gains
in domestic food production, and thereby meet the nutritional needs of their
populations. If LDCs do not, regardless of ideological debates about relations
of dominance and dependence, either international food aid will be used to address the nutritional needs of those segments of LDC populations lacking effective demand, or conditions of chronic malnutrition will fester, vulnerability to
food crisis will be enhanced, and famines will increase in frequency and scope.
In the short term, a vital role exists for international food aid in the development
of food security in LDCs.

In the longer term, given the inevitable political constraints of food import
dependence, among other factors, LDC food security must be generated from
within. The obstacles to developmental change posed by pervasive malnutrition
in populations are enormous, as Berg (1973) points out in great detail. The costs
in national development (Berg 1981) are felt in a host of crucial problem areas.
Productivity suffers because of diminished physical stature and strength, behavioral lethargy, attitudinal apathy, and heightened worker susceptibility to
disease. Education and skill development are diminished, not only by the behavioral consequences of malnutrition, but also by the intellectual retardation
and depressed learning curves of those who are nutritionally deprived during
childhood. The correlations of child and maternal malnutrition with infant and
child mortality and of infant and child mortality with high fertility place major
obstacles in the path of family planning and population control. The lifelong
effects of early malnutrition render affected individuals uncompetitive in a
modernizing society, place biological constraints on social mobility, and help
to cement class structure. Last, but by no means least, natural selection is at
work in populations under nutritional stress—in populations with high infant
and child mortality rates for selective subpopulation groups (Schubert 1983a).
There is no assurance that genetic changes will promote the long-term fitness
and adaptability of such populations—quite to the contrary. In short, the fundamental biosocial parameters of LDC societies in which food sufficiency and
security must be developed in the long term are undermined by pervasive
hunger and malnutrition. The achievement of food security and sufficiency in
poor societies may well depend in part on the effectiveness of food aid in promoting human welfare.

NOTES

1. Case study literature on famine includes Appleby (1978); Bhatia (1967); Edwards and Williams (1957); Mallory (1926); Robbins (1975); Shepard (1975); Stein
(1975); and Woodham-Smith (1962).

2. The Irish famine of 1845–1852 is a classic case of a famine whose causes are rooted in international political-economic relations of dominance and dependence. Thus, for example, the monocrop food dependence and vulnerability of the peasants (i.e., on the potato) must be understood in terms of Ireland's pattern of producing other food commodities for export to support the expanding industrial work force in England during the nineteenth century. Food continued to be exported to England in the midst of mass starvation in Ireland. Peasants raised cash crops on most of their land to pay rents and taxes; potatoes provided the peasants a large yield from a small plot and offered some security from landlords and tax collectors because potatoes grew underground (Carefoot and Sprott 1974).

3. Media accounts of Haitian riots at international food aid warehouses in May 1984 are quite typical of this type of aggressive participation (*Rochester Democrat and Chronicle* 1984).

REFERENCES

Aktan, R. *Analysis and Assessment of the Economic Effects of Public Law 480 Title I Program, Turkey*. Ankara: University of Ankara, 1964.

Appleby, A. B. *Famine in Tudor and Stuart England*. Stanford, Calif.: Stanford University Press, 1978.

Aykroyd, W. R. *The Conquest of Famine*. London: Chatts and Windus, 1974.

Banks, A. S. *Cross National Time Series Archive: User's Manual*. Binghamton: State University of New York at Binghamton, Center for Social Analysis, 1979.

Berg, A. *The Nutrition Factor: Its Role in National Development*. Washington, D.C.: Brookings Institute, 1973.

Berg, A. *Malnourished People: A Policy View*. Washington, D.C.: World Bank, 1981.

Berkowitz, L. "Whatever Happened to the Frustration-aggression Hypothesis?" *American Behavioral Scientist* 21 (1978):691–708.

Bhatia, B. M. *Famines in India: A Study in Some Aspects of the Economic History of India (1860–1965)*. London: Asia Publishing House, 1967.

Carefoot, G. L., and E. R. Sprott. *Famine on the Wind: Plant Diseases and Human History*. Sydney: Angus and Robertson, 1974.

Currey, B. "Famine Forecasting: Fourteen Fallacies." *Ceres F.A.O. Review on Development* 14 (1981):20–25.

Currey, B., M. Ali, and N. Khoman. *Famine: A First Bibliography*. Honolulu: East-West Resource Systems Institute, 1981.

Dando, W. A. *The Geography of Famine*. New York: V. H. Winston and Sons, 1980.

Davies, J. C. "Toward a Theory of Revolution." *American Sociological Review* 27 (1962):5–19.

Davies, J. C. *Human Nature and Politics: The Dynamics of Human Behavior*. New York: Wiley, 1963.

Dirks, R. "Social Responses During Severe Food Shortages and Famine." *Current Anthropology* 21 (1980):21–44.

Dirks, R. "Relief-Induced Agonism." *Disasters* 3 (1979):195–198.

Dollard, J., L. W. Doob, and N. Miller. *Frustration and Aggression*. New Haven, Conn.: Yale University Press, 1939.

Edwards, R. D., and T. D. Williams, eds. *The Great Famine: Studies in Irish History 1845–52*. New York: New York University Press, 1957.

Dougherty, J. E., and R. L. Pfaltzgraff. *Contending Theories of International Relations: A Comprehensive Survey*. New York: Harper and Row, 1971.

Food and Agriculture Organization. *The Fourth World Food Survey*. Rome: FAO, 1977.

George, S. *How the Other Half Dies: The Real Reasons for World Hunger*. Montclair, N.J.: Allanheld, Osmun and Co., 1977.

Goering, T. J., and L. Witt. *United States Agricultural Surpluses in Colombia: A Review of Pl 480*. East Lansing: Michigan State University, 1963.

Green, S. J. "Afterword." In J. Shepard. *The Politics of Starvation*. New York: Carnegie Endowment, 1975.

Green, S. J. *International Disaster Relief: Toward a Responsive System*. New York: McGraw Hill, 1977.

Gurr, T. R. *Why Men Rebel*. Princeton, N.J.: Princeton University Press, 1970.

Keys, A. B., J. Brozek, A. Henschell, G. Mickelson, and H. Taylor. *The Biology of Human Starvation*. Minneapolis: University of Minnesota Press, 1950.

Mallory, W. H. *China: Land of Famine*. New York: American Geographical Society, 1926.

Marden, P. G., D. G. Hodgson, and T. L. McCoy. *Population in the Global Arena*. New York: Holt, Rinehart, and Winston, 1982.

Mitchel, H. et al. *Nutrition in Health and Disease*. 16th edition. Philadelphia: Lippincott, 1976.

Muller, E. N. *Aggressive Political Participation*. Princeton, N.J.: Princeton University Press, 1979.

O'Neill, T. P. "The Organization and Administration of Relief, 1845–52." In R. D. Edwards and T. D. Williams, eds. *The Great Famine: Studies in Irish History 1845–52*. New York: New York University Press, 1957.

Reutlinger, S., and M. Selowsky. *Malnutrition and Poverty: Magnitude and Policy Options*. Baltimore, Md.: Johns Hopkins University Press, 1976.

Robbins, R. G. *Famine in Russia, 1891–1892: The Imperial Government Responds to a Crisis*. New York: Columbia University Press, 1975.

Rochester Democrat and Chronicle, May 29, 1984.

Schmandt, J. S., R. A. Shorey, and L. Kinch. *Nutrition Policy in Transition*. Lexington, Mass.: Lexington Books, 1980.

Schubert, J. N. "Hunger and the Problem of Politics." In H. Flohr and W. Tonnesmann, eds. *Politics and Biology*. Berlin: Verlag Paul Parey, 1983a.

Schubert, J. N. "Famines in World Historic-Political Retrospect." *Quarterly Journal of International Agriculture* 22 (1983b):27–45.

Schubert, J. N. "Toward a Psychobiological Model of Malnutrition and Political Violence." XII World Congress of the International Political Science Association, 1982a.

Schubert, J. N. "Food for Peace? The Political Impact of U.S. PL 480 Food Aid." International Studies Association Annual Meeting, 1982b.

Schubert, J. N. "The Impact of Food Aid on World Malnutrition." *International Organization* 32 (1981):329–354.

Sheets, H., and R. Morris. *Disaster in the Desert: Failures of International Relief in the West African Drought*. Washington, D.C.: Carnegie Endowment for International

Peace, 1974.

Shepard, J. *The Politics of Starvation*. New York: Carnegie Endowment for International Peace, 1975.

Shuman, C. B. "Food Aid and the Free Market." In P. G. Brown and H. Shue, eds. *Food Policy: The Responsibility of the United States in the Life and Death Choices*. New York: Free Press, 1977.

Sorokin, P. A. *Hunger As A Factor in Human Affairs*. Gainesville: University of Florida Press, 1975.

Srivastava, U. K. et al. *Food Aid and International Economic Growth*. Ames: Iowa State University Press, 1975.

Stanely, R. G. *Food for Peace: Hope and Reality of U.S. Food Aid*. London: Gordon and Breach, 1972.

Stein, A. *Famine and Human Development: The Dutch Hunger, Winter 1944–45*. New York: Oxford University Press, 1975.

Toma, P. A. *The Politics of Food for Peace*. Tucson: University of Arizona Press, 1967.

Walford, C. *The Famines of the World: Past and Present*. New York: Burt Franklin, 1970.

Wallerstein, M. B. *Food for War—Food for Peace: United States Food Aid in a Global Context*. Cambridge, Mass.: MIT Press, 1980.

Weissman, B. A. *Herbert Hoover and Famine Relief to Soviet Russia, 1921–23*. Stanford, Calif.: Stanford University Press, 1974.

Woodham-Smith, C. *The Great Hunger: Ireland 1845–49*. New York: Harper and Row, 1962.

14 Public Policy and Interdependence

Don F. Hadwiger

The world food partnership to which this book refers, like many other partnerships, is forged from past circumstances and current opportunities as much as from the preferences of the partners. The advantages that lead to a reluctant partnership are demonstrated in recent U.S.-USSR interactions—for example, the Soviet Union's decision to purchase much of its technology from the West because Western technology will increase efficiency. The decision to purchase was made without regard to whether it is ideologically or structurally "appropriate." So, too, was the momentary rejection of partnership during the U.S. agricultural food embargo against the Soviet Union, which caused a regrettable disruption within the U.S. agricultural economy and stimulated the Soviet Union to seek more dependable food sources both within its own economy and from other countries. Two great nations whose respective governments regard each other as imperialists and that spend a major portion of their budgets seeking military security from one another have nevertheless become partners in food production, not by necessity but because of enormous mutual advantage.

World food linkages or partnerships include not only those among governments but among other actors as well. Agricultural industries or agricultural subgovernments play leading roles, and sometimes the linkages extend beyond agriculture to other sectors. In U.S.-Mexican trade, as Gustavo del Castillo points out, the U.S. agricultural industry is an active agent, both directly and as it influences the policies of the U.S. government. In Mexican agriculture, the commercial or large-scale sector of Mexican agriculture, whose product is largely for export, animal food, or industrial uses, is the major policy beneficiary. The other agricultural sector, in which Mexican small farmers are organized into long-standing cooperatives, produces mainly for domestic human consumption. This second sector poses a predicament for the Mexican government, which recognizes that the country's roots are in peasant revolutionary activity and that there is still reason to fear small farmer discontent. But, at the same time, the government must react to the fact that the small farm sector no longer yields an adequate "surplus" to feed the expanding Mexican population, which is not well represented within the political system. As James Schubert points out, governments have good reason to avoid food shortages. The Mexican government has turned to the United States and to other exporting countries for incremental imports of basic food. Resulting new linkages include an international barter system that involves the U.S. agricultural industry and the Mexican oil industry. Castillo suggests that there may be too many linkages now, which frustrate the basic task of producing food and delivering it to the Mexican people.

THE ROLE OF GOVERNMENTS

Indeed, there is reason to ask whether the involvement of governments in food production is on the whole constructive. Historically, in both national and feudal systems, the government's relationship to the farmer has often been one of exploitation. In colonialism, obviously, imperial governments sought an extremely favorable balance of trade between the colonizing country and colonial agriculture. The communist countries have used and abused rural people. Recently, in developed countries, governments have been inclined to neglect their agriculture or to exploit it on behalf of diplomatic or general economic goals—witness the U.S. government's embargo on farm products to the Soviet Union. This exploitation of farmers was once possible, even in the 1970s, because traditional rural populations have been politically marginal, occasionally disrupting the system but unable to influence it on a day-to-day basis. Paradoxically, agriculture has become politically stronger when it has been transformed from a way of life for the majority of people into an industry with relatively few participants. During this transformation in the United States, a farm bloc was formed within Congress in the 1920s, supported by a large new farm organization. Working through the U.S. Department of Agriculture, this agricultural sector or subgovernment was able to enact price stabilization programs and also to finance large public research and extension agendas that had the goal of reducing production costs and improving demand. In France more recently, a comparable "corporatist" subgovernment was formed around a farm organization representing larger farmers, and it has obtained enormous developmental subsidies. Nicholas Butler finds that in the European Economic Community generally, farm groups are quite influential in determining farm policy. Japanese farmers, David Balaam states, have been able to dictate high prices for rice through their influence within the ruling political party. Hyam Gold and Ramesh Thakur showed the power of agricultural groups in Australia and New Zealand to make final decisions on agricultural trade policy. According to Anton Malish, even the Soviet Union is now stressing the development of an agro-industrial complex "as its agricultural development agent."

THE ROLE OF SUBGOVERNMENTS

Within developed nations, subgovernments often plan, decide, and implement food policy. These industry subgovernments are, of course, self-interested. In fact, it is their virtue that they do give first priority to agricultural interests. Also, they possess the knowledge and communicative abilities to make and implement effective food policy. These subgovernments may not choose to act in a developmental way, but experience suggests that in developed countries the policies these governments pursue do generally lead to increased agricultural productivity and often even to an embarrassment of surpluses. It may be this corporatism that explains the recently burgeoning food production within developed countries. Once industry has gained influence over policy, the role of national and provincial governments may be transformed from exploitation to support for food production.

Industry influence in food policy distresses Marxist analysts as well as conservative agricultural economists. Marxists are properly concerned that in poor countries, national and multinational industries supported by government are usurping choice agricultural resources and ignoring the needs of domestic citizens both as producers and consumers. Conservative economists are concerned that the agricultural sector will seek restraints on trade through monopolistic strategy or more likely by obtaining public policies protecting domestic markets and subsidizing agricultural exports, as indeed they have done in democratic developed countries. Yet, these agri-industrial sectors that obtain protection are responsible for much of the present and projected growth in world agricultural productivity. Typically, these sectors seek a protected domestic market, but in their efforts to export commodities, machinery, agricultural technology, and other products they are principal supporters of world food interdependence.

DEVELOPED AND DEVELOPING COUNTRIES

Agriculture in developed countries has been enormously responsive to public policy. As Nicholas Butler points out, price subsidies and incentives within the European Economic Community (EEC) have increased production to the point where both West Germany and the United Kingdom are becoming self-sufficient in basic commodities. France is becoming a major food exporter. Current experience in developed nations does not clearly reveal a preferable agricultural structure, or even a preferable political system. Labor-intensive small farms can be quite productive and efficient; so also can the moderate-to-large farm systems, characterized by few workers and even fewer managers, that are taking over in the industrialized democracies. The Soviet socialist system, now that it is committed to agricultural growth, may be improving its previously disappointing record.

Regardless of system or structure, developed countries have the capacity to finance and implement innovation, drawing upon an expanding body of adaptable technology. The democratic countries, moved by their subgovernments, have the political will to expand production. Even while supporting luxury diets at home, developed nations will likely maintain a positive balance of agricultural trade with the rest of the world.

Many developing countries have not been successful in agricultural development, as Louis Picard points out for governments in sub-Saharan Africa, where food need grows. Countries in the Middle East examined by Marvin Weinbaum have a mixed record. The record of Latin American countries is also questionable; Mexico is a case reported here. New technologies, particularly those of the so-called Green Revolution, have not lessened hunger substantially in Latin America, according to Michael Roberts and co-authors.

It has been suggested that agricultural change in developed countries produces, at some point, political support for agricultural development. But changes at earlier stages may actually increase the political constraints upon growth. One of the paradoxes of agricultural development is that it separates most people from the land. These separated people, having arrived in the city as food dependents, gain more political influence there than they possessed as subsistence producers. The political importance of urban populations within developing countries who are seeking cheap food is a political constraint upon agricultural development, as discussed by Louis Picard.

Even governments that make a strong political commitment to agricultural development may lack the structural capability and administrative skills to implement that change. In general, developing governments not only fail to make a strong commitment to developing their agriculture but tend to be parasitic upon it, and their traditional agricultural sector may play a part in that exploitation. It should be noted, however, that several governments that have undertaken aggressive industrial development in linkage with advanced economies have experienced agricultural growth as well: South Korea, for example, produces more food than it did a few years ago and also buys more food abroad. A few developing countries do have developmentally oriented agricultural subsectors, which could be led by service industries or bureaucrats who have a personal stake in agribusiness success. In the nineteenth century United States, for example, the railroads were developmental agents, although farmers were not likely to consider them friends.

Developing countries find it difficult to make developmental decisions. Picard and Weinbaum listed some political constraints that typically lead these countries to exploit rather than develop their agriculture. However, difficulties in decisionmaking are no greater than difficulties in implementing these decisions. Whereas in developed countries, implementation is by the same knowledgeable subgovernments that also make the decisions, the LDCs rely for implementation on a public bureaucracy that may lack knowledge of agriculture and also lacks administrative skills and institutional infrastructure. Institutions and skills evolve during many years and even through several generations.

POLICY OPTIONS

The challenge to create adequate world food production may be met, although no one should escape the sense of desperation with which we confront that challenge. The more difficult problem is to provide roles and income for those people displaced by agricultural change. Although it is to be hoped that developing countries will find ways to provide their own people access to adequate food, the reality of their dependency upon developed countries, and upon agricultural industries headquartered in developed countries, will surely continue.

Disappointment in the progress of developing countries surely stems in part from impatience, although the point is made frequently that developmental achievements require time. National and international policies designed to promote development directly have failed to concede the time needed to teach skills and values, develop institutions, and create technologies. Thus, much of the development that has occurred may be an unintended consequence of developed country policies initiated many years ago with other ends in mind. An example might be agricultural research policy. Some unintended benefits may occur even from dependence. The United States, in its earlier stages, accepted a heavy dependence on British capital, and several developed countries currently rely on United States agricultural technology in the pursuit of their own development. Dependence, even in its more repulsive forms, may prove to be an early stage of development.

For developed countries, it is a paradox that agricultural growth has often been achieved behind trade barriers, as in Europe. As Nicholas Butler points out, U.S. economists and agricultural leaders do not appreciate EEC policies that stimulated domestic production with high prices inside the community and then subsidized the sale of "surpluses" in international markets. In the United States, there is little support for joining Europe and others in a worldwide agricultural cartel comparable to the oil cartel—the Organization of Petroleum Exporting Countries (OPEC)—that stimulated energy exploration throughout the world. It is feared that a cartel's high prices would soon result in a worldwide glut of major agricultural commodities and would, therefore, be harmful to agriculture. So, on the one hand, agricultural subgovernments have played a major role in increasing their own agricultural production, meanwhile providing food exports and new technology adaptable elsewhere. On the other hand, their concern about "too much food" results in an unwillingness to join in international policies that would further stimulate world food abundance.

The challenge of food policy decisionmaking in developed countries is to work out a set of policies that will be acceptable first to the subgovernments that are the agricultural policymakers; second, that offer a mix of cost and benefits acceptable to national governments; and, third, that improve food production and equitable distribution. Examples of creative decisions embodying these goals include agreements worked out between New Zealand and Australia, as reported by Thakur and Gold, which rely on a long-run adjustment of these various interests. Another example is the agricultural policy of the government of Japan, as reported by Balaam, which absorbs producer interests in the short run while pursuing longer run production goals that are more appropriate to the needs of the Japanese people.

U.S. LEADERSHIP IN INTERDEPENDENCE

Perspectives offered in this book should be helpful in the task of evaluating U.S. food policy, if not necessarily in suggesting specific directions. Judgments about the virtues of food policies are usually made on the basis of whose interests are being sought and whose are being served, whether programs are efficient and effective, and whether they meet current world needs. Also to be considered in evaluating policies is the prospect of second order and unintended consequences because these are proving to be the most significant. Further, the psychological impact of policy orientation is often overlooked; gifts of food and interchange of education and technical training have enhanced the self-concept of a cooperative and humane race. For the United States, the facts that food aid has been, in large part, an outgrowth of unintended surpluses and that there is uncertainty as to whether food aid has been beneficial to recipients do not negate the benevolent feelings and good intentions that surround these programs. U.S. technological creativity, shared broadly through the medium of our public agricultural experiment stations, has enhanced the image of the United States as a benevolent and effective nation. Happily, our agricultural industry nowadays is rarely moved to squelch agricultural development elsewhere, though like other subgovernments it seeks to restrict competitive foreign products from U.S. markets. The impulse of U.S. agriculture is still to expand production and trade, despite the distress that has lately accompanied this growth.

The role of the United States in the world food economy has been and will continue to be that of leader. U.S. leadership in agricultural development is one of its great but relatively unheralded foreign policy initiatives, perhaps equaling or surpassing in impact such policies as the Monroe Doctrine, the Open Door to China, and the political leadership of the Free World. During the past fifty years, world war, then burgeoning world population and many other catastrophes have made world food supplies uncertain. The United States has shown the capacity and will to provide adequate food through food aid, through large exports in trade, through world market stabilization of major commodities, and through technology development. Although U.S. educational and technological leadership may be exaggerated, there are facts to provide perspective, such as Anton Malish's that the world's largest farm machinery manufacturer—the USSR—is increasing its imports of U.S. agricultural technology as a major step in its own development. China and India as well as countries whose agricultural systems are smaller than that of the United States have in one way or another acknowledged a large debt to the innovative U.S. system.

The United States and its agricultural industry are now in a position for leadership in a new developmental wave based on biotechnology. It seems likely that policies can be designed, again, that will serve the interests of the industry, the government, and the consumer. This will be the challenge of agricultural policy in the wake of the initial change signaled by the 1985 farm bill. But, given the slowly incremental pace of those 1985 redirections, it appears that any future deliberations along the lines of adjustment to biotechnology will be long and difficult ones.

Contributors

David N. Balaam is assistant professor of politics and government at the University of Puget Sound in Tacoma, Washington. His work includes *Food Politics: The Regional Conflict*. He is currently engaged in research on agricultural trade policies and relations between industrialized nations.

Rosario Barajas de Vega is coordinator of the U.S. Studies Program at the Programa Universitario Justo Sierra, Mexico's National Autonomous University. He is currently doing research into the role of the Commodity Credit Corporation and the 1984 Mexican purchase of U.S. grains.

William P. Browne is professor of political science at Central Michigan University. He has done consulting work on public policies, including agriculture and trade issues in the United States and Middle East. He has taught policy development, evaluation, and analysis courses and has written on various policy and administrative issues. Browne is currently on leave from the Economic Research Service, U.S. Department of Agriculture.

Nicholas Butler is a consultant to a private sector firm. He previously worked on EEC food trade issues for the United Kingdom and has published related articles in such journals as *Foreign Affairs*.

Gustavo del Castillo is assistant director, Centro de Estudios Fronterizos del Norte de Mexico (Center for the Study of North American Frontiers), Tijuana, Baja California. He is also a postdoctoral fellow at the Center for U.S.-Mexican Relations, University of California, San Diego. He has published a book on the forms of political control in rural Mexico, and a second book on U.S. trade policy is currently in print.

Hyam Gold is a senior lecturer in the Department of Political Science, University of Otago, New Zealand. His research and teaching interests are in trade and development with a particular emphasis on agriculture and Tasmanian relations. He has several related publications.

Don F. Hadwiger is professor of political science at Iowa State University. He has worked in Congress and both the Agriculture Research Service and Economic Research Service of the U.S. Department of Agriculture. He has taught national, comparative, and international policy. His writings are on agriculture and rural policy including an edited book on U.S. food trade and the recent *Politics of Agricultural Research*.

Anton F. Malish is former chief of the Eastern Europe and USSR branch of the U.S. Department of Agriculture's Economic Research Service. Before joining USDA, Mr. Malish served on the U.S. delegation to the Multilateral Trade Negotiations in Geneva, with the U.S. International Trade Commission, and as an officer in the U.S. Army Quartermaster Corps. He has written extensively on the agriculture of the Soviet Union.

Leo V. Mayer is associate administrator of the Foreign Agricultural Service, U.S. Department of Agriculture. He formerly was senior specialist for agriculture, Congressional Research Service, Library of Congress; senior agricultural advisor for trade negotiations, Office of the U.S. Trade Representative; Senior Staff Economist, Council of Economic Advisors; and associate professor of economics, Iowa State University. He has written several articles on world food and related agriculture policy.

Louis A. Picard is associate professor of political science at the University of Nebraska-Lincoln. He has published articles on development administration, political economy, arms control and arms transfers. Recent articles have appeared in *Polity, Comparative Political Studies, Comparative Politics, Journal of Modern African Studies,* and *Journal of Political and Military Sociology.* He is editor of a forthcoming book on the political economy of Botswana. Picard is now on leave from the National Association of Schools of Public Affairs and Administration.

Michael K. Roberts is a graduate student in sociology at Purdue University. He is working primarily in the area of the sociology of religion. He has presented conference papers on the dimensions of religious commitment.

Fred H. Sanderson is a senior fellow, National Center for Food and Agricultural Policy, Resources for the Future, Washington, D.C. He has published widely on European agriculture.

C. Micheal Schwartz is a graduate student in sociology at Purdue University. He is writing a dissertation on the world food system and hunger, and has presented a conference paper on the Marxist tradition and theories of population growth.

James N. Schubert is associate professor of political science at Alfred University with interests in food and nutrition politics and policy. He has published several related articles.

G. Edward Schuh is an administrator at the World Bank, International Agriculture. His research, teaching, consulting, and governmental services experiences have brought him into contact with all areas of agricultural trade. He has an extensive list of publications related to issues of world food.

Michael S. Stohl is associate professor, Department of Political Science, Purdue University. He has published books and journal articles on the politics of terrorism and violence and global political economy. Stohl is currently doing research on violence in the United States.

Ross B. Talbot is professor of political science, Iowa State University. He has published extensively on all aspects of U.S. agriculture and trade and teaches agricultural policy. He is author of *The Chicken War: An International Trade Conflict Between the United States and the European Economic Community, 1961–1964*.

Harry R. Targ is associate professor, Department of Political Science, Purdue University. He has published books on international relations theory and articles on international political economy. He is currently doing research on foreign policy and struggles between capital and labor after World War II.

Ramesh Thakur is senior lecturer in the Department of Political Science, University of Otago, New Zealand. He has followed closely the politics and impact of the Australian-New Zealand trade agreement as well as other aspects of Tasman agriculture. His publications have appeared in several journals.

Marvin G. Weinbaum is associate professor of political science, University of Illinois-Urbana. He has conducted field research throughout the Middle East and is author of *Food, Development and Politics in the Middle East* and several related articles.

Index